D0857625

THE VIKING LEGACY

THE VIKING LEGACY

The Scandinavian influence on the English and Gaelic languages

John Geipel

DAVID & CHARLES : NEWTON ABBOT

DISCARD

Southern State College Library
Magnolia, Arkansas

107204

0 7153 4960 0

COPYRIGHT NOTICE
© John Geipel 1971
All rights reserved. No part of this publication may be reproduced, stored in a retrieval system, or transmitted, in any form or by any means, electronic, mechanical, photocopying, recording or otherwise, without the prior permission of David & Charles (Publishers) Limited

Set in 10/12 pt Times
and printed in Great Britain
by William Clowes & Sons Limited, London, Colchester and Beccles
for David & Charles (Publishers) Limited
South Devon House   Newton Abbot   Devon

Contents

List of illustrations

In text

Introduction

In 1851, the young Danish archaeologist, Jens Jacob Asmussen Worsaae, returned home after a year in Britain to write his survey *Minder om de Danske og Nordmændene i England, Skotland og Irland.* The project, carried out on behalf of the Royal Danish Commission for Antiquities (Hans Majestæts Oldsagscommission) was an investigation into 'the surviving relics of the Danes and Northmen in Scotland and other parts of the British Isles'.

During the eight centuries which lay between Worsaae's visit and the extinguishing of the Anglo-Danish state by the Normans, the histories of the British Isles and the Scandinavian countries, once so intimately intertwined, had grown far apart. There had been time enough, one would have thought, for every vestige of the Northmen in Britain to have been completely expunged. Yet Worsaae, quarrying deep into all the available archaeological, linguistic and documentary material, succeeded in demonstrating to his countrymen that, despite this long separation, there was still palpable evidence of their forefathers to be found, not merely on British soil but, even more abundantly, on the tongues of the islanders themselves.

Stimulated by Worsaae's initial disclosures, and by those contained in his second seminal study, *Den danske Erobring af England og Normandiet* (The Danish Conquest of England and Normandy), a succession of Scandinavian scholars, starting with the Dane, Johannes Steenstrup, in the 1860s and continuing up to our own time, applied themselves to the task of elucidating the Norse linguistic legacy 'West over Sea'. Particularly valuable contributions were made by the Danes, Otto Jespersen and Jakob Jakobsen, the Swedes, Erik Björkman, Harald Lindkvist and Eilert Ekwall, and the Norwegians, Alf Sommerfelt, Nils Holmer, Carl Marstrander, Magnus Olsen and A. W. Brøgger. The findings of these authorities, and of their followers, will constitute the main substance of this survey. As the Scandinavian element in English and Gaelic has so far been somewhat neglected by British scholars (who have tended to concentrate more on the archaeological remains of the Vikings), much of the material presented in the following chapters is likely to be unfamiliar to the English speaking reader.

Although I have tried to keep technical terms and phonetic symbols to a minimum, a certain number are inescapable in a survey of this type, and glossaries of both are provided. A few details of usage should, however, be explained at the outset. The term 'Northmen' is employed as a catch-all for Gothonic-speaking Scandinavians, whereas 'Norsemen' refers specifically to Norwegians. Gudmund Schütte's rubric 'Gothonic' has been used in preference to 'Germanic' or 'Teutonic' as the name of the group of languages to which English and its northern relatives belong; the two older terms tend to give the erroneous impression that the Gothonic languages first took shape within the confines of the present Germany before spreading to Scandinavia.

Wherever they exist, established English forms of Scandinavian proper names have been used, e.g. Canute, Olaf and Guthrum rather than Knútr, Óláfr, Guðþormr. Otherwise, Scandinavian names are given in their conventional Old Icelandic spelling.

I should like to thank Richard Perkins, of the Department of Scandinavian Studies at University College, London, and my cousin, Nicholas Driver, for their constructive comments on two earlier – and much bulkier – versions of this survey. Thanks also to Anne Sole for her help with the typing, and especially to my wife, Eileen, who has been my helpmeet every inch of the way. Tilslut vil jeg rette en hjertelig tak til alle mine venner i Norden, der har været mig til hjælp under bogens bearbejdelse.

JOHN GEIPEL, May 1970

Abbreviations

adj.	adjective
app.	apparently
conn.	connected
corr.	corresponding
Dan	Danish
dial	dialect
Dut	Dutch
E	English
Faer	Faeroese
Fr	French
Gael	Gaelic
Gmn	German
HGmn	High German
Icel	Icelandic
lit.	literally
M	Middle. Middle English (ME) refers to the period c 1100–1500, Middle Danish (MD) and Middle Swedish (MSwe) to the period c 1300–1500
mod.	modern
N	Norse. In the context of this book, Norse (N) and Old Norse (ON) refer to the Old Icelandic form of Scandinavian, spoken c 1150–1350.
n	noun
Norw	Norwegian
O	Old. Old English (OE) refers to the period c 450–1100. Old Danish and Old Swedish to the period c 1050–1300.
obs.	obsolete
orig.	origin, original
pl.	plural
poss.	possibly
prob.	probably
rel.	related

Scand	Scandinavian
Shet	Shetlandic
Swe	Swedish
vb	verb

* (before a word) = a hypothetical or reconstructed form
> = developed into
< = developed from

Pronunciation guide

Approximate sound values of phonetic symbols and other characters.
(Except where languages are indicated, the characters are those used
in the International Phonetic Alphabet.)

A   As in northern English and Scots *man*
Á   (ON) As in southern English *aunt*
Á   (Icel) As Eng ow in *how*
Á   (Faer) Approximately as the diphthong oa in English *oar*
Ā   (OE) As in southern English *aunt*
Å   (Dan, Swe, Norw) As in English *awe*
AA   (Older Danish) As in English *awe*
Ä   (Gmn, Swe) Approximately as English ai in *air*
Æ   (ON, Dan, Norw, Faer) Approximately as English ai in *air*
Æ   (Icel) As English y in *my*
Æ   (OE) As in modern English *hat*
AI   As English y in *eye*
AU   As English ou in *house*
AU   (Icel) As Ø + I
AU   (Norw) As Ø + Y
Č   (Czech) As English ch in *chin*
Đ, ð   (OE, ON, Icel) As th in English *this*
Đ, ð   (Faer) Mute, or as English V in *vine*
Ē   (OE) As in Scots *eh?*
É   (Icel) As English ye in *yes*
É   (Gaelic) As English ay in *day*
EI   As English ay in *day*
EY   (ON, Icel) As English ay in *day*
HV   (ON) As H + V
HV   (Icel, Faer and some varieties of Norw.) As K + V
HV   (Dan) As v
HW   (OE, Jutland Dan) As Scots and American English wh in *what*
Í   (ON, Icel) As English ea in *eat*
Í   (Faer) Approximately as English oy in *boy*

Ī	(OE) As English ea in *eat*
Ó	(ON, Icel, Faer, Gaelic) As southern English oa in *boat*
Ō	(OE) As southern English oa in *boat*
Ò	(Gaelic) As southern English o in *job*
Œ	(ON) As Scots ö in *öwer*
Ø	(ON, Dan, Norw, Faer) As Scots ö in *öwer*
Ö	(Swe, Gmn.) As Scots ö in *öwer*
Ǫ	(ON) As in English *awe*
Ɔ	As in English *awe*
OU	As in southern English *cold*
Š	(Czech) As English sh in *ship*
Þ	(ON, OE, Icel) As English th in *thin*
U	As in English *cook*
U:	As in English *boot*
Ú	(ON, Icel) As in English *boot*
Ū	(OE) As in English *boot*
Ù	(Gaelic) As in English *boot*
Ü	(Gmn) As in Scots *puir*
Y	(OE, ON, Dan, Swe, Norw) As in Scots *puir*
Ý	(ON, Icel) As ea in English *eat*
Ý	(Faer) Approximately as English oy in *boy*
Ž	(Czech) As English z in *azure*
ZH	(English rendering of Cyrillic ж) As English z in *azure*

One

The common roots of English and Norse

Of the many peoples who have settled in Britain since the coming of the Anglo-Saxons, only two, the Normans and the Scandinavians, have exerted any appreciable influence on the languages and place-names of these islands.

The Normans were a conquering aristocracy, a powerful and influential minority who imposed their alien institutions on the English and brought with them a Latin-based language that differed radically from the various Gothonic and Keltic idioms of the established island peoples. The imprint of Norman French on English is, in the main, quite unmistakable. Most of the French ingredients in our language still bear the earmarks of their extraneous origin, either in the concepts they describe or in the sounds they contain, and few are to be found in the deeper and more elemental levels of our vocabulary. The meagre French contribution to English placenaming habits similarly reflects the negligible impression made by the French language on the colloquial speech of the English peasantry.

The Scandinavians, who had been in Britain for at least a couple of hundred years at the time of the arrival of their Frenchified kinsmen, the Normans, were, unlike William's followers and their immediate descendants, speakers of a language that resembled that of the Angles and Saxons in so many ways that the incorporation of large quantities of Norse elements into English was able to be effected without the slightest violation of the structure or the sound-system of the recipient language.

'Cultural borrowing', of the kind typified by the French loanwords in English, occurs when a language regarded as representative of a superior culture is imposed upon the existing language of an alien people, either forcibly or by imitation. Foreign terms derived from the superimposed language are first adopted, together with the concepts that they describe, by a bilingual upper class, and only later find their way into the vernacular of the ordinary people. Even when established, they tend to remain characteristic of certain specialised sections of the borrowing language; the French loans in English are, for example, typical of the terminology of government, religion, law, hunting, sport, social relationships and etiquette, morals, fashion and cuisine. The assimilation by one language of such intimate items as 'structure words' (i.e. conjunctions, prepositions and personal pronouns) and even of phonological features from another language, can, by contrast, only take place when the speakers of the two languages live together for a prolonged period as a single, closeknit community. Just such a community, in fact, as existed between the Scandinavian settlers and their English hosts some thousand years ago.

The symbiosis that grew up on English soil between the resident population and the immigrants after the initial Viking settlements was evidently so intimate that a complete fusion of the native with the implanted language was achieved in the remarkably short space of five or six generations. So thorough was the integration of Norse constituents into English that many of these remained undetected until philologists using the comparative method began to investigate our language during the second half of the nineteenth century.

The thoroughness of this assimilation is largely due to the fact that the two languages were very similar to start with. Even to an untrained observer, the close kinship between English and the Scandinavian languages (Icelandic, Faeroese and the many varieties of Danish, Swedish and Norwegian) must be obvious. The most superficial comparison is enough to demonstrate that English shares not only a substantial portion of its native vocabulary but also many basic grammatical constructions with its northern cousins.

English and the Scandinavian languages are, in fact, all representatives of the Gothonic family, which embraces such other living members as High and Low German, Frisian and Dutch, and formerly included such languages as Gothic, Langobardic and Burgundian – all long extinct.

The similarities between all these languages are far too many to be coincidental, and lead one irresistibly to the conclusion that they stem from a common progenitor – a source language that no longer exists. Such a language appears to have taken shape in north-west Europe – the Gothonic heartland – during the last millennium BC. It seems that, by about the sixth century BC, most, though probably not all, of the important sound-changes that were to distinguish the Gothonic languages as a group from their more distant relatives in the Indo-European phylum had taken place, the basic stock of root-words on which the surviving Gothonic languages continue to draw had accumulated, and the fundamental grammatical constructions which they have all inherited were already well established.

It is at about this time, too, that the many-stranded lines of descent leading backwards from the historically attested Gothonic languages appear to converge into what must have been their fairly homogeneous mutual ancestor.

Although there are no written records of this primordial Gothonic, there is sufficient evidence in its historical descendants to enable some pretty well-founded inferences to be made about its probable nature. When this material is augmented by the thousands of demonstrably archaic Gothonic loans found in such languages as French, Italian, Spanish, Lithuanian, Russian, Finnish and Lapp (whose ancestral speakers are known to have been in regular contact with the early Gothones), we have a fairly comprehensive body of information about the most salient features of Primitive Gothonic. Still more evidence is to be found in the writings of Greek and Roman historians and geographers, who recorded the names of many early Gothonic chieftains and nations, and of locations in Gothonic tribal areas, at a time when the Gothonic dialects were still only slightly differentiated from each other.

Tantalisingly, the Roman Iron Age is as far back as the comparative method will allow us to trace the roots of the Gothonic languages, and any theories concerning their evolution prior to that period must be purely speculative.

Most scholars, however, agree that the indigenous inhabitants of north-west Europe spoke, at some inaccessibly remote period, languages that were not Gothonic, and possibly not even Indo-European, at all. Only such a conclusion can account for the enormous number of idiosyncrasies in pronunciation, vocabulary and syntax that are shared by all forms of Gothonic yet are wholly unattested outside that group of languages. While there is considerable discord about the ultimate wellsprings of Gothonic, it is now widely accepted that at any rate its Indo-European component was introduced from outside, either by invaders or by some other people with whom the proto-Gothones were in contact.

It is clearly impossible to state, even approximately, when – let alone how – this Indo-Europeanising process took place. Some authorities favour the theory that the Gothonic languages began life in the early Iron Age as a kind of 'pidgin Keltic'; others claim for them a Bronze Age genesis; while others would put back the implanting of Indo-European in the north by at least four thousand years.

Sigmund Feist has suggested that Gothonic may have evolved out of a 'contact vernacular' between the 'Hyperboreans' and Indo-European-speaking traders from southern or south-eastern Europe. The resulting jargon, a rough-and-ready mélange of aboriginal and Indo-European ingredients, may thus have resembled, in its infancy, such latterday lingua francas as Swahili and Fanagalo in Africa and, in its adolescence, the various half-breed Creoles of the New World.

Whatever the case, it seems more than likely that the deepest taproots of English and the Scandinavian languages lie buried in some prehistoric mongrel, a hybrid tongue whose genealogy was anything but pure.

Many of the most striking peculiarities that finally came to mark off Gothonic once and for all from other forms of Indo-European seem to have been further accentuated during the last few centuries BC. This may have been a direct result of the increased isolation of the proto-Gothones in their remote northern homeland, an isolation that was made all the more effective by the solid belt of belligerent Keltic tribal aggregations that held sway across the whole of central Europe between the sixth and the last century BC, and sealed the Gothones from direct contact with the Mediterranean civilisations.

The period of Gothonic linguistic unity – which, if it ever existed, must have been short-lived – had long since passed away by the time the historical Gothonic languages were committed to writing, and the first written records of these languages suggest that diversification into distinctive regional forms had been going on since well before the Christian era. Indeed, the break-up of the once fairly homogeneous Gothonic speech community may have been initiated as early as the fourth or fifth century BC by the migration from Scandinavia to the

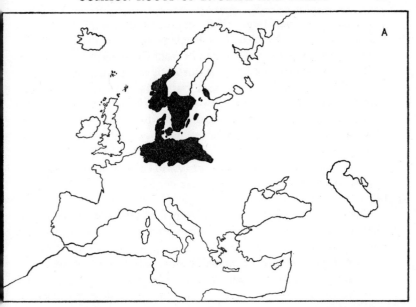

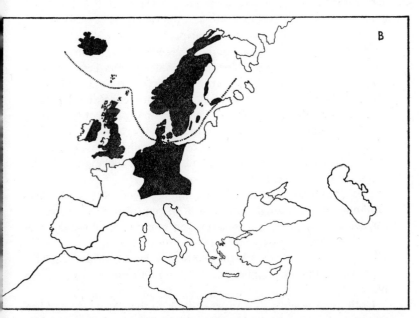

FIG. 1. Gothonic-speaking Europe: (A) during the last century BC; (B) today.
The dotted line divides North from West Gothonic languages.

2

south Baltic of such large tribal confederations as the Goths and Langobards from Sweden, the Rugians from Norway, and the Vandals, Burgundians and Sillingians from Denmark.

The languages spoken by these northern expatriates appear, from their scant remains, to have been transitional between the 'West' Gothonic ancestral to English, Frisian, Dutch and German and the 'North' Gothonic forerunner of the later Scandinavian languages. Their removal from southern Scandinavia evidently left something of a hiatus between the two remaining varieties of Gothonic, and it was not until perhaps as late as the fourth century AD that these two clearly differentiated siblings of a once common tongue came face to face.

Where did this confrontation take place? One thing is sure: the earliest line of demarcation between North and West Gothonic did not coincide with its present location across the neck of south Jutland.

The grounds for such a confident claim are purely linguistic. It was from southernmost Sweden that the Langobards (Longbeards) migrated to the Lower Elbe during the third and fourth centuries AD, and from the southern part of the present Denmark that the Angles left for England in c AD 450. Both these migrant peoples spoke dialects of a demonstrably West Gothonic stripe, whereas the Vikings, and all subsequent inhabitants of southern Sweden and Denmark, were North Gothonic speakers. The initial confrontation between North and West Gothonic must therefore have occurred somewhere to the north of the historic province of Skåne in southern Sweden after the departure of the Langobards. Only gradually was the resulting linguistic watershed pushed south and west – perhaps as the result of unrecorded ethnic movements – across the Danish Isles, not reaching its historical location in south Jutland until after the migration of the Angles in the fifth century.

This secondary line of demarcation between North and West Gothonic has persisted right down to our own time. From the Zuyder Zee in the west, an unbroken continuum of purely West Gothonic dialects stretches north-east into Slesvig. Here, a few kilometres south of the present Danish border, an abrupt transition to North Gothonic – unbridged by any intermediate form – takes place.

Until quite recently, it was generally held that Denmark had been the original nucleus of this North Gothonic, the centre from which the language was diffused to other parts of Scandinavia. This supposition was based on the use in pre-thirteenth-century Scandinavian texts of the expression *dǫnsk tunga* (Danish tongue) as a catch-all for every form of North Gothonic. Modern opinion, however, favours central Sweden as the North Gothonic cradleland – for reasons that must, in the light of the foregoing facts, be obvious.

As a remote, marginal and isolated dialect, this nascent Norse was stamped both with archaic traits that had long since been discarded by the more centrally situated members of the Gothonic moiety and with aberrant forms of its own. During a protracted gestatory period, which spanned the first half-dozen centuries AD and is attested by some two hundred runic inscriptions (the oldest written memorials in any Gothonic tongue), the language acquired many of its most distinguishing earmarks. These were added to during the brief maturational, 'syncope' or pre-Viking stage (*c* AD 600–800) by a mass of further adjustments, the cumulative effect of which was irreversibly to sever the Scandinavian dialects from their West Gothonic relatives in Britain and Germany.

An acquaintance with the most salient of these peculiarly northern characteristics is obviously essential for the task of pinpointing possible Scandinavian loans in our own language.

Many of the diagnostics that mark off the North Gothonic languages from their Western congeners are phonological, and it is safe to say that, if the phonic shape and content of an English term is found to conform more to the Scandinavian than to the West Gothonic, norm then there is a fair chance that it reached Britain with the crews of the longships.

In most cases, Norse phonology – even after the numerous mutations and adjustments it had undergone during the 'syncope' period – had remained more faithful than had English to the apparent prototypes in their mutual progenitor, the hypothetical 'Common Gothonic'.

In the realm of the consonants, Norse preserved the 'hard' articulation of G and K even before the front vowels, E, I and Y – whereas English palatalised these initial consonants before front vowels, making them Y and CH respectively. Even when preceded by S, followed by R, or both, K appears to have retained its occlusive quality in Norse, although the clusters SK and SKR were 'softened' in English to SH and SHR. We thus find such correspondences as Norse *garn, kista, skǫmm, skruð* and English *yarn, chest, shame, shroud.* When, in English, we encounter words displaying an occlusive G or K (whether or not the K is preceded by S) before a front vowel, we may reasonably suspect Norse influence to have been at work. Either the term itself may turn out to be of Scandinavian derivation (as are *get, kid,* and *skin*) or it may be a Norse remodelling of a native word (as are *give, kettle* and the placename Skipwith – which, had they escaped the Nordicising process, might well have come down to us as 'yive', 'chettle' and 'Shipwood').

Common Gothonic vowels and diphthongs, too, were inherited differently by the ancestral forms of English and Scandinavian. Here, again, the Norse forms are more often closer to the underlying Common Gothonic prototypes. Common Gothonic Ā, AU and AI were retained as Á, AU and EI in Scandinavian, but became Ē, ĒA and Ā in Old English, yielding such doublets as Norse *hár, lauss, steinn,* and Old English *hēr, lēas, stān.* In the modern English equivalents of these three examples (*hair, loose, stone*), *loose* is the odd man out; its vowel sound, *oo,* clearly reflects the Norse *lauss* rather than the native *lēas* and it may safely be regarded as a Scandinavian borrowing. The same may be said for *weak* and *swain,* which are modelled, not on the native *wāc, swān* (which would have given as 'woak' and 'swoan') but on the Norse forms, *veikr* and *sveinn.*

Although such instances of Norse sound substitution are comparatively rare in standard English, they abound in the dialects of Scotland and the north, where direct Scandinavian influence was most intense and enduring. Medieval writers from the Scottish Lowlands and the old Danelaw shires tended to favour the Scandinavian *bleik, heil* and *leith* at the expense of the native *blāc* (pale), *whole* and *loath* (-some), *coupe* and *loup* rather than *cheap* (to buy) and *leap, gra* and *har* rather than *grey* and *hair,* and *skere* and *harsk* rather than *sheer* and *harsh.*

This Scandinavian influence has left an indelible imprint on the pronunciation of Scots and northern English, and it is still possible in some areas to hear forms like *garth* and *garn* (for *yard* and *yarn*), *kist* and *kirn* (for *chest* and *churn*), *skift* and *skelf* (for *shift* and *shelf*) and *skrike* and *scrood* (for *shriek* and *shroud*).

The word-final 'hard' G and K characteristic of Norse are also preferred in some northern English dialects to the palatal English *-ch* and *-dge* in such terms as *rig* and *brig* (for *ridge* and *bridge*) and *benk* and *thack* (for *bench* and *thatch*).

Scandinavian vowels, too, have left their mark on most Scottish and northern forms of English. Norse AU, rather than English ĒA, shines through in *rowk* and *nowt* (for *reek* and *neat* = cattle), whilst Norse EI may have contributed to the retention by the northern dialects of such forms as *stain, hame, mair, ain,* and *aik,* for *stone, home, more, own,* and *oak.* It may be that the pure vowel, *oo,* familiar in northern English in words like *oot, hoose,* and *doon* (*out, house, down* = feathers) has been similarly reinforced by the identical sound in the corresponding Scandinavian words.

The influence of certain other Norse phonological tendencies in English – both standard and provincial – is far less pervasive.

The lack of a medial guttural H sound in Viking Norse may possibly have accelerated the shedding of this feature by medieval English. Such an inference seems to be supported by the fact that spellings indicating the loss of this medial guttural (e.g. *dowter* for *daughter, rite* for *right*) are attested from the late fourteenth century onwards from those parts of eastern England where the Danes settled most densely.

Somewhat more easily attributable to Scandinavian influence is the presence in certain English dialects of forms like *dag, hagg, yuggle,* and *sniggle* for *dew, hew, owl,* and *snail*; these appear to have been influenced by the sound development known as Holtzmann's Law, peculiar to the Scandinavian languages and to Gothic.

North-country forms like *i'* for *in, o'* for *on* and *drucken* for *drunken* (e.g. Mid Yorks 'Our Jack were drucken ageean last neet – liggin' o' t' flooer wi' 'is feet i' t' 'airth'), which lack a medial or final -*n*, are probably attributable to Scandinavian influence, as is the standard English Thursday, which has replaced an earlier native Thundersday.

We must, however, discount the 'Northumbrian Burr' – the guttural R characteristic of Tyneside English and Berwickshire Scots – as yet another example of enduring Scandinavian influence. This velar sound, identical with the 'Drøbel R' of Danish and the 'Skorrande R' of certain varieties of Swedish and Norwegian, is a relative newcomer to Scandinavia. It seems to have gained its first toehold in Copenhagen as a modish affectation among the francophile Prussian aristocracy at the time of Struensee, and is only now in the process of usurping the old apical R from some outlying Danish dialects. The Vikings are scarcely likely to have used the sound – let alone to have introduced it to the ancestors of the Geordies.

FIG. 2.   Isophones marking the approximate southern limits of: (A) the use of
EI in *stane*, *aik*, *hame*, for *stone*, *oak*, *home* (etc); and (B) the use of the 'pure'
vowel U: in *oot*, *hoose*, *coo*, for *out*, *house*, *cow* (etc.).

Investigation of the sound systems of provincial Danish, Swedish, Norwegian and Faeroese dialects has revealed that by no means all the phonological criteria formerly regarded as the most reliable earmarks of the Scandinavianisms in English are universal to all forms of North Gothonic. Indeed, many Scandinavian dialects make use of sounds that are closer to their English counterparts than to their equivalents in medieval Icelandic – the sound system of which was traditionally regarded as the archetypal Scandinavian norm. Thus, one may hear a Scanian countryman pronounce the Swedish words *rygg* and *bänk* almost as their English counterparts, *ridge* and *bench* (with 'soft' final *g* and *k*); a Jutlander say *worm* and *Wonsda* (with initial *w-*) for standard Danish *orm* and *Onsdag*; and a Norwegian from Setesdal or Telemark drop the *l* before labials or *-k* (just as in most forms of post-sixteenth century English), sounding *folk* and *halv* as *fo'kk* and *hå'v*.

The discovery of such startling convergences between English and dialectal Scandinavian phonology meant that many of the words once regarded as 'indisputable Norse loans' in our language have had to be relegated to the status of uncertain, borderline cases.

It was not, of course, merely in details of sound that the North Gothonic languages came to differ from their more southerly relatives. By the Viking period, the Norse vocabulary had amassed a substantial number of lexical items that were either completely unknown in the West Gothonic languages or had long since been discarded by them. Among the apparently home-grown Scandinavian terms that were carried by the Vikings to Britain were *drengr* = a bold man, *griss* = a pig, *kjọt* = flesh, *lyng* = heather, *sild* = a herring, and *elska* = to love, all of which have found a place in the regional dialects of England and Scotland.

Just as with phonological influences, however, it is necessary to sound a caveat or two in connection with Norse lexical loans in English. First, it should be remembered that the vocabularies of English and the Scandinavian languages were even closer a thousand years ago than they are today, and that hundreds of terms that were once common to Old English and Norse have – although still used in Scandinavia – long since dropped out of our vocabulary. Such are: *barn* (child), *cwen* (woman), *wynstra* (left), *cweld* (evening), *gamol* (old), *gnidan* (to rub) and *tygel* (a bridle), which, while meaningless to a modern Englishman, are instantly recognisable to a Scandinavian (cf Danish *barn, kvinde, venstre, kveld, gammel, gnide, tøjle*).

Hundreds, if not thousands, of other lexical cognates in the two languages must have gone unrecorded, so that the mere absence from Old English vernacular texts of a term attested from a Scandinavian source is obviously no proof that it was unknown to the English. We suspect that lexical convergences between Norse and the Anglian dialects of Northumbria must have been particularly plentiful – although this is difficult to substantiate, for, as a result of Viking activities, there was a complete break in the old Northumbrian literary tradition from the eighth century to the twelfth.

Even when all these acid tests are ruthlessly applied, however, the inventory of probable Scandinavian phonic and lexical influences in English remains impressive, and it is still reasonable to assume that, if a form is undocumented in Old English but attested in some Scandinavian idiom, and if that form occurs in Middle English from an area known to have experienced intense Scandinavian influence, then there is a strong likelihood of its being a Norse loan.

Finally, what of the Scandinavian influence, if any, on the syntactical structure of English? This has been the subject of much heated contention, with opinions ranging from those of W. Keller, who argues in favour of a strong and very early Danish influence on English (particularly the Northumbrian variety), to those of E. Einenkel, who vehemently denies any such influence.

Somewhere in between stands Otto Jespersen, who has cogently demonstrated that although Norse cannot be shown to have exerted any direct influence on English syntax, its presence on British soil may well have accelerated the rapid disintegration of the elaborate inflectional apparatus of Old English. He makes the point that, although a large proportion of the basic lexicon was common to English and Norse, the grammatical processes of the two languages were in many respects divergent. In those areas where both languages were spoken side by side, and where a substantial proportion of the population would have been bilingual, words tended to be shorn of their affixes and other superfluous morphological appendages and used in their root form (e.g. 'I see the bird in the tree' rather than the more highly inflected: *Ic se þone fugol in þæm treow*). It is significant that this process of grammatical simplification first got under way in precisely those districts where Danes and English lived side by side.

Jespersen also cites many examples of syntactical convergences between modern colloquial English and the living Scandinavian languages, developments which English does not share with any of its West Gothonic congeners. Such are: 'You're a fine one to talk', 'He has someone to work for', 'It's me', 'The best of two', and even the vulgar 'this here', 'that there' and 'them little apples' – each of which is mirrored word-for-word in various forms of idiomatic Scandinavian but completely alien to Dutch or German. The Scandinavians also seem to have shared with English-speakers a certain bewilderment concerning the correct accusative and dative forms of the personal pronoun 'who' ('The man who (whom?) I met') – although the Danes, Swedes and Norwegians long ago gave up the unequal struggle and opted in favour of the inflected form 'whom' (*hvem, vem, kvem, kem,* etc) in every context.

Whether the hundreds of such convergences between English and Scandinavian usage are the result of direct Norse influence on our language, or whether we should regard them as a legacy from the time when Anglians and Danes lived cheek-by-jowl in Jutland, it is impossible to decide. But although it is difficult to demonstrate conclusively that the language of the Vikings exerted any influence on the grammatical structure of English, there is, as Professor Baugh remarks, 'nothing improbable in the assumption that certain Scandinavian turns of phrase and certain popular usages should have found their way into an idiom of a people in no small part Danish in descent, and living in intimate contact with the speakers of a Scandinavian tongue'.

While vestigial Scandinavian flexional processes are frequently found in British placenames, very few have been preserved in spoken English.

The suffix *-sk* to the English verbs *bask* and *busk* is such a relict form; attached to the root of a Norse verb, it indicated the reflexive aspect (i.e. *baða* = to bathe, *baða-sk* = to bathe oneself, or 'bask'). Another survival is the neuter suffix *-t*, which has been retained as an ossified appendage by the English *scant* and *want*; *scant* is merely *skammt* – the neuter form of the Norse adjective *skammr* = short, whilst *vant* was the neuter of *vanr*, meaning defective.

One more vestigial Norse inflection is the genitive plural affix *-ar*, which survives only in the Scots expression 'by nichter tale' = in the middle of the night. The phrase was evidently more widespread in former times, and Chaucer used it in his *Canterbury Tales*. It is merely a corruption of the Norse *á nattar þéli*, literally 'on the strength of the night'.

A perennial preoccupation of the investigator on the qui-vive for Scandinavian borrowings in English is: which loans can be hailed as Danish, and which were introduced by the Norwegians? The question is more than merely academic, for if the comparative proportions of Danish to Norwegian loans in English could be determined, we should be in a position not only to evaluate the extent of the influence exerted on our language by these two species of Northman but also to make some pretty responsible calculations about the relative numbers of Danes and Norwegians who settled in Britain.

Unfortunately, however, every attempt so far to winnow the 'Danish' from the 'Norwegian' (let alone the 'Swedish') ingredients among our Scandinavian loans has met with one frustration after another. One of the biggest problems is sound distortion: not a single one of the Scandinavian terms still used in English has escaped some form of erosion or other phonic disfigurement during the thousand or more years of its British circulation. In this way, a term whose existing form suggests that it is of unbroken Danish descent may well have started on its rounds with a distinctly Norwegian cast of feature.

An even greater problem, however, arises from the misguided attempt on the part of certain authorities to categorise the Norse of the Viking period into entities bearing such modern national-language labels as 'Danish', 'Norwegian', and 'Swedish'. These literary standards are artificial enough even today; a thousand years ago they would have been quite meaningless. Admittedly, spellings in Scandinavian texts from the ninth century indicate that two broad geographical groupings of dialects were already taking shape – a 'Western' variety embracing the forms of Norse spoken in much of Norway and its Atlantic outliers and an 'Eastern' group comprising most of the budding forms of Danish and Swedish – but the outlines of these two regional clusters were still extremely ill-defined. By the eleventh century, it may have been possible for an experienced listener to distinguish between an Icelander and a Sealand Dane, a Gaut and an Uppland Swede, by their speech, and we read in Harald Hardráði's Saga of a Danish-speaking carter in Yorkshire who, when addressed by the fleeing Earl Marshal of Norway after the battle of Stamford Bridge, had no difficulty in identifying his interlocutor as a Norwegian.

By that time (1066), however, the major absorption of Scandinavian terms into English had long since taken place. The bulk of the Norse expressions in our language entered it at a time when regional discrepancies within the Scandinavian speech community must have been scarcely perceptible, and it is fair to say that the Vikings, regardless of their place of birth, brought with them to Britain in the ninth and tenth centuries what was in all essentials a homogeneous language – a language known throughout the north as *dǫnsk tunga* – the Danish tongue.

Two

The Northmen in Britain

It is essential, when examining the influence of one language on another, to see that influence in its correct social setting and historical perspective. For this reason, and before proceeding with the task of reviewing the extent of the Norse linguistic legacy in Britain, it is necessary to reiterate in the broadest outline the story of the activities and settlements of the Scandinavians 'West over Sea'.

Although the arrival of the Vikings brought the inhabitants of these islands into abrupt and violent contact with the Scandinavians, the rascally crews of the longships were by no means the first northerners to set foot in Britain. Indeed, the archaeological evidence speaks unambiguously of an intermittent two-way flow of cultural influences – and so, presumably, of human beings – between Britain and the lands to her north and east that began long before the final rupture of the islands from the parent continent and continued throughout the Neolithic period and into the age of metal.

While the Belgic invasions during the first century AD are thought to have carried a certain number of continental Gothones to Britain, it was not until the end of the Roman occupation that the linguistic ancestors of today's English-speaking Britons began to arrive in substantial numbers. The languages brought across the North Sea by the Angles, Saxons, Frisians and Jutes during the fifth century AD were wholly West Gothonic in type. They were, however, all representative of an assemblage of closely kindred dialects – collectively known as Ingvaeonic, Maritime or North Sea Gothonic – that had more in common with Norse than had any other form of West Gothonic. Besides sharing a number of terms not generally favoured by the more southerly Gothones – words like *of*, *from*, *first*, *hare*, *tree* and *rye* – Norse and Ingvaeonic also had certain phonological tendencies in common. Such convergences were doubtless due to the close geographical proximity of Ingvaeonic to Scandinavian Gothonic, and they were greatly to facilitate the fusion of English and Norse when these two languages were brought together in Britain at the time of the Viking settlements.

West Gothonic dialects of Ingvaeonic type appear to have been spoken in parts of Jutland right up to – perhaps even for a short time after – the departure of the Angles for England. The Anglian migration seems to have coincided with the first infusion of Norse into the peninsula from across the Danish islands, so that Jutland was one of the last corners of Gothonic Scandinavia to be nordicised in speech. Even today, the Jutland dialects of Danish display a number of wholly un-Norse characteristics reminiscent of English – particularly Scots and northern English. These extend from pronunciation and intonation to word usage, and have led some scholars to postulate an Ingvaeonic substratum underlying Jutland Danish. As a random, and superficial, example of the often striking similarity between Jutland Danish and Scots, note how Jutland 'Hur manne skal A gi æ børn næst ug?' ('How many shall I give the children next week?') is almost as close to the old style Aberdonian 'Hoo monna sal Ah gie the bairns neest ook?' as to the Copenhagenese 'Hvor mange skal jeg give børnene næste uge?'

It was not only in their language that the Angles and other Jutland expatriates in England retained their connection with their ancestral homeland. Their traditions – as recorded in *Beowulf*, *Widsith* and the *Finnesburh Fragment* – kept fresh for many generations the memory of their legendary heroes and their former intimate association with the Scandinavian world, an association that was eventually to be renewed by the coming of the longships to Britain.

Although more than three hundred years were to elapse between the planting of the first Gothonic settlements in Britain and the arrival of the Vikings, the people of the north were no more homebound during this time than they had ever been. Throughout the fifth, sixth and seventh centuries, whilst the Angles, the Saxons and their fellows were energetically extending their territories west across Keltic Britain, Scandinavian seamen continued to be active, both as merchants and pirates, along the coasts and up the rivers of Frisia, Saxland (north Germany) and the fledgling kingdom of the Franks. It was on such a plundering expedition to Frisia that Hugleikr, king of the Gauts (a south Swedish people) met his death some time early in the sixth century, an event recorded by the contemporary Frankish chronicler, Gregory of Tours (who called him 'Chlochilaicus'), and by the composer of the Old English epic of *Beowulf*, in which, under the anglicised name of Hygelac, he is identified as Beowulf's uncle.

Long before the Northmen turned the prows of their longships 'West over Sea' towards Britain, the dwellers of the inner Baltic – Wends, Letts, Kurlanders, Ingrians, and Finns – were well acquainted

FIG. 3.   The main Scandinavian trade routes in Viking times.

with the crews of the coast-hugging vessels who came from Denmark, Gautland and Sweden to trade, or, just as frequently, to pillage.

However, these early northern seamen were not Vikings in the strictest sense, for they had not yet the robust sailing ships that were to enable their successors to become true salt-water mariners, and although it is impossible to pinpoint the precise moment when 'proto-Vikings' became Vikings proper, most Scandinavian historians define what they call *Vikingetiden* – the Viking Age – as the 250 years between AD 800 and 1050, the era of the long-range peregrinations that carried men of Danish, Swedish and Norwegian birth as far abroad as Baghdad, Byzantium and Labrador. Such excursions only became possible after the spectacular improvements in the technique of shipbuilding that took place in Scandinavia during the eighth century; by the late 700s, northern vessels were being fitted with masts and sails, their sides heightened and their hulls deepened and lengthened, until they were fit to undertake ocean voyages that would previously have been unthinkable.

What prompted the Northmen, from about 780 onwards, to take to their ships and plague the coasts and riverways of Europe for a full 250 years? Famine, pestilence, cataclysmic natural disasters in their native land, over-population as a result of the widespread practice of polygamy, the custom of driving out younger sons to fend for themselves, the cutting off by the Arabs of the old trade connections with Byzantium, an obsessive mania to destroy other people's property, a fanatical loathing of Christianity, and an insatiable appetite for high adventure – these and many other suggestions have been put forward as likely explanations for the prodigious outboiling of people from the north that is part of the conventional concept of the 'Viking eruption'.

However, whilst each of these factors may have induced individual Scandinavians to adopt the Viking life, they can hardly have been as universal throughout the north, or have exerted so protracted a stimulus, as past generations of Viking scholars would have had us believe. Certainly there may have been local cases of overcrowding in Scandinavia, certainly polygamy was popular among those who could afford it, certainly the northern weather could be as appalling a thousand years ago as it can today, but the traditional concept of an excessively fecund, volatile, rain-sodden population bursting at the seams and then erupting outwards in all directions – and continuing to erupt for 250 years – is nowadays critically regarded as reflecting too literal an interpretation of the early records.

'The history of the Vikings', says Viggo Starcke, 'was written by their enemies', and few of the British, Frankish, Byzantine and other chroniclers whose compatriots had experienced the depredations of the ungodly northern marauders would have been disposed to eulogise their exploits. It is doubtful whether many of the contemporary annalists were eyewitnesses to the events they recorded and some, in the heat of their outrage, may have been moved to exaggerate the size of the Viking 'hordes' and to overdramatise the atrocities accredited to them.

This is not to deny the ferocity of the Vikings: they were clearly an insufferable menace, an ever-imminent danger, and, having the advantage over those of their contemporaries who also favoured the predatory life in being the best seamen in Europe, they were likely to show up where and when they were least expected. But they certainly did not monopolise the brutalities that characterised their turbulent era; Franks, Saxons, Burgundians, and Wends, not to speak of Bulgars, Magyars, Avars and Moors, all showed themselves to be capable of bestial behaviour – the only difference between them and the Vikings being that most of them were landlubbers. The Anglo-Saxons are by no means exempted from this general indictment, for there is plentiful evidence that during the four centuries following their settlements in Britain, their treatment of the native Kelts was no less harsh than that which they themselves were to suffer at the hands of the Northmen.

The Vikings were active during one of the most restless periods in recorded history; large-scale tribal movements and ethnic displacements were the order of the day, and it was only their superior seamanship that distinguished the Scandinavians from all the other footloose and land-hungry peoples who swilled about Europe at this time. As farmers from a meagre-soiled country, the Northmen craved fresh arable; as ordinary human beings, rapacious but no more so than human beings before or since, they were acquisitive for material wealth, which they would obtain by force if they could not procure it by trade. As superlative mariners, they had the means of procuring both these commodities – land and loot – more easily than most of their contemporaries.

As far as Britain is concerned, the Viking Age may be said to have begun one day in the year 787, when, according to the *Anglo-Saxon Chronicle*, three shiploads of 'Danes' from 'Horthaland' (like all Vikings, they carried no passports and were more likely Norwegians than Danes) landed at Portland in Dorset and butchered Beaduheard, the king's reeve, who, thinking them to be peaceable traders of the sort who often beached on the Wessex coast, had ridden down to ask them to identify themselves.

'*Þat wæron þa ærastan scipu Deniscra manna þe Angelcynnes land gesohton*' ('These were the first ships of the Danish men to attack England') concludes the *Chronicle* for that fateful year, and it seems likely that the scoundrels involved had come the short sailing across

the Channel from the coast of Frankland, where they and their kind
had for many seasons past been prodding, with considerable success,
the fat commercial centres that stood, bloated with booty and often
pitifully defended, at the river mouths of Charlemagne's burgeoning
empire.

Vikings are not mentioned in the *Chronicle*, either under that name
or under the equally familiar sobriquets, 'Pagans', 'Heathens' and
'Strangers', until 793, when the following dismal entry was made:

> 'In this year terrible portents appeared over Northumbria and
> miserably frightened the inhabitants. There were exceptionally
> high winds and flashes of lightning and fiery dragons were seen
> flying in the air. A great famine soon followed and a little while
> after that in the same year on 8th January the harrying of the
> Heathen miserably destroyed God's church on Lindisfarne by
> rapine and plundering'.

Wrote Simeon of Durham:

> 'They laid everything waste with grievous plundering. They trampled
> the holy places with polluted steps, dug up the altars and seized all
> the treasures. They killed some of the monks, took some away with
> them in fetters; many of them they drove out and some they drowned
> in the sea.'

The Vikings had arrived in Britain, and from now on the chronicles
are punctuated more and more with entries recording Viking raids –
entries that, for all their terseness, speak plainly enough of the horrors
that accompanied these brutal assaults.

Sometimes there were casualties on both sides, as in 794 when:
'Northumbria was ravaged by the heathen and Ecgfrith's monastery
at Jarrow looted, and there one of their leaders was slain and some of
their ships besides were shattered by storms: and many of them were
drowned there, and some came ashore alive and were soon slain at the
river mouth'. More often than not, however, the raiders were able to
escape, scot-free and with little danger of pursuit, in their fast-moving
ships. In that same year, 794, Columba's church on the Holy Island of
Iona was pillaged and the following year Lambey off Dublin, the isle of
Skye, and several of the little holms off Wales all suffered the first of
many visitations. In 797 it was the turn of Kintyre in western Scotland,
of Rathlin off Ulster and then, in the spring of 798, of the Isle of Man.

'We and our forefathers have lived here for about 350 years',
lamented Alcuin, Charlemagne's Northumbrian-born librarian,

'and never have such terrors as these appeared in Britain, which we must now suffer from the pagans: it was not thought possible that such havoc could be made!' To Alcuin, and to many another devout Christian of his day, these visitations were a judgement on the English for the lax and immoral ways into which they had lapsed, and Alcuin recalled a fitting quotation from Jeremiah that seemed to him to be the prophecy that was now being fulfilled: 'Out of the North an evil shall break forth upon all the inhabitants of the land'.

These early raids were, for the most part, lightning affairs. The Vikings would descend, usually with no warning and often under the cover of darkness, on unprotected islands, exposed headlands, quiet estuaries or stretches of undefended coast – many of them the sites of monasteries run by small communities of anchorites. The sequence of events on such occasions soon became predictable: monks were put to the axe, chapels and shrines stripped of their gold, relics, and other finery, the more comely of the womenfolk carried off into slavery or concubinage, cattle slaughtered or driven on board the longships, and barns robbed of their grain before being set alight. Vicious though they were, such acts of *strandhǫgg*, as the Northmen called them, were mere pinpricks compared with what would shortly follow.

The delinquents responsible for these early raids seem to have been for the most part – if not exclusively – Norwegians. During the closing decades of the eighth century, Norwegian *bønder* (peasant farmers) and their families had been settling in substantial numbers on the northernmost British islands, the Shetlands and Orkneys, where they established their language and institutions and assimilated the remnants of an earlier Pictish-speaking population. Although the assailants of Lindisfarne, Jarrow, Iona and other monastic sites were – unlike their compatriots who were peaceably colonising Orkney and Shetland – out for loot rather than land, their sudden appearance in British waters may be seen as part of the same westward movement from Norway as that which led to the Scandinavian settlement of the Scottish Isles and Ireland, and eventually to the colonisation of Iceland and Greenland and the discovery of North America.

Early chroniclers seldom troubled to discriminate between Norwegian, Swedish and Danish Vikings, and all northern marauders were liable to be dubbed 'Danes' as, for example, were the Norwegians who had axed Beaduheard at Portland in 787. The activities of demonstrably Danish, rather than Norwegian, pirates in Britain seem not

FIG. 4.   The Viking approaches to Britain. The shaded areas are those principally colonised by the Scandinavians and where Norse placenames and other linguistic influences are most strongly in evidence. The dotted line marks the boundary fixed by Alfred and Guthrum at Wedmore to divide their two kingdoms. The Five Boroughs (Dan: Femborgene) of the Danelaw are: (1) Derby; (2) Nottingham; (3) Lincoln; (4) Leicester; (5) Stamford.

to have begun in earnest until the third decade of the ninth century, and their appearance in England was largely the result of involvements between Denmark and the Frankish empire of Charlemagne and his successors, involvements that had drawn the interest of the Danes more and more towards those continental coasts nearest to British shores.

In order to understand the reasons that were eventually to bring the Danes to Britain, it is necessary to cast a brief backward glance at some of the increasingly frequent encounters that had been taking place between them and the Franks during the opening decades of the ninth century.

The first of these confrontations was occasioned by Charlemagne's brutally systematic depopulation of eastern Holstein, from which those of the Saxon inhabitants who had not been annihilated in the preceding 'crusade' against their nation were herded south to the Rhineland while their former lands were resettled by the Abodrites, the emperor's Slavic vassals from Mecklenburg. This action brought the gargantuan empire right to Denmark's southern doorstep and the Danes justifiably began to fear that the emperor would sooner or later deal with them in the same unequivocal manner in which he had, to all intents and purposes, wiped their old neighbours, the East Holstein Saxons, from the map.

Border incidents, in which it was claimed that Abodrites had violated Danish territory, provoked the impetuous Danish king, Godfred, into launching a hugely successful punitive expedition to Mecklenburg against these trespassers, a campaign to which Charlemagne retaliated by setting up a powerful garrison at Itzehoe, just south of the earthen rampart, the Danevirke, which Godfred had thrown across the neck of south Jutland to seal his lands against future invasions. Apart from manning the Itzehoe garrison with a large Frankish force, Charlemagne, it appeared, did not intend any further reprisal action against the Danes for their rough handling of his Abodrite vassals – at least, not for the time being – and in 810 Godfred launched an audacious assault on the coast of Frisia. The crews of his 200 longships axed and burned until they were bought off by the emperor's Frisian subjects with 100 pounds in silver – the first recorded instance of the extortion by Danes of *geld* – the kind of protection money that was soon to drain the coffers of the English kings.

Godfred's son and successor, Hemming, doubtless apprehensive that Charlemagne would decide to avenge himself on the Danes for their onslaught in his inimitably ruthless fashion, made peace with the emperor and vowed to contain his people within their native lands north of the Ejder.

When Charlemagne died, in 814, his son, Louis the Pious, inherited an empire whose shores and river mouths were protected by an efficient system of coastal defences established by Charlemagne explicitly to keep such marauders as the Danes from striking any distance inland. Throughout his reign, Louis maintained these fortifications and, by supporting the pretender, Harald Klak, and his party in their claims to the Danish throne, attempted to dislodge the sons of Godfred, who still held sway in Denmark. Louis even ceded large tracts of Frisia to Harald and his supporters in return for their oaths of allegiance, an unthinking act that was to have far-reaching and, as yet, unimaginable consequences both for his successors and for England. Despite the emperor's continued support, however, Harald was unable to assert himself in Denmark; although he and his borrowed Frankish armies struck repeatedly into Jutland, they could not oust the sons of Godfred from their fastnesses on the Danish islands, whence, protected by their superior sea force, they continued to raid across to Holstein and along the shores of Mecklenburg. Thanks to Charlemagne's littoral defences, however, the Frisian and Frankish coasts were little molested during Louis' reign.

Early in the 830s, when the emperor's sons rose up against him, Danish pirates were quick to take advantage of the inevitable weakening of the imperial defences and, whilst Louis' sons were engaged in their internecine squabbling, were able to launch a series of damaging attacks along the Frisian coast, an onslaught which culminated, in 833, in the capture and disembowelling of Dorestad, the plumpest mart in north Europe. The following year, Louis the Pious died and three of his sons, Charles the Bald, Lothar, and Louis the German, divided the empire among themselves at the Partition of Verdun.

From now on, Danish Vikings harried annually down the coasts of the three kingdoms, from the Elbe to the Garonne, pillaging such important trade centres as Rouen, Nantes and Quentovic, and making occasional lightning raids across the Channel to the south coast of England. Charlemagne's fine coastal defences were neglected and the pirates were able for the first time in a generation to romp up-river in their quest for plunder. In one year, King Horik Godfredsson sailed up the Elbe with 600 ships to sack Hamburg, whilst his most notorious subject, the redoubtable Viking Ragnar Hairybreeks, led his warriors up the Seine to assail Paris itself. Soon, the brutal assaults of these 'Wild Beasts', as one Frankish eyewitness called them, threw dwellers along the entire Atlantic littoral of western Europe, and eventually the Mediterranean, too, into a perpetual state of apprehension, and a new verse, an unbridled howl of terror, was added to the Litany: 'From the fury of the Northmen, good Lord, deliver us!'

This intensification of Danish activities in western Europe meant that the waters off southern and eastern England were now infested with pirates as seldom before, and for the people of Kent, Wessex and East Anglia, these were anxious times.

The first Danish assaults on the English coast seem all to have been directed from Viking roosts across the Channel, especially from those strategically placed in the many gullets of the Rhine. The Danes who had been granted land hereabouts by the emperor Louis and his son Lothar, in return for their aid in repelling others of their species, had rapidly reverted to type, and it was probably these Frisian-based Vikings who were responsible for the series of stabbing raids along the south coast of England from Sheppey to Cornwall that punctuated the 830s. It was not until 850, however, that a large force of Danes – possibly dispatched by the Walcheren chieftain, Rørik – established a permanent toehold on English soil when they captured and dug themselves in for the winter on Thanet, which was then an island on the Kentish lip of the Thames estuary. From here, they were able to strike up-river to fillet London and south to storm Canterbury.

Ensconced on their twin eyries in the throats of the Thames and the Rhine, Danes now had complete mastery over the narrow northern approach to the Channel, a position which, for a rabble of unprincipled hooligans, could hardly have been bettered.

Even before these initial assaults by Danish intruders on southern England, the Irish had been rudely introduced to the Northmen and their ungentlemanly ways when, during the ten years between 820 and 830, according to the *Annals of Ulster*: 'The ocean poured forth torrents of foreigners over Erin, so that not a harbour or landing, fort or stronghold, was without fleets of Scandinavians or pirates'. In 836 the Northmen established a fortified base at Dublin and dispatched two large fleets up the rivers Boyne and Liffey to harry Meath. Soon, other Viking garrisons were set up at Carlingford, Linn Duachail in Louth and Liam Roio.

The 'foreigners' who were pouring into Ireland were Norwegians, rather than Danes, and their coming was a part of the general westward impetus from Norway that had brought so many others of their kind to Shetland, Orkney, the Hebrides, Man and western Scotland during the preceding half century. The Northmen found Ireland a disorganised and disunited country, torn by dissenting petty kings, fat with farmland, well-placed for trade and for plundering the coasts of Scotland, Wales and western England and, most irresistible of all, studded with fine monasteries and churches that were often crammed with fabulous treasures. Small wonder that more and more of them were attracted to Ireland.

In 839 the 'Sea King', Turgeis, proclaimed himself 'King of all the Strangers in Ireland' and attempted, according to legend, to enforce the worship of Thor on the Christian Irish, defiling their sacred places and having his wife, Aud, shriek heathen incantations from the high altar at Clonmacnois. As a result of this blasphemous behaviour, Turgeis' reign was predictably short, and in 843 he was waylaid by a party of Irishmen who, on the orders of the king of Meath, drowned him in Loch Owel.

This appears to have been the signal for a general uprising throughout Ireland against the 'foreigners' and, in 847, Hákon, Þórgeirr and the 'heathen of Derry' were routed by a native force. News of this and subsequent Norwegian defeats reached Denmark and, in 850, the Danish chieftain, Gorm, hell-bent on taking advantage of the weakened position of the Norsemen in Ireland, arrived with a great fleet. Vicious fighting broke out immediately between the newcomers – called by the Irish 'Black Strangers', perhaps on account of the colour they painted their shields – and the 'White Strangers', or Norwegians, still in Ireland; wide tracts of country were laid waste in the ferocious brawling that followed. When the Norwegians sprung an attack on Gorm's fleet as it lay in Carlingford Lough, the Danes invoked St Patrick, patron saint of Ireland, and won the day.

For a year or so it seemed as if Gorm and his Danes would be the masters in Ireland, but their suzerainty was effectively snuffed by the coming from Norway of Olaf the White, who brought with him so formidable a force that Gorm and his followers fled to Wales, leaving the remainder of the Vikings in Ireland, Black and White Strangers alike, to submit to Olaf, who, it appears, rapidly extended his rule to take in the Vikings roosting in the firths of west Scotland and on the Hebrides and Man.

There were, however, renegades in Ireland, notably the Gall-Gael, a godless rabble of mixed Irish and Scandinavian parentage, who refused to kowtow to the new paramount Viking chief, and it took Olaf the best part of three years to bring the most recalcitrant of them all, one Ketill Finn, to heel at Munster. During the brief peace that followed, the ports that the Northmen had established around the coasts of Ireland – Dýflin (Dublin), Hlymrekr (Limerick), Veisufjǫrðr (Wexford), Vatnafjǫrðr (Waterford), and Víkingaló (Wicklow) – prospered and grew fat on trade, for the Ostmen (N: *austmenn* = eastmen – their name is remembered at Oxmantown, now a suburb of Dublin) as the Scandinavians came to be known in Ireland, were as skilled in the arts of commerce as they were as fighters and mariners.

In England, by contrast, the Viking menace was about to take a turn for the worse. In 860, three sons of Ragnar Hairybreeks – Halfdan, Ubbe, and Ivar the Boneless – arrived unheralded in East Anglia at the head of what the *Chronicle* describes as a *mycel hæþen here* (great heathen army) which, although its numbers may not have exceeded a thousand men, turned out to be a singularly aggressive and well-disciplined force.

Although it is unnecessary, for the particular purpose of this survey, to give a blow-by-blow commentary on the encounters between the English and the *mycel here*, to catalogue the names of its leaders and to plot in detail its erratic movements across the map of England, it would be well to remind ourselves of the most significant events that took place during the fifteen-odd years when this force was active, for they were to culminate in the colonisation by the Danes of extensive tracts of northern and eastern England and, consequently, in the first implanting on English soil of the Norse language.

Precisely what brought this Danish force to England can only be guessed at. Scandinavian tradition has it that the sons of Ragnar had come to avenge their father who had recently been captured whilst on a raid to Northumbria and foully put to death in a snake pit by Ælla, unlawful ruler of that kingdom. 'The porkers', the old Viking is reputed to have howled as he lay dying of multiple adder bites in Ælla's pit, 'would grunt if they knew the fate of the boar!'

The 'porkers' – his sons – did more than merely grunt when they heard the news of their father's death. After wintering in East Anglia, they acquired horses and, side-stepping the Fens, struck north through Lincolnshire towards York, capital of Northumbria.

Having achieved their mission of revenge – which they did by 'carving the blood eagle' on Ælla's back – and having secured the submission of the people of Deira, the sons of Ragnar led the 'host' south into the Midland kingdom of Mercia. For the next fifteen years, this remarkably cohesive and well-organised body of warriors crossed and recrossed England at considerable speed, spreading terror before them and dragging in their wake an ugly swath of carnage and destruction.

From Nottingham, their initial Mercian base, they turned back to East Anglia (whose king, Edmund, was brutally murdered on the orders of their sadistic chieftain, Ivar) before proceeding, with unbridled savagery, to despoil the countryside. In the spring of 870, Halfdan led them on the first of many thrusts into Wessex, richest but, as they soon learned, best defended of the English kingdoms. Driven from Wessex by King Ethelred and his younger brother Alfred, the Danes returned to London, extorted geld and, next spring, moved north to a new base at Torksey in Lindsey. From here they stormed Mercia, whose king fled before them and left them free to set up a puppet governor, Ceolwulf, to rule from Repton on their behalf.

Halfdan next led part of the *here* into Bernicia, northernmost Northumbria, where, having exchanged blows with the Picts and the Strathclyde Welsh, he established Danish overlordship in the Tyne region and retired to Ireland, where his brother Ivar, who now ruled as 'King of all the Northmen in Britain and Ireland', was feverishly tearing open prehistoric tumuli in his insatiable quest for treasure. Those of Halfdan's henchmen who remained in Northumbria now laid down their axes and set about 'ploughing and making a home for themselves'. This was the first permanent settlement of Danes in England.

Another portion of the *here* moved south from Repton to Cambridge and it was from here that their chieftain, Guthrum (N: Guðþormr), led them on a rampage that carried them, in the spring of 875, as far into Wessex as Wareham in Dorset. Alfred, now king in Wessex, was there to meet them; the ships that had been dispatched from Ireland to reinforce them were dispersed in a storm off Portland

Head and Guthrum was forced to give up hostages to Alfred and agreed to leave his kingdom for good and all. True to form, however, the Vikings broke their word; sidestepping Alfred's army in the dark, they slipped away to Exeter, where, sheltered by the town's stout defences, they were able to winter. The following spring, harassed by Alfred and with their supply lines cut, they had no alternative but to capitulate and allow themselves to be herded north to the Mercian border under heavily-armed escort. Once in Mercia, they split into two detachments, one remaining under Guthrum at Gloucester, the other turning back to take possession of the parts of eastern Mercia now embraced by the counties of Leicester, Nottingham, Lincoln and Derby.

At midwinter 878, Guthrum's section of the *here* slipped out of Gloucester and made a final attempt to overrun Wessex. Although their numbers were far fewer than when they had reached Wareham and Exeter the previous summer, their arrival caused widespread panic in the south-west and they were able to penetrate Somerset with little opposition.

Alfred now withdrew into the swamps of Athelney, to which fastness fighting men from all over Wessex streamed to his side. In the spring of 879, Alfred was strong enough and confident enough to come out of this lair and engage the Danes at Edington, a few miles south of their winter quarters at Chippenham. A sea-force under Ubbe Ragnarsson, fresh from viking in Wales, attempted to reach Guthrum through Devon, but was turned about at Countisbury Hill. Alfred routed the Danes at Edington and, after the battle, had Guthrum baptised into the Christian faith. The *mycel here*, or what was left of it, now withdrew under escort to East Anglia, whence a substantial number of Guthrum's warriors left to join others of their kind on a plundering spree that carried them down the Rhine as far as Cologne.

Many of Guthrum's henchmen, however, chose to remain in England. In 886 a treaty was drawn up between Alfred and Guthrum at Wedmore in which the Danish leader swore to confine the activities of his followers to the parts of England lying east of Watling Street and north of the Thames – an area later known as the 'Danelaw', for it was here that Danish, as opposed to Saxon, law and custom came to prevail – and to leave the kingdom of Wessex undisturbed. The districts where Guthrum's followers settled are still liberally freckled with Danish placenames and, although many of these certainly date from a much later period than the original *landnam* (settlement), they give a fair indication of the density of Scandinavian colonisation in the east Midlands and East Anglia. The distribution of these names clearly indicates that the Danes, far from displacing the established Anglian population from the best farmlands, found themselves homes in less favourable, more sparsely populated areas, such as the thin-soiled flanks of the Lincolnshire Wolds and the low bottomlands of Kesteven and the Wreak valley in Leicestershire.

The two thousand wholly Scandinavian placenames that have so far been identified in England obviously reflect a far more substantial settlement than that which can have been effected by the disbanded Danish armies of invasion. The *mycel here* is now estimated to have been composed of barely a thousand warriors, many of whom did not settle in England after Edington but moved on to Ireland or back to the Continent. Moreover, the distribution patterns of the Scandinavian parish names themselves imply, in certain parts of the Danelaw, movements of colonists pressing inland from the Lincolnshire coast and the Humber estuary rather than radiating outwards from the Danish garrisons at Lincoln and Nottingham. The impression of large influxes of newcomers crossing from Denmark after the cessation of hostilities between Alfred and Guthrum – although based on little but placename evidence – seems perfectly valid. Indeed, it is only by postulating such an influx that we can account for the thick blanketing of Scandinavian names in, for example, Lindsey, which, in the late ninth century, 'assumed the character rather of a Danish province than of an English shire' (Rev G. S. Streatfield, *Lincolnshire and the Danes*, 1883, p. 7).

Although the most conspicuous social difference between the parts of England granted by Alfred to Guthrum's disbanded armies and the remainder of the country was the fact that a Danish legal system eventually replaced its English counterparts in the Danelaw, other distinctively Scandinavian institutions were soon established in the north and east Midlands. Here, a Danish monetary system, based on the *øre* and the *mark*, was to prevail, as were Danish measures of land, including *oxgangs* and *ploughslands*, such administrative districts as the *wapentake* and, in Yorkshire and Lindsey, the *thirding* (later Riding), and the governing of such districts by jarls and their twelve *lǫgmenn* or lawmen.

FIG. 5. Counties whose minor administrative districts are called by the Scandinavian term 'wapentake' instead of, or as well as, the native 'hundred'.

After Wedmore, Alfred took no further chances with the Danes.
He kept a weather eye on those in the Danelaw, built fortresses at
strategic points throughout his kingdom, improved his navy until it
was efficient enough to intercept several subsequent attempted
Viking raids, and when, in 892, two large fleets fresh from marauding
in the Mediterranean landed in Kent and struck inland towards
Wessex, his levies were ready for them. The leader of this new invasion
was Hásteinn, a bullyboy of Bjørn Ironside, yet another of the many
sons of Ragnar Hairybreeks, and his exploits were well known to
those of Guthrum's Danes who had lately settled in England. Many
of these now broke faith with Alfred and hurried to swell the ranks of
Hásteinn's invading army. Alfred's previous encounters with the

Danes, however, had familiarised him with both their tactics and their weaknesses. For four years his armies dogged and grappled with an assortment of fast-moving Danish forces across the south and centre of England from Exeter to Thames-mouth and west again to the Welsh marches. The fighting was ferocious and protracted, but each successive attempt by the Danes to overrun Wessex and Mercia was frustrated and, after suffering a series of crippling and decisive defeats at Alfred's hands, they finally gave up all hope of conquest and dispersed, some to Northumbria, others to East Anglia, but the bulk across the Channel to Normandy.

Whilst Alfred and the kings of English Mercia were attempting to contain the Danes in the eastern parts of England, Scandinavian kinsmen of these untrustworthy colonists, the bulk of them from Norway, were intensifying their activities in the northern and western extremities of the British Isles.

In this westward overspill from Norway, the Orkney and Shetland archipelagoes played the part of stepping-stones as, somewhat later, did the Hebrides, called by the Northmen *Suðreyjar*, the Southern Isles, to distinguish them from *Norðreyjar*, the Northern Isles of Orkney and Shetland. The proportion of Scandinavian settlers in the Hebrides had been growing rapidly since the islands were first visited by the Northmen, probably in the 780s and 790s, so much so that they had come to be known to the mainland Scots as *Innsi Gall*, the islands of the foreigners. By Shetland, Orkney and the Hebrides, the Norwegian homeland was linked, albeit tenuously, with the Viking outposts in Ireland and on Man.

Although the earlier settlers on the Scottish isles and along the ragged western fringe of the mainland were, for the most part, peaceful, law-abiding folk, they were joined from about 850 onwards by newer immigrants of a less docile breed – outlaws, robbers and malcontents, amongst them a number of Norwegian chieftains who, together with their often sizeable retinues, had struck 'West over Sea' to escape the tyrannical rule of the crusading Christian king, Harald Fairhair. The constant viking of these exiles along the coasts of Norway eventually goaded Harald into action and he sailed to Scotland with a large war fleet and proceeded to quell the 'Island Beardies' (N: *eyjarskeggjar*) in a most decisive fashion.

Before leaving Scotland, Harald appointed as his jarl in Orkney one Rǫgnvald, who straightaway handed over control of the islands to his brother, Sigurðr. It was this Sigurðr who, in the company of Þórsteinn the Red, a scion of the old Hebridean Viking, Ketil Flatnose, began, in King Harald's name, the conquest of the northernmost Scottish mainland, opening up the area for Scandinavian colonisation. The Gaelic language, injected into Scotland from Ireland at about the time of the Anglo-Saxon landings in England, had barely penetrated the remote north-east, and the Norse that was implanted here by the Orkney landnamsmen, and which survived until the 1600s, no doubt replaced Pictish rather than Gaelic, as it had done in the Northern Isles some generations earlier.

The Scandinavian colonists in Orkney were not, it would seem, of exclusively Norwegian parentage, and one of Jarl Sigurðr's successors, his nephew Turf Einar (so nicknamed because, according to local tradition, it was he who first taught the islanders to cut peat for fuel), won himself distinction by ejecting from Orkney a nest of Danish pirates, who, under their leaders, Þórir Treebeard and Kalfr the Scabby, had been using the islands as a base. That the Scandinavian population of the Northern Isles at one time contained a Danish, as well as a Norwegian element, is also suggested by the linguistic and placename evidence presented by Dr Jakobsen.

Early in the tenth century, both western Scotland and north-west England received substantial influxes of Scandinavian settlers from Ireland, whence the Vikings had been driven after the Irish capture of Dublin. A large proportion of these newcomers were evidently Gall-Gaels, halfbreeds of Irish/Norse extraction, and they settled densely along the west coast of Scotland – bequeathing their name to the district of Galloway. Those who arrived in the English north-west, under their leader Ingimundr, obtained permission from the Lady Æþelfled, daughter of Alfred the Great, to settle near Chester – a not altogether wise concession, for they were to prove a troublesome brood.

During the years following the treaty between Alfred and Guthrum and the ejection of Hásteinn, Æþelfled and her brother, Edward, had been gradually and systematically reclaiming those parts of east and central England ceded to the Danes. The colonists were nowhere extirpated, they seem to have offered scant resistance to the reclamation of their lands, and their absorption into the fabric of the English nation appears to have taken place without undue violence. By 921, following the defeat by Edward of Jórik Guthrumsson, Danish overlord of East Anglia, almost the whole of England was back in native hands.

England's Danish population, who had almost entirely abandoned their predatory ways to become diligent husbandmen, now stood to suffer as much from any further Viking irruptions as did their Anglian neighbours, and it is hardly surprising that the arrival in Yorkshire of a powerful force of Dublin Vikings under Rǫgnvald caused the inhabitants of eastern England, Angles and Danes alike, to take up their weapons and rally to King Æþelstan's side.

The Norwegians based in Ireland had recovered from the defeat that had caused many of their fellows to emigrate to England and Scotland at the turn of the century, and a powerful Scandinavian dynasty had reestablished itself in Dublin. The Vikings from this quarter who had begun to attempt the reconquest of Northumbria were abetted, not only by the Scots and the Strathclyde Welsh, but also by those of their Norse and Irish kinsmen who had settled in north-west England less than twenty years previously.

Rǫgnvald took York, where he ensconced himself as king, and on his death left the throne to his son, Sigtryggr the Mad. Sigtryggr's successors, however, Guðrøðr, Olaf Kvarán and Erik Bloodaxe, were each ejected from York and by the middle of the tenth century the whole of Northumbria was in English hands again, enabling the new king, Edmund, to proclaim himself 'King of all England and ruler of the islands and the Sea Kings' (i.e. the Scandinavian petty chieftains).

Another hundred years were to pass before the Norwegians made a final bid to reinforce their rule in Northumbria; this, however, was even less successful than previous attempts and Harald Hardráði, King of Norway, was defeated at Stamford Bridge a few days before his vanquisher, Harold Godwinson, himself lost life and kingdom to the Normans at Senlac Field. But this is jumping far ahead.

The relatively untroubled conditions that characterised Edgar's reign and earned him the nickname of 'The Peaceful' were shortlived. Early in the reign of his successor, Æþelred – whom men were later to call 'Unræde', the unprepared – Viking fleets began once more to molest the southern coasts of Wessex from Dorset to Cornwall, and in 991 a fleet of ninety-three warships arrived in Essex direct from Denmark under the veteran Varangian, Olaf Tryggvasson. Æþelred's levies were routed at Maldon and, many hundredweight in geld the wealthier, the invaders swaggered north towards York. On their march through the Danelaw, they were joined by large numbers of second- and third-generation Danes, many of them descendants of the men of the *mycel here* who had come here with Halfdan and Guthrum; this act of treachery so incensed Æþelred that he ordered the massacre of all the foreigners outside the Danelaw. This impetuous, and wholly characteristic, act was to bring the direst of consequences on Æþelred, for one of the victims slaughtered in the pogrom was none other than Gunnhildr, sister of the Danish king, Sveinn Forkbeard.

King Sveinn, receiving the news of his sister's murder at his court at Jelling in Jutland, was stung into action, and during the winter of 1007 assembled a great fleet of warships which he led to East Anglia the following spring. Sweeping inland, the Danes axed and burned their way across country, ransacking every village and town that would not accede to their demands for geld.

In 1009, reinforcements from Denmark arrived at Sandwich under the renowned Jomsvíking, Þórkill the Tall and his Norwegian comrade-in-arms, Olaf the Stout. They entered the Thames where, finding their passage blocked by London Bridge, they bodily dismantled this obstruction and thrust up river to eviscerate Oxford. They encountered little resistance other than that offered them by the mettlesome Ulfkel Snilling, himself of Danish stock, whose East Anglian levies were quite unable to stem the invaders' momentum.

Þórkill's unexpected desertion to Æþelred, whose bodyguard he became, doubtless influenced King Sveinn in his decision to step up the attacks on England; he invaded Northumbria again, scorched what was left of Oxford and took Winchester, the old Wessex capital, by storm. In 1014 – the year in which Brian Boru finally broke the Norse stranglehold on Ireland by defeating the Vikings, under the Orkney jarl, Sigurðr the Stout, at Clontarf – Sveinn Forkbeard died at Gainsborough. Æþelred, who had fled to France at the height of

OPPOSITE: Replicas of twin golden horns found at Gallehus in South Jutland. The horns are believed to date from the early fifth century AD – the time of the Anglian migration from South Jutland to England. The language of the runic inscription on the left-hand horn is a form of Gothonic so archaic that it may be regarded as ancestral either to English, the Scandinavian languages, or both. It was this common base that would, some five centuries and more later, facilitate the fusion of English and Norse on British soil. The inscription reads: 'Ek HlewagastiR HoltijaR horna tawido' (I, Lægæst, made the horn of Holt).

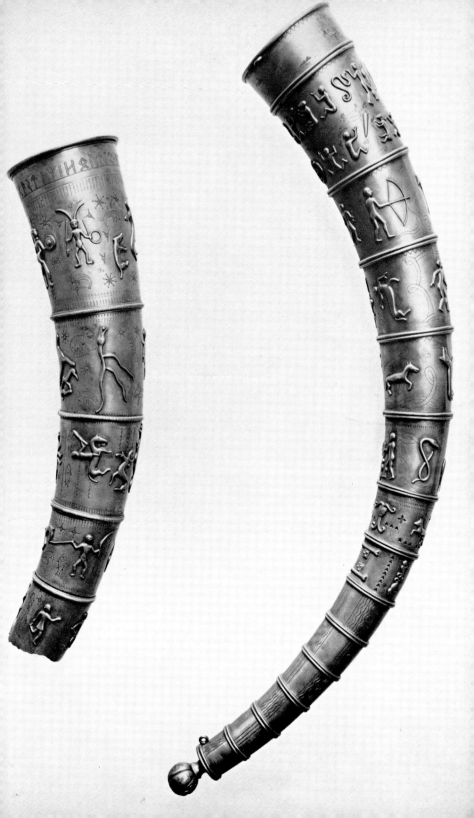

the invasion, returned briefly to deal, with malicious brutality, with the vociferous pro-Danish element in the north and east. These Danophiles were now clamouring that Sveinn's son, Canute (N: Knútr), lately driven from England on account of his youthful record of atrocities, should return from Denmark as their king.

In the high summer of 1015, Canute's fleet, mustered from all over Scandinavia, landed in the mouth of the Frome and swept almost unimpeded north through Wessex and Mercia towards York. In a matter of months, the whole country, save for London, was in Danish hands. Æþelred died in 1016 and Edmund Ironside, champion of the Londoners, offered the Danes a spirited resistance until his own defeat at Ashingdon in Essex. Although it was agreed after the battle that Edmund should hold Wessex and Canute the rest of the country, Edmund died that autumn and Canute was proclaimed king of all England. Whilst many of the rank and file of his force were paid off and returned to Scandinavia, as many elected to remain on English soil, becoming, as had their predecessors, farmers, landowners and traders – not merely in the Danelaw, but also further to the south and west.

By 1028, Canute ruled over the most far-flung empire in northern Europe, embracing England, Denmark and Norway. This *Danevæld*, however, was pitifully short-lived and, under his sons, Harald Harefoot and Hardeknud, the North Sea Empire fell apart. After Hardeknud's death at a Lambeth aleboard, and despite the threat of reinvasion from the new Danish King, Magnus Olafssøn, the English elected the half-French, half-Saxon Edward the Confessor, son of Æþelred the Unready, to rule them – although many Danes continued to hold the high positions to which they had been appointed by Canute.

This Anglo-Danish state was brought to an abrupt end by the arrival early in 1066 of William the Bastard, Duke of Normandy. After defeating Harold Godwinson's Anglo-Danish force, the Normans –

OPPOSITE: Two Scandinavian runestones referring to Viking activities in England. Although Swedish Vikings probably played a less active role than their Danish and Norwegian kinsmen in the Scandinavian campaigns in Britain, several Swedish runic inscriptions, such as this one from Orkesta in Uppland (*above*), testify to their occasional participation. The runes read: 'Ulf has taken Danegeld three times in England. The first was that which Tost gave. Then gave Thorkil [Thorkil the Tall – see p. 48]. Then gave Canute.' (*Below*) The runestone from Valleborga in Scania was raised by Sven and Thorgot 'in memory of Manne and Svenne. God will help their souls well. But they are lying over in London.'

many of whom were descended from Rolf the Ganger's Scandinavian followers who had been granted land in northern France some 140 years before – proceeded systematically and ruthlessly to bring the whole of England under their sway. The Danes in the north and east, rightly fearing that they would lose their traditional status as freemen under the Norman feudal barons, organised local resistance groups and appealed to the Danish King, Sveinn Ulfssøn, for help.

In 1069, Sveinn's brother, Asbjørn, arrived with a Danish fleet in the Humber, but was driven back within sight of York by the Norman cavalry. Although bribed by William with silver to quit the country, Asbjørn's crews remained in the Humber that winter, and many of them streamed south through Lindsey to join Hereward's resistance movement in the Ely marshes.

King Sveinn, however, doubtless realising the futility of trying to liberate his Danelaw kinsmen from the oppressors, sailed from Denmark to the Humber, where he persuaded Asbjørn to call his men out of Ely and return home.

The fate of the Danes in England was sealed. Continued resistance on the part of the Northumbrian earls, Edwin and Morcar, the latter of Scandinavian family, led to William's brutal reprisal action known as the Harrying of the North, in which large areas were depopulated and scorched black; many hundreds of free Danish peasants and their families, rather than remain on their lands as villeins under the Normans, fled north into the Lothians of Scotland.

Placename evidence suggests that much of the northern Danelaw was eventually repopulated by settlers of mixed Scandinavian/Irish parentage coming east through the Pennines from the old Norwegian colonies in Cumberland and Westmorland. Aside from an abortive attempt in 1080 on the part of the Danish King, Canute the Holy, to reclaim the Danelaw, there were no further attempts by the Danes to reestablish the lost portions of the Danevæld 'West over Sea'.

In Scotland, however, Scandinavian chieftains continued to hold sway over the islands and a portion of the mainland – although even in the erstwhile preponderately Norse areas the links with the motherland were eroding fast, only Orkney and Shetland remaining as integral parts of the kingdom of Norway. Caithness and Sutherland were gradually reclaimed by the Scottish kings and Gaelic speech spread north almost to the Pentland Firth.

Scandinavian influence in Man and the Hebrides was also ebbing and although Jarl Þórfinn the Mighty, who died the year before Hastings, was reputed to hold sway over a domain embracing all the Northern and Southern Isles and large bites of mainland Scotland and Ireland, this was almost certainly an exaggeration.

The three naval expeditions undertaken by King Magnus Barefoot to western Scotland, the Hebrides and Man reaffirmed Norwegian sovereignty 'West over Sea', but only briefly, and the belated attempt by King Hákon Hákonsson to regain a toehold in Scotland ended with the ignominious routing of his troops – first by foul weather and then by King Alexander III – at Largs. In 1266, three years after this skirmish, Hákon's son, Magnus, renounced all Norwegian claims to the Hebrides and Man. Despite this change of hands, however, certain of the Western Isles remained Norse in speech for another hundred years and more, whilst a corrupt Scandinavian vernacular seems to have persisted on Man until the early 1400s. Traditional legends and folktales – many involving actual historical personages from the period of Norse occupation, such as the chiefs of Lochlin (Norway) and Gorry (or Orry), a twelfth-century Scandinavian king of Man – have survived in Manx and Hebridean lore down to our own day.

The two northern island groups, Orkney and Shetland, remained in Scandinavian hands for a further two hundred years after Largs. They were, however, subjected throughout the fourteenth and early fifteenth centuries to the ever intensifying influence of Scots language and culture. This process began with the appointing of Scots ministers (known in Orkney as *utlendske menn* or foreigners) and continued through the period of overlordship of the Angus, Strathearn and Sinclair families – who had succeeded as governors or 'fouds' (Dan: *fogder*) from the Norse jarls as early as the 1230s. According to the history books, both island groups were pledged by Christian I, the impecunious king of Denmark and Norway, to James III of Scotland as part of the dowry of Christian's daughter, Margrethe – Orkney in 1468 and Shetland in 1469. In fact, the islands continued to be recognised as Norwegian for a full two hundred years after this transaction. Scotland's rule was understood by all parties concerned as being a purely temporary arrangement, and the contract expressly stipulated that the Scots were to make no changes to the traditional Scandinavian laws and institutions in the earldom. On three occasions after the transfer, Dano-Norwegian kings offered to pay the sum necessary to release the islands, and as late as 1667 Norway's right of ownership was acknowledged by Scotland in a document that also carried the signatures of the kings of France and England. This was the last to be heard of Orkney and Shetland's ambivalent position until early in 1968, when the discovery in the British Museum of a copy of the original 'Impignoration' – the document containing the conditions of Shetland's transfer to Scotland – reopened the question and at the same time triggered off a great deal of antiquarian polemic.

The document is said to state quite unambiguously that King Christian pledged to King James only his royal estates in Shetland, not the sovereignty of the islands. It therefore reinforces the argument that, technically, Shetland has never been a possession of the Scottish crown. Christian's habit of referring in the document to himself and his successors as Kings of Norway (not of Denmark), however, makes somewhat equivocal the question of which of these two Scandinavian kingdoms has the right of redemption. Despite its intrinsic fascination, this obscure historical problem has little bearing on the fortunes of the old Scandinavian vernacular in the Northern Isles; the story of the disintegration of the 'Danska Tongue' – as it was called in Orkney – will be recounted in some detail in the next chapter. All we need note at this juncture is that, some four hundred years after the transfer of Orkney and Shetland to Scotland, a Scandinavian idiom of West Norwegian affinity was still being spoken in some of the remoter Northern Islands.

Although it would be reasonable to assume that the Scandinavians, who lived in identifiable linguistic communities in Britain for almost a thousand years, must have left behind them an extensive legacy of material remains, there are in fact disappointingly few relics anywhere in British soil that can without reservation be attributed to them. This is entirely due to the fact that they had so little of cultural value or distinctiveness to offer the islanders. Unlike the Romans who preceded them, the Vikings constructed neither aqueducts nor highways; unlike the Normans who followed, they built neither castles nor permanent military fortifications. Of the dozen or so 'burhs' or earthworks that the *Chronicle* has the Danes throwing up during the campaigns of Guthrum, Hásteinn and Sveinn Forkbeard, only a dubious two, at Tempsford and Shoebury, have left any trace. Otherwise, apart from an uneven scattering of coins, weapons and other artefacts, an occasional grave-field or single barrow, half-a-dozen pagan ship burials and the odd habitation site, there are precious few visible reminders of the Scandinavians in Britain. Even the last of the grisly 'Dane's Skins' – the flayed hides of captured Vikings nailed as trophies to the doors of English parish churches – disappeared more than a hundred years ago.

Elements of Scandinavian superstition and folk belief may have been woven into Highland, North Island, Manx and even Channel Island lore, though it is well-nigh impossible to disentangle such threads from their surrounding matrix. Even that most outwardly 'Viking' of British festivals, Shetland's Up-Helly-Aa, owes neither its name (which is Lowland Scots) nor its pseudo-Scandinavian trappings (grafted on to the old Antonmass by romantics last century) to the Northmen.

While it can hardly be doubted that Scandinavian practices had some effect on the legal procedures and social structuring of early medieval England (and of later Scotland and Man), there is little agreement among scholars about the precise nature or extent of these influences.

As for such impalpables as the British 'commercial acumen' and 'maritime prowess', which historians delight in attributing to the Scandinavians, there is no evidence either for or against such an influence.

Most difficult of all to determine is the Scandinavian contribution to the ethnic composition of the British people. Neither the classical 'Nordic' physical earmarks (blonde hair, blue eyes, long skulls and lofty stature) nor more sophisticated serological criteria have yet proved of the slightest diagnostic value to those hoping to find evidence of 'Viking blood' in Britain. Apart from certain details of their dress, and the distinctive way in which the Danish braves seem to have worn their hair, there can have been little to distinguish the Scandinavian landnamsmen from the established island stocks with which they were so completely integrated.

It must, in short, be ruefully admitted that any material, cultural, biological or other tangible evidence of the Scandinavians in Britain is extremely meagre, and it is only by turning to the languages and placenames of the British Isles that we find abundant and unambiguous proof of their presence 'West over Sea'.

Three

The Norse invasion of the languages of Britain

The Norse language was spoken in various parts of the British Isles for a thousand years and more, of this there can be no doubt. In Shetland and Orkney, Scandinavian dialects, implanted perhaps as early as the eighth century AD, were spoken until as recently as the late eighteenth century – in Caithness until the sixteenth – whilst others survived in the Hebrides and parts of Sutherland until the thirteenth and early fourteenth centuries. A form of Norse persisted on Man until the early decades of the fifteenth century, and Norse-speaking communities were still living in the old 'Ostman' ports of Ireland when Henry II of England despatched Richard Strongbow to establish the Dublin Pale in 1169.

Elsewhere, however, it seems likely that Norse yielded to English – although not before leaving an enduring imprint on that language – at a considerably earlier date than in these peripheral northern and western areas. Indeed, the process of its absorption by English may have begun very soon after the initial landnam of Guthrum's de-mobilised Danes in the second half of the ninth century, soonest of all, no doubt, in the southern extremities of the area assigned to them by Alfred at Wedmore; hereabouts – in Essex, Hertford, Bedford, Huntingdon, Buckingham and Cambridge – and even in Rutland and west Suffolk, the Danish settlement seems to have been sparse.

Further north, in the 'Land of the Five Boroughs' (Stamford, Lincoln, Derby, Leicester and Nottingham) and in the parts of Yorkshire occupied by Halfdan's henchmen in 870, the density of Danish placenames suggests that the Scandinavian settlers must have preserved their language – as they seem to have preserved many of their native customs and institutions – in *bygds* (villages, hamlets or homesteads), where they outnumbered, or were at least equal in number to, Anglians. It is reasonable to assume that Danish 'cope-men', or merchants, who were active in commercial centres through-out the north and east (and, during the reign of Canute, throughout the entire country) carried on their transactions, both with others of their kind and with Scandinavian traders visiting ports along the Danelaw coast, in their mother tongue. Nor can it be doubted that fresh influxes from the homeland, before, during, and after the reign of Canute, must have reinforced the Danish language in certain districts.

All the same, communication between the Danes and the native English was of crucial importance and it would clearly have been an advantage for the Scandinavians living in Britain to have become bilingual as rapidly as possible. Although the *Anglo-Saxon Chronicle* suggests that some of the early raiding parties included women, these are more likely to have been captives or slaves than Viking wives from Scandinavia, and there can be little doubt that intermarriage between Danes and local Anglian and Saxon women must have begun soon after the initial Danish landwinning. This being so, the Danes would sooner or later have found it expedient to acquire at least a smattering of English for everyday purposes. The learning process need not have involved undue effort, and in the Anglian north and east, where the language was somewhat closer to Norse than was Wessex Saxon, communications between settlers and natives must have been par-ticularly simple. Perhaps not quite as simple, however, as implied in the Saga of Gunnlaugr Serpent's Tongue, where we read: 'The language in Norway and England was one and the same when William the Bastard won England'.

Scandinavians abroad have never been particularly faithful to their mother tongue, and they were probably no more so a thousand years ago than they are today. Among the European immigrants to Canada and the USA, it is the Danes, Swedes and Norwegians who are the most willing to part with their native languages. This was demonstrated most strikingly in 1934, when William A. Prescott conducted a survey of first-language usage in Baltimore; Prescott found that first- and second-generation Danes resorted to their old language only in a fifth of the situations under consideration, whereas Germans used theirs in a quarter, Poles, Czechs and Italians in half, and Greeks,

Spaniards and Ukrainians in at least two-thirds of the situations surveyed. If this is the case today, when English and the Scandinavian languages are no longer mutually intelligible, then how much easier must it have been a thousand years ago for a Danish landnamsman to switch to a language that was, in so many details, interchangeable with his own.

The disintegration of Norse in the Danelaw was doubtless further accelerated by the fact that the offspring of mixed Anglo-Danish marriages would have been much more likely to grow up speaking their mother's than their father's language, although the presence in certain districts of so many Danes certainly resulted in varieties of English that were strongly tinged with Norse accentuation and stiff with Scandinavian turns of phrase.

In the remoter north-west of England – the old Norwegian settlement area – Scandinavian speech appears to have retained its integrity for considerably longer than in the Danelaw. Its longevity hereabouts was largely due to the Norwegian settlement pattern; compared with the well-integrated Anglo-Danish communities that grew up in and around the Five Boroughs, the Norwegian fell and dale *bygds* tended to be small, isolated and self-contained. Another factor contributing to the resilience of Norse in the north-west was the relative weakness of competition from English. The anglicisation of Cumberland, Westmorland and Furness was still in its infancy at the time of the Norwegian settlements in the tenth century (the Norsemen may even have encountered a few shreds of the old 'Strathclyde Welsh' in some of the more sequestered dales) so that the process of contamination and erosion from English was insidious and protracted rather than rapid and wholesale. It is, appropriately enough, in this part of the country that we find actual written evidence, in the form of runic inscriptions, which show that the interpenetration of English and Norse was still incomplete hereabouts as late as the twelfth century.

The most significant of these inscriptions is that found over the door of Pennington church in Lancashire – both church and inscription appearing to date from about AD 1100. The runes have been transliterated as: 'Kamial seti þesa kirk. Hubert Masun uan.' (Gamal endowed this church. Hubert the Mason (or Má's son) built it.)

Another inscription, found at Carlisle Cathedral during restoration work in 1885, reads: 'Tolfihn wrait þis runar a þisi stain.' (Dolfin wrote these runes on this stone.) This inscription is believed, like that at

Pennington, to date from the early twelfth century, and the language of both inscriptions is purely Norse, as yet unsullied by contact with English.

Contemporary, or possibly slightly earlier, runic inscriptions from Yorkshire confirm that the assimilation of Norse by English had reached a more advanced stage in the Danelaw than in the north-west by the time of the Norman Conquest. Although most of the personal names in the following two Yorkshire inscriptions, the first from Kirkdale in the North Riding, the second from Aldborough in the East, are Scandinavian (Ormr, Gamal, Tosti, Hávarðr, Brandr, Ulfr and Gunvǫrr), the language itself is overwhelmingly English, with only two Norse forms, 'solmerca' and 'hanum'. Interestingly, however, no attempt was made to anglicise any of the personal names.

The Kirkdale inscription reads:

Orm Gamalsuna bohte Sc̄s Gregorius minster þonne hit wes æl tobrocan [and] tofalan [and] he hit let macan newan from grunde. Chr[ist]e [and] Sc̄s Gregorius. In Eadward dagum c[y]ng and [i]n Tosti dagum eorl. þis is dages solmerca æt ilcum tide and Haward me wrohte and Brand pr̄s.

(Orm Gamalson bought St Gregory's minster when it was all broken and fallen down and he had it renewed from the foundations to Christ and to St Gregory. In the days of Edward the King and Tosti the Earl. This is the day's sunmark (sundial) at every hour and Hávarðr made me and Brandr the Priest.)

The Aldborough inscription runs:

Ulf het aræran cyrice for hanum and for Gunware saula.

(Ulfr had the church hallowed for himself [N: *hanum*, dative of *hann* = he] and for Gunvǫrr's soul.)

A further Yorkshire inscription, from St Mary's Castlegate in York, possibly also of eleventh-century date, likewise contains Scandinavian names (Grim and Ási), although the language is otherwise wholly English:

þis mynster set[ton] ... rard [and] Grim and Æse o[n] [na]man drihtnes Hæl[endes] Christes.

(...rard and Grim and Ási endowed this minster in the name of the Lord Saviour Christ.)

The inscriptions from Harrogate, Skelton-in-Cleveland, Thornaby-on-Tees and Bingley, all in Yorkshire, are, although written in

Scandinavian runic characters, too fragmentary to decipher. On the Harrogate example, for instance, only the sequence '...suna s...' can be made out, whilst the Norse conjunction *ok* (and) is the only legible word in the Skelton specimen.

The eleventh-century comb case found at Lincoln, bearing the Norse inscription 'kamb kothan kiari Thorfastr' (Thorfast makes a good comb), is believed not to have been made in England – it is more likely a Danish import – whilst the inscription on a memorial slab (plate p. 68) formerly in St Paul's churchyard, London, and dating from about 1030, almost certainly commemorates two Danes, possibly 'Butsecarls' or members of the Danish commercial community that flourished in London during the reign of Canute. It reads: 'Gina leta stin þensi auk Toki' (Ginne and Toke had this stone set up). The single vowel of *stin* (stone) adds weight to the supposition that this inscription was the work of Danes rather than Norwegians,

FIG. 6.   An early example of Danish advertising? The bone comb case from Lincoln.

whose variety of Norse preserved the diphthong EI – as, for example, in the 'stain' (N: *steinn* = stone) of the Carlisle inscription mentioned above.

A post-Conquest date (*c* 1073) has also been given to the magic formula against 'matter in the veins' that was jotted in runic characters in the margin of an ecclesiastical document from Canterbury (plate p. 68). The language is pure Norse and reads: 'Gyril sarþuara. Far þu nu, funtin is tu. þur uiki þik, þarsa trutin, Iyril sarþuara' (Gyril Wound-stirrer. Vanish at once, thou hast been discovered. Thor slay thee, Gyril Wound-stirrer, thou lord of the ogres). Neither the Scandinavian language nor the invocation to the most popular of the heathen gods need surprise us unduly. To judge from the many hundreds of Scandinavian personal names listed in early medieval monastic registers, large numbers of Danes were members of religious communities in Britain, and it is logical to assume that, where there were many of them under one roof, they would continue to converse together in their mother tongue. In this way, Norse may conceivably have been kept alive longer in the monasteries than out in the Danelaw countryside. As for the curse 'Thor slay thee', here uttered by a churchman, it would be perfectly natural for the name of Thor, last of the old pagan gods to be forgotten, to be preserved in such an imprecation. 'Thor slay thee' would, at this time, when the memory of the old gods was still fresh in the minds of those whose grand-fathers had venerated and feared them, have been even more forceful an oath than one invoking the Devil of Christian belief.

Although it seems likely that, by the time of the Norman Conquest, the variety of Norse implanted in the Danelaw had almost completely lost its structural integrity, it is equally reasonable to assume that the assimilation by English – more specifically by the north-east Anglian dialects – of most, if not all, of the large body of Scandinavian lexical elements that begin to occur, from the mid-eleventh century on, in English contexts, was now complete.

It is of course impossible to pinpoint with any precision the moment when Scandinavian terms first began to be adopted by the English. Few, if any, can have been borrowed during the pre-settlement phases of the Danish invasion, when forces such as those led by Guthrum and the sons of Ragnar moved rapidly about the land. Indeed, the only Norse words to appear in the *Anglo-Saxon Chronicle* during the eighth, ninth and tenth centuries were the names of the important Danish leaders – and even these are either anglicised (e.g. Hinguar for Ívarr, Halfdean for Halfdanr, etc.) or Latinised (e.g. Hastingus for Hásteinn). It was probably not until the latter part of the ninth century, after Guthrum's ex-warriors had taken land and wives between the Welland and the Tees, that the invaders and the natives were on terms permanent and intimate enough to allow the reciprocal exchange of lexical items to take place.

The adoption of large quantities of Scandinavian terms by English – as reflected in eastern and northern Middle English texts from the 12th century onwards – is an unambiguous indication of the extremely close relationship that rapidly grew up between the speakers of Norse and of Anglian. It seems that, just as the Danes who took land in predominantly Anglian areas found it necessary for practical purposes to acquire some English, so there must have been other districts – especially parts of Lincoln and Yorkshire – in which the immigrant

Danish population was large enough and socially important enough to necessitate the acquisition by the local English of at least the rudiments of the settlers' language.

Be this as it may, few demonstrably Scandinavian words seem to have found their way into vernacular English texts until after *c* 1016, and the items that do occur prior to that date refer to specifically Danelaw concepts, such as various familiar kinds of Scandinavian vessel (*barða, cnearr, floege, scegð*), units of currency (*ōran, marc*), social grades (*dreng* = warrior, *hold* = a high-ranking Danelaw official, *liesing* = a freedman, *bonda* = a farmer), administrative divisions (*wæpentæc* = wapentake – a unit corresponding to the native hundred – and *socn* = a type of estate) and, most frequent of all, legal terms (*hamsocn* = housebreaking, *sacleas* = innocent, *withermal* = defence, and *stefnan* = to summon). The fact that so few of these terms are attested from Denmark itself has been attributed to the retention by the Danes in England, isolated from their fellows in the old country, of archaic terms that had become obsolete in Scandinavia itself by the time of the earliest medieval vernacular records there. This situation is identical to the survival in North America of earlier English terms that have long since passed out of common use in the mother country.

Of the handful of Norse terms recorded in English texts prior to 1016, only the following have survived to our own time: *husband, fellow, thrall, outlaw, husting, wrong, call,* the verb *to egg* (meaning 'incite') and – most significant of all – *law*, which appears to have ousted its native English equivalent, *æ*, from our vocabulary at a very early date. The Norse prototype of the English *law* was **lagu*, a very archaic form of what later became, in the literary Old Icelandic of the sagas, *lǫg*, as a result of a process known as 'U Mutation'. The presence of the unmutated form, *lagu*, in early English adds weight to the supposition that U Mutation may not have been particularly characteristic of the variety of Norse carried to the Danelaw. Indeed, documentary evidence in early medieval texts from the Scandinavian motherland confirms that this development was much less widespread in Denmark and southern Sweden – the area from which the bulk of the Danelaw colonists hailed – than in Norway and Iceland (compare Old East Norse: *allum mannum* = to all men, with Old West Norse: *ǫllum mǫnnum*).

Unfortunately for our purpose, almost all the surviving documents in Old English dating from before the eleventh century are of southern and western provenance, and texts from the north and east of the country, where Scandinavian influence was strongest, are scarce. The once flourishing and highly productive literary tradition of Northumbria had been almost completely snuffed by the coming of the Vikings in the eighth century.

During the late eleventh and the first half of the twelfth century a further thirty-odd Scandinavian terms appear for the first time in vernacular manuscripts, and of these, about half the total number have survived to our own time: the nouns *knife, root, rag, score, snare, skin,* and *haven,* the verbs *die, hit* and *take,* the adjective *crooked* and the personal pronoun *they* (with its accusative and genitive forms, *them* and *their*) which appears to have spread fairly rapidly from the Danish areas towards the south and west, eclipsing, as it went, the native forms *he, hem* and *hire.* The triumph of the Scandinavian form is almost certainly due to the fact that the native equivalent was close enough to the third person singular pronoun (*he,* masculine, *heo,* feminine, *him* and *her,* accusative) to be confused with it. The corresponding Norse paradigm *they, them, their,* provided, by contrast, a most acceptable alternative, with which it was impossible to confuse *he, him* and *her.*

In due course, some of these Norse borrowings elbowed their native equivalents out of the English vocabulary, *die* replacing *swelt, skin* replacing *fell, root* replacing *wyrt* and *take* replacing *nim.* More terms referring to specifically Danelaw concepts also made their appearance at this time, e.g. *lithsman* = a warrior, *huscarl* = a member of the king's *hird* or bodyguard, *hofding* = a chieftain, *fylcian* = to marshal, *manslot* = the portion of land allotted to the head of a family, *sceppe* = a measure of grain, and *tapor-æx* = a small hand axe – a term borrowed by Varangians in Russia and later brought by the Vikings to England.

From the middle of the twelfth century onwards, texts from the north and east become increasingly common and most of these contain substantial numbers of Scandinavian terms hitherto unattested in written English. From now on, even manuscripts from the south and west begin to have their share of Norse expressions, which presumably drifted south from the Danelaw – although these southern texts cannot, of course, be regarded as such rich repositories of Nordicisms as can those from further north.

The terms *both* and *till* are first attested at this time from the *Peterborough Chronicle*, *birth* soon follows in the *Hymns of St Godric*, and *gape*, *cast* and *want* occur, in the company of many others that have long since fallen by the wayside, in the legends of Saints Katherine, Margaret and Juliana.

The Lincolnshire writer, Orm, used some 120 words of indisputably Scandinavian origin in his *Ormulum*, and of those which have come down to us may be cited: *anger*, *awe*, *aye*, *bait*, *band*, *bloom*, *boon*, *bound*, *bull*, *flit*, *fro*, *gain*, *guest*, *hail*, *ill*, *kid*, *kindle*, *loft*, *low*, *meek*, *raise*, *root*, *scare*, *scathe*, *skill*, *sleuth*, *though*, *thrive*, *till*, and *wing*, besides dozens of others – many of which are still used in the regional dialects of the north and east. Some of Orm's terms, such as *rad* (afraid), *leyten* (to seek), *occ* (and), *rowst* (voice), *ros* (praise), *sum* (as), *ro* (peace), *usel* (wretched), *gal* (mad), *skil* (to divide) and *allesamen* (altogether), although nonsensical to most Englishmen, are instantly recognisable to a Dane.

The composer of the *Lay of Havelok the Dane* – the legend of the founding of Grimsby – was, like Orm, a Lincolnshireman, and his English was similarly stiff with Danish terms. Indeed, there are passages in *Havelok* that are almost as Danish as they are English:

'Bernard *stirt* (leaped) up, that was ful *big*,
And *cast* a *brinie* (mail coat) on his *rig* (back).'
'Slo mine *sistres* with hise *hend* (hands).'
'Hwen he *felede* (put to flight) hise foos,
He made hem *lurken* and crepen in *wroos* (corners).'
'*Dreng* (free tenant in the Danelaw) and thayn, kniht and *bondeman* (peasant farmer) and *swain*.'

Havelok and the *Ormulum* were composed in the very heart of the old Danelaw, an area where, because of the dense Scandinavian settlement, we should naturally expect an abundance of Norse terms to have been assimilated into the local variety of English. But even away from the north and east, more and more words of unambiguously Norse derivation were finding their way at this time into the general English vocabulary. Laghamon (whose name is the Norse *Lǫgmaðr* = lawman) composed his *Brut* in the late twelfth century dialect of Worcestershire, and it was he who first committed to writing the Norse *leg* and *Thursday* in place of the corresponding English *shank* and *Thundersday*, whilst Chaucer, a fourteenth-century Londoner, made use of some twenty-five Scandinavian words in his *Canterbury Tales*. It is in Chaucer's 'Nonnes Prestes Tale' that we meet the adage 'Wommennes conseils ben ful ofte colde', which may be the sole example in English of the retention of an old Scandinavian proverb. It appears to have been calqued on the Norse 'Kǫld eru kvenna ráð', and mirrors both the Danish 'Koldt er altid kvinde raad' and the Norwegian 'Så kalle er kvennerå'.

From the thirteenth century onwards, dozens of fresh Norse words begin to sprinkle the English texts, often at the expense of their native counterparts. Thus the Scandinavian *cast* triumphed over the English *werp*, *neck* over *halse*, *window* over *eyethirl*, *sister* over *swester*, *anger* over *ire* and *cut* over *snith*. Sometimes, the native and Scandinavian forms have survived side by side in such doublets as craft/*skill*, sick/*ill*, rear/*raise*, whilst, at an earlier period, it was possible to witness two synonymous terms – one Norse, the other English – jostling for position for many generations until one or the other passed out of use. This happened to the English *bā*, which, after a protracted struggle, was finally jostled out of our vocabulary by its Scandinavian equivalent, *both*.

There were, of course, plenty of instances in which it was the Scandinavian form that was usurped; *naken*, for example, was eventually reovertaken, even in the most heavily Nordicised dialects, by the English *naked*, *haithen* by *heathen* and *stern* by *star*. In the north and east, however, where Norse influence was strongest, it is still possible to hear the Scandinavian, rather than the English, forms of a whole range of commonplace terms; in parts of Scotland and the English north country, for example, *grass*, *worse* and *goat* are pronounced 'gress', 'waur' and 'gait' to this day.

Occasionally, a native term, while retained intact, acquired a new meaning through the influence of its Scandinavian counterpart. Our words *bread*, *bloom*, *dream*, *dwell*, *gift*, and *plough*, for example, although thoroughly English in derivation, no longer mean the same as they did before the coming of the Vikings. In Old English, they signified a fragment, a mass of metal, joy, to make a mistake, a dowry and a measure of land respectively; their present meanings are those of the Norse: *brauð*, *blóm*, *draumr*, *dvelja*, *gipt* and *plógr*.

Eorl (earl), too, which signified a minor official in pre-Scandinavian Britain, was later upgraded as an obvious result of its kinship with the Norse *jarl*, meaning a highborn nobleman. Occasionally, a Norse term would survive in anglicised garb: the verb *shift*, for example, began life as the Norse *skipta*, whilst Norse *þjónusta* (service), *tíþandi* (news) and *brúðhlaup* (wedding) became, in Middle English, *theonest*, *tithende* and *brydlop* respectively.

The transition from the English to the Norse form of a word common to the two languages must often have caused confusion, especially when the Norse form was still in the process of eclipsing its English counterpart. There was, for example, a time when the Norse noun *egg*, imported to London from the Danelaw, was used side by side with the native *ey* – some speakers favouring one form, some the other. William Caxton, writing as late as 1490, recounted an amusing anecdote in this very connection. A north-country merchant named Sheffield goes into a London shop to buy some eggs, but the 'good wyf' can make no sense of his request and 'answerde that she coude speke no Frenshe. And the merchaunt was angry, for he also coulde speke no Frenshe, but wolde haue hadde egges and she vnderstode hym not. And thenne at last a nother sayd that he wolde haue eyren. Then the good wyf sayd that she vnderstod hym wel. Loo, what sholde a man in thyse dayes now wryte: Egges or Eyren?'

It was, incidentally, in Caxton's day that two Scandinavian inflections of the present tense of the verb to be – *thou art* and *they are* – reached London from the Danelaw on their way south and west. It says a great deal for the continuing influence of Norse that such intimate structural items as these were able to usurp their native equivalents (*thou bist* and *he sind*) in districts far removed from the main Scandinavian settlement areas.

By this fairly advanced date, all but a few of the Scandinavian words that have been carried forward into standard modern English had been assimilated. The few that were still to find a place in our vocabulary (a mere trickle compared to the large number that were already established) came mostly from the dialects of the old Danelaw shires.

OPPOSITE: (*Above*) This stone from St Andreas, Isle of Man, bears a representation of Odin with one of his ravens. Other Manx crosses inscribed with figures enacting scenes from heathen Scandinavian mythology are those from Jurby, Malew, Maughold and the famous 'Thor' stone from Bride. (*Below*) Stone from Bressay, Shetland. Although the inscription (down the right-hand side), which dates from the eighth or ninth century, is in 'Pictish' Ogham characters, one term – *dattrr* – possibly represents the Norse word *dóttir* = daughter.

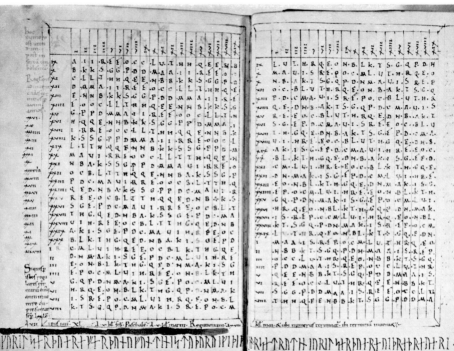

In the sixteenth century, *batten, scrag, wad, slag, skit, snag, scuffle, simper* and *snug* were admitted to literary English, where they were joined in the seventeenth century by *oaf, keg, squall, skewer,* and *smut,* in the eighteenth by *cosy* and *muggy* and in the nineteenth by *vole, nag* and *ski. Bawl, clip, slouch, slop, bungle, gawk, spud, niggle, mawkish, dowdy, gawmless, wizen* and *scrawny* are all comparative newcomers to our standard vocabulary – although they have been used for generations in the north country. They still look and sound as if they have some of the mud of the farmyard clinging to them and no one would call them elegant.

Indeed, grace and elegance are not typical of any of our Scandinavian loans; it can hardly be claimed that *big, bag, scab, scum, nasty, clumsy, odd, blink, toss* and *prod* make as great an impression on the intellect as do such classical concatenations as verisimilitude, procrastination or agoraphobia, yet what would our language be without them? We should surely miss *lump* and *muck, drip* and *drown, flit* and *fog, sniff* and *snort,* for they fit so snugly and unobtrusively into our everyday language that it is difficult to think of them as imports. As Otto Jespersen remarks, 'An Englishman cannot *thrive* or be *ill* or *die* without Scandinavian words; *they are* to the language what *bread* and *eggs are* to the daily fare'.

It is precisely because of their unassuming character that these Norse loans were for so long overlooked by scholars. Admittedly, once the presence of Scandinavian items in our vocabulary had been detected, etymologists tended, in their zeal, to identify rather more than actually existed. For example, more than a third of the 600-odd items claimed by Professor Skeat in the 1882 edition of his *Etymological Dictionary* as Norse have since proved, on further examination, to be of alternative – frequently Low German or Dutch – derivation. Nonetheless, some 400 items whose origins are incontestibly Scandinavian or whose closest affinities seem to be with forms otherwise peculiar to the northern languages, are still in daily use in standard, literary English. Now, while 400 words make up a mere fraction of the 20,000–30,000 that comprise the vocabulary of the educated English

OPPOSITE: (*Above*) Memorial plaque from Old St Paul's Churchyard, London. The inscription, which dates from about the time of Canute the Great, still bore traces of blue colouring when it was rediscovered in 1852. It is now in the Guildhall Museum (see p. 60). (*Below*) The foot of folios 123v–124 of the Cotton Manuscript, Caligula A XV, which bears a footnote (c 1075) written in runes in the Norse language (see p. 60).

speaker, it must be realised that most of these Scandinavian terms are part of the very bedrock of our lexicon and among the most frequently occurring words in colloquial English. If we add to these 400-odd Nordicisms in standard English the hundreds of others that continue to flourish in the rural dialects, we quickly arrive at a total far in excess of 2,000 items, sufficient to allow us, if we so desired, to carry on an elementary conversation using almost entirely Scandinavian forms.

By no means all the apparent northern loans in English were immediately traceable to classical Icelandic or to the modern Scandinavian standard languages. Gradually, however, the ultimately Scandinavian derivations of such bothersome items as *gaze, glint, lurk, pixy, rug, sag, slouch* and *tangle* began to be elucidated. This was largely thanks to the activities of such pioneer Scandinavian lexicographers as the Danes, Matthias Moth, Christian Molbech and Henning Feilberg, the Swedes Hof, Ihre and Rietz, and the Norwegians, Aasen and Ross, whose investigations into the peasant dialects of their respective countries revealed a wealth of hitherto unsuspected cognates between standard, archaic and provincial English and uncultivated, non-literary forms of North Gothonic.

Among the most recent of the Scandinavian loans in English are those terms that refer to specifically northern concepts, such as Norse antiquity and mythology (*saga, troll, skald, berserk, valkyrie, Valhalla, Ragnarok* – all of them lifted from Old Icelandic literature); natural and topographical features (*fiord, fjell, skerry, jokull,* (ice)*berg, floe, maelstrom, geyser*); and fauna (*auk, lemming, eider, narwhal, rorqual, elk,* the extinct *garefowl* (or great auk) and the mythical *kraken.* (*Reindeer,* however, has been a part of the English vocabulary since medieval times.) Norwegian skiing terms, such as *slalom, telemark* and *christiania* (or, more often, *christie*), have, although they are less widely known, also found a place in our vocabulary. So have the Swedish terms *dahlia* (from the botanist, *Dahl* – the plant is more often called '*georgine*' in Scandinavia), *tungsten* (*tung =* heavy + *sten =* stone), *smörgåsbord* (with or without diacritics) and *sloid* (a system of manual training, consisting of wood carving, employed in schools: the word goes back to the Norse *slægd,* and is thus identical with the English *sleight*). To the English-speaking housewife accustomed to shopping in the delicatessen, the names of such traditional Norwegian crispbreads as *flatbrød* and *knekkebrød* and of the popular *geitost* (goat cheese) are also becoming familiar. Sea-food devotees are especially likely to recognise the Norwegian *torsk* (cod), *klippfisk* (dried, or split, cod), *laks* (salmon) and *sild* (herring) from container labels, whilst a whole host of Scandinavian brand-names are well-known throughout the English-speaking world, from the various cheeses – *Danbo, Samsø, Esrom, Fynbo* and *Jarlsberg* to the famous Danish lagers, Carlsberg and Tuborg (lager, incidentally is known as *pilsner* in Scandinavia). So familiar are these last two, that one – doubtless apocryphal – anecdote tells of an English schoolboy who, when asked to name the king and queen of Denmark, replied 'King Carlsberg and Queen Tuborg'.

Somewhat less widely known are the names of certain species of bird. Such are *skua*, a name picked up by British seafarers from the Faeroe islanders, who call these birds '*skúgvar*', *loon* (or *loom* – an old Orkney and Shetland and now a North American name for the Great Northern Diver) from ON: *lómr*, and *siskin*, whose ancestry seems to have begun with the Czech *čižek* (diminutive of *čiž*). This Czech word passed into North German dialect as *Siesek* and *Siesken*, and thence into Danish as *sisken* – the form on which the English name seems to be based. Other English bird names of Scandinavian provenance (apart from *eider, auk* and *garefowl* mentioned above) are *tern* – which, with its initial 'hard' *t*- is obviously based on the modern Danish *terne* rather than the original Norse *þerna*, with its initial fricative; and, possibly, *shrike* and *erne*. In Old English, *scríc* appears as a gloss of the Latin *turdus* (thrush), although its modern 'hard' final -*k* smacks of Norse influence (compare Norwegian *skrike*, Swedish *skrika* = the jay); whilst *erne* (used in northern Britain of the white-tailed sea eagle) is more likely to reflect the Norse *ǫrn* than its Old English counterpart, *earne*.

Knot, the name of a small wading bird of the sandpiper family, has a curious history in English, and has somehow become confounded – through sound-association – with the Danish king, Knútr (or Canute) the Great. It was William Camden who seems to have recorded the earliest version. Writing in 1607, he defined the 'Knott' as 'Canute's bird, I suppose, for it is believed to fly here from Denmark'. (In fact, the knot is a regular winter visitor to Britain from the high Arctic, and is known in Denmark as the *Islandsk ryle* – Icelandic sandpiper.) Drayton, however, offered an alternative explanation, assuring us that knots were first brought to Britain 'Canute's appetite to please'. Others have sought for an explanation in the fact that knots are found on the seashore, and even that they allegedly make periodic attempts to prevent the waves from coming in by forming themselves into a tight phalanx along the surfline – just as Canute himself is supposed to have commanded the tide to cease. The association between the bird and the ancient Anglo-Danish monarch is solely one of folk-etymology – although it has even become enshrined in the knot's scientific name, *Calidris canutus canutus* – and the primal connection is more likely to be with 'gnat' and 'gnat-snap' – two provincial English names for this species.

Little known outside ornithological circles are the taxonomic, mock-classical names based on Scandinavian originals that are applied particularly to those members of the auk family which, because of their relative rarity in the Mediterranean, have no indigenous names in either Greek or Latin. The systematic names of the Guillemot (*Uria aalge*), Brünnich's Guillemot (*Uria lomvia*), the Black Guillemot (*Cephus grylle*) and the Razorbill (*Alca torda*) are all Scandinavian, although they are now part of the international language of science. *Lomvia* is based on the Danish and Norwegian name, *lomvie*; *grylle* is the Gutnish (Gotlandic) name for the Guillemot (*grissla* in standard Swedish); *aalge* is, like the generic name, *Alcidae*, merely the Swedish *alka* = auk; whilst *torda* is from the Gutnish *torda* (standard Swedish: *tordmule*). The Little Auk's specific name, *Plautus alle*, is the name given to the bird by the people of the Swedish Baltic island of Öland.

Our latest linguistic acquisition from Scandinavia is *Ombudsman*, an alternative name for the Parliamentary Commissioner. The title, borrowed from the Danes, was first used in English in New Zealand on 1 October 1962, and was adopted in Britain in March 1967. The Danish term itself had been calqued, in 1953, on the corresponding Swedish *Ombudsman*, although the word had been used in medieval Danish in the sense of 'an official appointed by the King to administrate a Herred [shire]' – whilst its Old Icelandic counterpart, *Umboðsmaðr*, likewise referred to a steward or commissary. The term is not as strange to Britain as one might suppose; the Norse word *umboð* = a stewardship, survived in Shetland and Orkney usage, in the sense of 'commission', as *Umboth, Umbith* or *Oumbotht* until the end of the sixteenth century, although the title *Umbothsmann* had passed out of the North Island vocabulary at an earlier date.

A minority of the Scandinavian loanwords in English were introduced into Britain through the agency of Norman French: *flounder* (the fish), *faggot, frown, equip, blemish, target, tryst, scutch, jolly, elope, brawl* and *waive* are a few that survive from the large number brought across by the followers of William the Conqueror.

A few Scandinavian terms have reached us by even more circuitous routes; *walrus* and *doit* (a small coin, from Old Norse: *þveit*, literally 'a piece cut off' – the origin of the English placename ingredient *thwaite*) come to us via Dutch, *knout* via Russian, and *scorbutic* through medieval Latin.

Although the number of Scandinavianisms that have found their way into standard English is impressive, the dialects of northern England and of Scotland continue to be the greatest repositories of Norse terms in Britain; the greater proportion of these terms have never been taken up by the literary language.

One of the first Danish scholars to draw attention to the large number of Scandinavian expressions in early and provincial English was Peder Hjort, whose book, *Om det engelske Konjugationssystem, med en Tillæg om Forholdet imellem Dansk og Engelsk* ('On the English conjugation system, with a supplement on the relationship between Danish and English'; 1843), contained extensive inventories of Scots and English dialect words, Chaucerian terms, etc, together with their Norse etymologies and corresponding forms in Danish.

A later list, compiled by Professor W. W. Skeat and published as an appendix to the second edition of Cleasby and Vígfússon's *Icelandic Dictionary*, filled eighty tightly packed columns; as Skeat himself confessed, however, the catalogue was 'by no means exhaustive, and it will require a careful search through the pages of the English Dialect Dictionary to do justice to the wealth of this Old Norse material'.

Worsaae, writing in 1851, observed that 'in the north of England, many words and phrases are preserved in the popular language, which are neither found nor understood in other parts, although they sound quite familiar to every Northman. These original Scandinavian terms are not only applied to waterfalls, mountains, rivulets, fords and islands, but are also in common use in daily life.... [They] are now chiefly found in the north-west of England among the remote mountains of Yorkshire, Westmorland, Cumberland and Lancashire' (Worsaae, pp. 80–81).

Again, the Norwegian-American investigator, G. T. Flom, who, in his *Scandinavian influence on southern Lowland Scotch* (New York, 1900) lists some 400 dialect terms of Norse derivation, admits that this inventory is 'probably far from complete'.

The earliest sources for Norse loans in the English dialects are, of course, medieval vernacular texts from those parts of the country where the Scandinavians had settled most densely, and documents in the Northumbrian dialect (which includes Lowland Scots) are particularly full of them. The fourteenth-century *Metrical English Psalter* swarms with Nordicisms, as do the works of the early Yorkshire poets, Lawrence Minot and Richard Rolle. A typical Rolle couplet runs: 'Thi lufe is *ay* last*and, fra* that we may it fele, Tharein make me byrn*and* that na thing *gar* it kele' (Thy love is everlasting, from that we may it feel, Therein make me burning, that nothing make it cool), with three purely Scandinavian terms and a possible Norse inflection (the gerundive suffix, *-and*).

The somewhat later alliterative poems, 'The Awntyrs of Arthur', 'The Destruction of Troy' and, especially, 'The Wars of Alexander', are also alive with Norse terminology, as are Blind Harry's 'Schir William Wallace' and John Barbour's 'The Bruce' (composed *c* 1375). The fifteenth-century Wakefield and York cycles of religious plays contain their fair share of Scandinavianisms, whilst certain passages in the medieval Scots poems of William Dunbar, Robert Henryson and Gavin Douglas are stiff with them. Dunbar's 'The Manere of the Crying of ane Playe', for instance, contains the lines:

> My forgrantschir height Fyn McKowle,
> That *dang* (smote) the Devill and *gart* (made) him *yowle*,
> The *skyis* rang quhen he wald *scowle*
> and trublit all the aire,

whilst one of the verses of Henryson's 'Robene and Makyne' runs:

> Robene ansert: 'Bi the rude,
> Na thing of lufe (love) I knaw,
> Bot keipis my scheip undir yone *wid*, (wood)
> Low qhair they *raik* on *raw*.' (wander in a row)

More recent Scots and north-country dialect writers have continued to tap this rich vein of Scandinavian expressions, and Robert Burns, for example, used dozens from his native Ayrshire dialect:

Duncan Gray cam here to woo,
Ha, Ha, the wooing o't,
On blithe Yule nicht when we were fu',
Ha, Ha, the wooing o't,
Maggie *coost* her head fu' high,
Look'd *asklent* (obliquely) and unco' *skeigh* (disdainful),
Gart (made) poor Duncan stand *abeigh* (aloof),
Ha, Ha, the wooing o't.

Apart from the five purely Scandinavian words in this verse from 'The Wooing of Duncan Gray', Burns makes use of the Scots *fu'* (full) in the same sense of 'drunk' as employed by the Scandinavian languages whilst his use of *Yule* (Christmas), a term still current in Scotland and the north of England (as in Yule clog, Yule tide, etc.), is an example of a native word (Old English: *geōl*) that was almost certainly reinforced in northern Britain by the presence of a corresponding Norse term, here: *jól*. There are several other instances from Scotland and the north of the reinforcement of native words by their Scandinavian counterparts; *bairn* (child) and *dale* (valley), for example, although of ultimately English derivation, undoubtedly owe their continued Scots and north-country usage to the influence of the Norse *barn* and *dalr*. The use in parts of Cheshire and Lancashire of the personal pronoun *hoo* for *she* (e.g. 'Th' owd tale', said hoo, an' laft her stoo' – a line from a dialect poem by Edwin Waugh) may also be due to the reinforcement of the Old English *heo* by Norse: *hón* (Norwegian: *ho*).

Scandinavian expressions sprout thickly in the dialect poems of such north-country writers as John Hartley, Ben Preston and Samuel Laycock, and in the Scots sketches and dialogues of R. L. Stephenson, J. M. Barrie, the Aberdonians George Macdonald and W. Alexander, the Galwegian S. R. Crockett, and the Edinburgh poet Robert Fergusson, and in the works of Sir Walter Scott. There are plenty, too, in Tennyson's Lincolnshire dialect verse, as in 'The Northern Cobbler', 'The Spinster's Sweet Arts', 'The Village Wife' and both the 'Northern Farmers'.

Many of the Scandinavian expressions in northern English have a wide distribution, being heard from Shetland to as far south as East Anglia and Northampton; such are: *havers* = oats, *bigg* = barley, *addle* = to earn, *clegg* = horsefly, *scarn* = cowdung, *ewer* = udder, *lea* = scythe, *skellum* = rascal, *kenspeck* = easily recognisable, *scrat* =

goblin, *howk* = to dig, *aye* = always, *ket* = carrion, *nay* = no, *toom* = empty, *steg* = gander, *mun* = mouth, *waur* = worse, *smoot* = narrow passage, *hoast* = to cough, *laithe* = barn, *ing* = meadow, *beck* = brook, and *sprot* = twigs.

The Scandinavian prepositions, *till* (to) and *fro* (from) seem almost ineradicably engrained in northern English; indeed, in many dialects which employ *till* in the locational sense (e.g. 'He's away up *till* Aunt Edna's'), the word has, in order to avoid ambiguity, been displaced in the temporal sense of 'until' by *while* ('I'll not have it ready *while* tea-time'). This northern usage of *while* has caused frequent confusion, as when notices carrying the injunction: 'Wait while the red light flashes' were recently set up by British Rail at level crossings in the north! Other dialects, however, employ the Scandinavian preposition in both its locational and its temporal sense; in Aberdeen, for example, it is by no means unusual to hear such expressions as: 'They sanna apen the kirk door *till* us *till* twal' o'clock'.

Other Scandinavianisms are much more restricted in their range: *frod* = frog, *scow* = noise, and *slem* = mud, are, for instance, now confined to parts of Yorkshire; *slood* = cart track, *glatten* = slippery, and *mawt* = moth, to Lancashire; *smere* = clover, and *gyde* = pour, to the Lake District; *skegg* = bearded oats, to Nottingham; *sniggle* = snail, and *stive* = dust, to Leicestershire; *swaul* = to gulp, to Lincoln; *kyle* = wedge, to Northumberland; and *reen* = to drop, and *scrail* = a puny creature, to Norfolk. (*Scrail* is the same as the Norse *Skraelingr*, the name given by the Northmen to the inhabitants of 'Vínland' – North America. *Skrælling* is still used in Denmark, and *skrellin* in Shetland, to signify a weakling.) Certain of these Scandinavianisms are now confined to Scotland, *risk* = to tear, *clowk* = to gurgle, *kae* = jackdaw, and *skoal* = drinking cup, being seldom heard south of the border. (Scotland, incidentally, was the only part of Britain where it was, until historically quite recently, possible to 'drink a man's *skoal*' (to drink his health) as in Scandinavia – compare Danish: *At drikke ens skaal*. Although this usage may have been popularised in 1589, when James VI was married in Norway to Anne of Denmark, the word – variously spelt *skul, skull, skoll, scoll, schole*, etc. – had been recorded in Scots in its original sense of 'drinking vessel' (N: *skál*) long before that date.)

The Ulster dialects of English – particularly those spoken in the north and east of the province, where Scots influence is marked –

abound in Scandinavianisms, although few, if any, of these are unique to Ulster. *Bouk* (belly), *shawp* (peapod), *fozy* (spongy), *gizzen* (a leaky boat), *dowf* (dull), *stroop* (gullet) and *snod* (smooth), for example, all occur again in various parts of England and Scotland. The obsolescent Ulster Gaelic appears to have bequeathed none of its Scandinavian ingredients to the modern English dialects of Northern Ireland.

A substantial proportion of the old Scandinavian terms that formerly thrived among the speakers of provincial English are now on the very threshold of extinction, and it would be difficult to find a member of even the oldest generation in the Lake District who still used – or even remembered – such expressions as *oast* = cheese curd, or *seng* = a bed (of straw).

There was a time, however, not so very long ago, when the Scandinavian component in the rural dialects of Scotland and the north was incomparably greater than it is today. To the great-great-grandparents of many of today's Yorkshire folk, pigs were *grice*, heifers *quees* and bullocks *stots*, yellow was *gool*, soft was *blowt*, large was *stor* and steep was *brant*; *bairns* would *laik* where nowadays children play, and a man would *risp* if he had a *lop* on his *rig* where today he would scratch if he had a flea on his back.

As little as ten years ago, I was astonished to hear an old Lincolnshire sexton refer to his '*forelders* as *ligs* oot i' th' *kirkgarth*' (forebears who lie out in the churchyard. Dan: Forældre [parents], som ligger ude i Kirkegården.). This old man would have been born around the 1880s, at about the time when the Rev G. S. Streatfield, Rector of Holy Trinity, Louth, was engaged in writing his *Lincolnshire and the Danes*, a comprehensive and – remembering the time when it was compiled – remarkably scientific investigation into the Norse relics – chiefly linguistic – in his county.

In Streatfield's day, rustic Lincolnshire speech was still rich in Scandinavian terminology, and a selection of the most commonly used words of Danish provenance occurs in the following extract from his chapter on 'The Lincolnshire Language'.

The *garthman* himself, by his very title, seems to bear witness to his Danish predecessors in his office. His work lies to a great extent in the *crewe-yard*, where he will be proud to show you, amongst other livestock, the *stots* (steers) and *quees* (heifers) of the establishment. As you turn from the *crew* (straw yard) you may pass the *midden* and the *staggarth* (stack yard), and should you follow him to his home of *stour* and daub, covered, it may be, with *starthack* (coarse grass used for thatching), you may hear his *bairns* ask after the *cush-cows*. If, however, we linger near the farm buildings, we may catch many other words that carry us back to the Norsemen of old, or over the sea to their descendants in Denmark. The farm lad will talk to you of the *cletch* of chickens by the *henstee* (ladder by which poultry ascend to roost) or feeding at the *lathe* (barn) door; he will call your attention to the calves *blethering* in the meadow, or show you the *kittlings* (kittens) *ligging* on the *secks* or playing in the *heck* (cattle rack). The cottage, like the farmyard, is full of these Scandinavian relics. The house-wife herself is a *heppen* (tidy) sort of body. She *addles* (earns) many a shilling besides what she saves by good management. If she is not *throng* with work, and her *bairns* are not *bealing* and *yammering* round her, she will be ready to show you her house-hold treasures. She will gladly cut you a slice from the *bread-loaf* she makes herself, and perhaps ask you to taste the cakes she has baked on her own *bakston* (iron plate for cooking muffins on), and to this she will generously add a slice from the *flick* that hangs from the *raf*. Here is the peck-*skep* in which she measures her potatoes and apples, there is the *soa* (cask) in which she keeps the milk, and yonder the *sile* (sieve) through which she *teems* (pours) it. Here is her *meal-ark* (large wooden chest), and there, *gainhand* (hardby), is the *kist* (chest) in which she keeps the *eldin* (kindling).

Then if you should chance to come across the shepherd we may find him *cledding* (covering) the *trays* (hurdles) against lambing time, because at the *fore-end* (beginning) of the year the winds are often *hask* (piercing) and *snyde* (cold). Among his flock he may draw your attention to the well-conditioned *gimbers* (two-year-old ewes). He will tell you how many sheep were lost last summer through *farwelting* (falling on their backs), how much his master *wared* (spent) in cake, and how many *tod* of wool were produced by last year's *clip*. If you go further afield you will find the same curious survivals. The *gare* (three cornered section of land which has to be ploughed in a different direction from the rest) at the head of the field, the *fleaks* (wicker hurdles) in the *gapsteads* (openings in the fence), the *moudiwarps* (moles) impaled on the blackthorn, the *gatrum* (rough by-lane) that leads from the road into the close, the cattle *rake* (pasture) upon the moor, the *screed* of grass that borders the *beck* (stream) on this side of the *car* (depression where rain water gathers) that stretches beyond it on the other; these and many other objects, by the names attached to them, most likely bear witness to the influence of the Northmen upon our provincial tongue.

Despite his sometimes over-zealous etymologising and the fact that he disregards certain Norse terms (e.g. *call* and *cake*) used in standard English, Streatfield evidently gives a reasonably accurate impression of the extent to which Scandinavian terms were still employed in farming communities in the heart of the old Danelaw some three or four generations ago.

Some twenty years before the appearance of Streatfield's book, another north-country parson, the Rev J. C. Atkinson, had compiled a *Glossary of the Cleveland dialect* (published by John Russell Smith in 1868). Scandinavian speech habits had left an even deeper imprint on the form of English spoken in this hilly and thinly populated part of the North Riding than on the folk speech of Streatfield's Lincolnshire, and Atkinson remarked in his introduction:

... it is impossible for anyone fairly familiar with the dialect spoken in Cleveland, and only moderately acquainted with the Scandinavian languages and dialects, or even with any one of them, not to be struck with the curious family likeness obtruded on his notice between no scanty portion of the Cleveland words and those in current use among the Danes, Norwegians and Swedes of our own day. And not only in the case of words – idioms, modes of expression, habitual phrases, proverbs or proverbial sayings are found to occur, which, in many cases, are so nearly identical that what is ordinarily called translation is scarcely requisite in order to enable the Clevelander to appreciate the Danish saying, or the Dane the Cleveland formula.

It is highly unlikely that the provincial speech of any part of the old Danelaw is today as replete with Nordicisms as was that of the North Riding in Atkinson's day, although some of the more sequestered dale communities of the far north and north-west of England appear to have retained a surprisingly substantial number of Scandinavian expressions right up to our own time. As recently as 1967 it was still possible for a Swedish investigator to remark of one particular West Riding dialect: 'a Scandinavian in Dentdale soon finds that the dialect is saturated with Norse words' (Bertil Hedevind, *The Dialect of Dentdale in the West Riding of Yorkshire*, Uppsala, 1967, p. 10).

Scandinavian loanwords in Britain are by no means confined to the various forms of English. When the Northmen settled here, a large proportion of the British population was still Keltic-speaking and plenty of Norse expressions found their way into these languages – although, mainly as a result of the dissimilarity between them and Norse, fewer Scandinavian terms were adopted than by English. Of the surviving Keltic languages of the British Isles, the various forms of Goidelic – Scots, Irish and Manx Gaelic – contain a great many more Scandinavianisms than does Welsh, an understandable state of affairs when we recall that permanent Norse settlements were fewer and more scattered in Wales than in the Gaelic-speaking north-west. As for Cornish, which at the time of the Viking invasions was probably still spoken over a fairly wide portion of the English south-west, the few Scandinavian terms recorded in this language doubtless found their way there at a much later date, through English.

The Isle of Man

Norse, which seems to have been spoken on the Isle of Man until as late as the 1400s, contributed a large number of terms to the local form of Gaelic (now, alas, moribund), and about a hundred of these have been carried over into the modern English dialect of the island. These include *braag* = a shoe, *dess* = a haystack, *margad* = a market, *winniag* = a window, and *skeerey* = a district, the last from *skíri*, the Norse rendering of the Old English *scíre* = a shire.

Apart from the Orkneys and Shetlands, Man has the largest concentration of Scandinavian runic inscriptions in Britain, thirty-six having been identified so far. Most of these inscriptions occur on Christian stone crosses, usually in association with reliefwork decorations depicting both Christian and heathen motifs, and most, like the following example from Kirk Michael, contain Gaelic as well as Scandinavian personal names: 'Mallumkun raisti krus þena efter Malmuru fustru sin en Tufkals kona as Aþisl ati. Betra es laifa fustra kuþan þan son ilan' (Mael Lomchon and the daughter of Dubh-Gael, whom Adils had to wife, raised this cross in memory of Mael-Muire, his fostermother. It is better to leave a good foster son than a bad son.)

Apart from Adils, all the names on this inscription are Gaelic; Dubh-Gael, incidentally, meaning 'Black Stranger', was the nickname given in Ireland to the Danes (to distinguish them from the 'White Strangers' or Norwegians), although by the time the Kirk Michael inscription was carved – probably during the twelfth century – the name Dubh-Gael (or 'Dougal' as it has since been anglicised) had no doubt lost its original ethnic connotation, and there is slim reason for supposing, as some have, that the Dubh-gael named here was necessarily a Dane.

Our second Manx runic inscription, also from Kirk Michael, reads: 'Gout cirþi þand oc Ala i Maun' (Gaut made this and Ali in Man). Here, both personal names are Scandinavian – Gaut being, in all probability, Gaut Bjarnarson, a famous runemaster and carver who is believed to have acquired his skill in northern England, where many of his most characteristic decorative motifs seem to have originated.

The final Manx example comes from St Andreas; it reads: 'Santulfr hin suarti raisti krus þana aftir Arinbiaurk kuinu sina' (Sandulfr the Black raised this cross after Arinbjǫrg, his wife).

Ireland

The Gaelic of Ireland, like that of Man, made copious borrowings from Norse, some 150 of which, including some possible placename elements, have been recorded. These Scandinavian loans doubtless found their way into Gaelic through the agency of the hybrid Hiberno/ Norse Gic-Gog jargon spoken by the Gall-Gael (see p. 40 above). To date, few Scandinavian inscriptions – a meagre three – have been located in Ireland. These comprise the runic legend carved on a stone cross at Killaloe Cathedral – 'Thorgrim erected this cross' – the Ogham inscription (also at Killaloe) – 'Beandac(h)t (ar) Toreagr(im)' (A blessing on Thorgrim) – and the twelfth-century Viking sword found in a grave at Greenmount, Co. Louth, which bears the inscription: 'Tomnal Selshofoþ a soerþ þeta' (Domnal Seal's Head owns this sword). The name Domnal is Gaelic (although the nickname Selshofoþ is Norse) and we may suspect that the owner of the Green-mount sword may have been one of the mongrel Gall-Gael himself.

Western Scotland

The variety of Gaelic that received the greatest infusion of Scandin-avian terms was that spoken in western Scotland, more specifically the dialects of the Hebrides which were spoken alongside Norse for generations. Some three hundred Norse expressions have survived in Scots Gaelic, typical examples being: *rómag* (a mixture of meal and whiskey), *staing* (a pole used for carrying peat creels), *siolag* (a sand eel), *sorgha* (a fish hook) and *udabac* (an outhouse, from the Norse *út í bak* = out at the back). Most of these Norse borrowings in Gaelic are found, as in English, in those parts of the vocabulary concerned with such everyday activities as fishing, farming and running the home.

Owing to the highly dissimilar sound-systems of Gaelic and Norse, many of these Scandinavian loans have been distorted almost beyond recognition, e.g. *arspag* = the greater black-backed gull (N *svartbakr*), *ealbhar* = a good-for-nothing (N: *álfr* = an elf), *cuidh* = an enclosure (N: *kví*). A minority, however, are fairly recognisable, e.g. *droig* (N: *dregg* = dregs), *faedhail* (pronounced 'fuil') = a ford (N: *vaðill*) and *cleitt* (N: *klettr* = a cliff). As an example of the relative proportions of Norse to Gaelic items in Hebridean seafaring terminology, the following lines from the poem 'The Bark of Clanranald', by the eighteenth-century poet, Alexander Macdonald, will serve:

> A Mhic beannaich fein ar n-*acair*,
>   [N: *akkeri* = anchor]
> Ar siùil, ar beairtean, 'a ar *stiùir*;
>   [*styra* = steer]
> 's gach *droinip* tha chrochta ri'r crannaibh,
>   [*reiði-reip* = rigging rope]
> 's thoir gu cala sinn le d'iùl.
> Beannaich ar *rachdan* 's ar slat,
>   [*rakki* = ring that ties the yard to the mast]
>
> Ar croinn 's ar taoda gu léir;
> Ar *stagh* 's ar tarriunn cum fallain,
>   [*stag* = a stay in the ship's rigging]
> 's ar leig-sa 'n ar caraigh beud.
> An Spiorad Naomh bi'dh air an *stiùir*,
> Seolaigh e 'n t-iùl a bhios ceart.
>
> (And thou, O Son, bless our anchor,
> Our sail, shrouds and helm do thou bless,
> Each tackle that hangs from our masts,
> And guide us to port in peace.

Our parrel and yards do thou bless,
Our masts and our ropes one and all,
Our stays and our halyards preserve,
And let no mischance befall.
The Holy Ghost be at the helm,
And show us the right track to go.)
(English translation by Dr Alexander Nicolson)

The possibility that Scandinavian speech-habits may be ultimately responsible for certain traits in the pronunciation of Scots Gaelic was first suggested by Carl Marstrander in his paper 'Okklusiver og Substrater', published in the *Norsk Tidsskrift for Sprogvidenskap* in 1932. Although Norse had no apparent effect on the phonology of Irish Gaelic, the presence in its Scottish offspring of certain articulatory traits having counterparts in provincial Norwegian dialects led Marstrander to postulate an enduring Scandinavian influence – an influence which may go back to the time when large numbers of Norwegians resident in northern and western Scotland were forsaking their native speech in favour of Gaelic.

One of the most conspicuous phonological similarities which Marstrander noted between Scots Gaelic and the dialects of southwest Norway was the occurrence of 'post-aspirated voiceless occlusives' after stressed vocals. Essentially, this means that the speakers of Scots Gaelic insert a short, spirant *h*-sound before the 'hard' final consonants of words like: *sop* (a handful of straw), *cat* and *mac* (son) – pronouncing them: 'sho*h*p', 'ca*h*t' and 'ma*h*k'. (The family name Mackenzie may thus sound like 'Ma*h*kónyich'.)

A parallel tendency in the Norwegian dialects centring on North Gudbrandsdal – a tendency which Marstrander links with the identical development in Scots Gaelic – gives rise to such pronunciations as: 'ka*h*tt' for *katt*, 'do*h*ter' for *dotter* (daughter) and 'ta*h*kk' for *takk* (thanks). 'Is it accidental', asks Marstrander, 'that *katt, kjepp* (stick) and *stokk* (log) are pronounced in Norway and Scotland – and only there – as 'ka*h*tt', 'kje*h*pp' and 'sto*h*kk'? Is it accidental that we should find so peculiar a development as this – of *post*-aspirates to *pre*-aspirates, which is unknown in any other Indo-European language – in two language areas which we know to have been neighbours and in linguistic and cultural contact for hundreds of years?'

He thinks not, and nor does he think, as many have, that the presence of this and certain other traits in Scots Gaelic is due to any lingering

'Pictish' influence – for our almost complete ignorance of Pictish phonology makes any such theory pure speculation. Marstrander reinforces his opinion by pointing out that the development in Scots Gaelic of preaspirated tenues can 'under no circumstances be older than the tenth century' – when Pictish had been extinct for at least 250 years, but at about the time when an identical tendency was beginning to take effect in southwest Norway.

While Marstrander has no hesitation in holding the Norsemen responsible for the implanting of this feature in Scotland, he is less confident in attributing certain other peculiarities of Scots Gaelic pronunciation to Scandinavian speech habits. The insertion by some Gaelic speakers in west Caithness (where the language was a late-comer) of a -t- into the consonant combination sr may, he speculates, reflect an attempt on the part of the Scandinavians to ease the articulation of this tricky Gaelic sound-cluster (e.g. 'struth' for sruth = stream, 'strian' for srian = bridle, etc). Caithness speakers also tend to pronounce the Gaelic falling diphthong ia like a 'broken' ya – saying 'sgyaan' for sgian (knife), much as the Norsemen made Bríann into Brjánn and Níall into Njáll. A similar treatment is given by north Inverness speakers to the diphthong ea, so that we hear 'yakh' and 'yarrub' for each (horse) and earb (fish roe). Although Marstrander does not claim that these, or any other, features of Scots Gaelic phonology – however suggestively 'Scandinavian' they may seem – are of direct Norse inspiration, it cannot, he points out, be denied that many of the phonological tendencies that distinguish the Gaelic of Scotland from that of Ireland are strikingly reminiscent of similar traits in provincial Norwegian, and that such resemblances may not be entirely fortuitous.

While the existence of a Scandinavian substrate underlying the sound system of Scots Gaelic as a whole can neither be proved nor entirely discounted, there is no doubt whatever about the Norse influence on one particular variety of that language – the Gaelic of Lewis. Marstrander's compatriot, Magne Oftedal, has made an intensive study of the Gaelic dialects of the Hebrides, and has no hesitation in attributing many of the differences that mark off the speech of Lewis from all the neighbouring varieties of Gaelic to the deeply engrained and persistent influence of Norse – which he believes to have been the predominant language on the island until the eleventh century. All the Gaelic placenames on Lewis, claims Oftedal, are relatively modern in appearance, and between 50 and 80 per cent of them are automatically dated as post-Norse by the Scandinavian elements they contain.

Of the decipherable Scandinavian runic inscriptions in Scotland, the eight found in the cell of St Molaise on Holy Island in the Firth of Clyde are, despite their brevity, among the most interesting, for it is thought that they may have been scribbled by some of the men who accompanied King Hákon Hákonsson on his ill-fated expedition to Largs in 1263. Typical examples from this site are: 'Onontr raisti rur ...' ('Qnundr carved [probably 'these runes']') and the signature: 'Olabr' (Óláfr). On a brooch found at Hunterston, West Kilbride, in Ayrshire – not far from Largs – was scratched this terse inscription in the Norse language: 'Malbriþa a stilk' (Melbrigda owns [this] brooch). Other Scandinavian personal names occurring in Scottish runic inscriptions include Ikulb (Ingólfr – found on a grave lid at Thurso in Caithness), Sikuik (the woman's name Sigveigr, from Knockando in Moray), and (Kri)mkitill (probably Grímketill, from Laws in Angus). From Kilbar on Barra comes what is possibly the oldest Scandinavian runic memorial so far discovered on Scottish soil. It dates from the early tenth century and reads '(Ep)tir Thurkirthu s(t)in(a)r(dotti)r is kurs sia r(ei)str' ('After Þórgerda, Steinar's daughter, this cross is raised').

FIG. 7. Norse runic inscription on a slab now in Knockando church, Scotland, but believed to have been moved c 1810 from an old burial ground called Pulvrenan in the same parish. The runes read, from right to left, KIUKIS, which, when reversed to SIKUIK looks remarkably like the Scandinavian woman's name, Sigveigr.

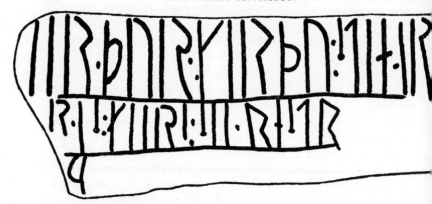

FIG. 8. Probably the oldest Scandinavian runic memorial in Britain: the Kilbar Stone from the Hebrides.

North-east Scotland

Gaelic was late in penetrating the north-eastern extremity of Caithness, and it seems probable that a Scandinavian idiom, similar, no doubt, to Orkney Norn, held out much longer here than elsewhere on the Scottish mainland. Dr Per Thorson of Bergen estimates that Norse finally gave way to Lowland Scots sometime during the sixteenth century. The Norse words in the modern Caithness dialect, Dr Thorson points out, 'bear no traces of having passed into Low Scottish through Gaelic', and other factors, such as the paucity of Gaelic placenames hereabouts, seem to substantiate his impression of Norse yielding, not to Gaelic as it did in Sutherland, Wester Ross and the Hebrides, but directly to Lowland Scots. Scandinavian terms in the Caithness dialect, recorded around the turn of the century by David B. Nicolson, a native of Wick, include: *birsk* = gristle, *elt* = to knead dough, *scroo* = a small stack of corn, *squaar* = a swath in mowing, *cassie* = a basket made of twisted straw, *ingy* = to bring forth lambs, *ug* = the pectoral fin of a fish, *maak* = the milt of a fish, *scorie* = a young gull, *glaep* = to gulp, *scravvle* = to scramble or crawl, *waan* = hope, *clype* = to scratch with the nails, and *skyle* = to shade or shelter. The Caithness terms *brithersin* and *britherdochter* for (fraternal) nephew and niece are, although wholly Scots in sound, strikingly reminiscent of their Icelandic and Faeroese counterparts *bróðirsonur* and *bróðirdóttir* = brother's son and brother's daughter. Although Thorson makes no mention of Norse phonological traits in Caithness Scots, it is possible that certain archaic features of this dialect – notably the retention of the initial K before N in such words as *knife*, the fortis articulation of initial HW as F (e.g. 'fat' for *what*, 'faar' for *where* and 'filk' for *which*), and the 'breaking' of the initial vowels of words like *earth* (pronounced 'yürd' in Caithness) may reflect Scandinavian influence. The substitution of *f-* for English *wh-* is not, of course, confined to Caithness; it is fairly general throughout north-east Scotland – and occurs as far south as Dundee. This feature is absent, however, from both Sutherland and Ross and Cromarty, and, although there is some evidence that it was formerly used in certain varieties of Shetland Norn (e.g. the placename Fitful Head – from ON: *Hvít fugl* = white bird?), it is no longer characteristic of North Island Scots.

The Northern Isles

The densest concentration in Britain of both runic inscriptions in the Norse language and surviving Scandinavian expressions in colloquial speech is to be found in the northernmost Scottish islands, the Orkneys and Shetlands. It was here that Norse was first implanted in Britain – some time during the eighth century AD – and here that a Scandinavian vernacular persisted until the eighteenth or even into the early nineteenth century.

This idiom, sometimes referred to in Orkney as the 'Danska Tongue', was more generally known to its speakers as 'Norn', from the Norse: *norrœnn*, a contraction of *norðrœnn* = northern.

Of the Orkney runic inscriptions, the most interesting are the two dozen-odd graffiti scratched on the stone interior walls of the pre-historic tumulus at Maeshowe. Most of these are mere jottings of the 'Kilroy was here' variety (e.g. 'Thorny was bedded – Helge says so', 'Ingeborg, the fair widow', 'Ingegerd is the best of them all' and 'Many a woman, for all her airs and graces, has had to stoop to get in here'), but the following is the longest and most complete fragment of Norse so far discovered on a runestone in Britain: 'Iorsala fara brutu Orkøugh. Ut norþr er fe folgit mikit þat er lo eftir uar fe f folgit mikit sael sa ir fina maþan øuþ hin mikla' (The crusaders to Jerusalem [N: Jorsalafarar] broke open the Orkney mound. Out north is the great treasure hidden. Happy is he who can find this great wealth). Close at hand, another inscription reads: 'Þisar runar rist sa maþr er runstr er fyrir uæstan haf mæþ þæiri øhse er ati Køukr Trænils sonr fyrir sunan land' (These runes were cut by that man who is most skilled in runecraft west over sea, with that axe which Gauk Trandilsson from the south country owned).

Both the style of the runic characters and the form of the Norse language in which the inscriptions are written suggest that they were carved early in the twelfth century, when Rǫgnvaldr II was jarl in Orkney. It is believed that the Gauk Trandilsson named in the second inscription as the owner of the axe which carved the runes was a known historical figure, an Icelander whose killing, at the hands of one Ásgrím, is related in Njál's Saga. When Jarl Rǫgnvaldr sailed home to Orkney from Iceland on one occasion, he travelled in a vessel owned by one Þórhall Ásgrímsson, a grandson of the Ásgrím who had slain Gauk Trandilsson.

In addition to these runic inscriptions, we know that a certain amount of skaldic poetry was composed by Scandinavians living in Orkney during the twelfth and thirteenth centuries, most notable being the 'Hattalykill' (described by Hugh Marwick as 'a kind of metrical key to Old Norse prosody') – partly composed by Jarl Rǫgnvaldr – and Bishop Bjarni Kolbeinsson's famous poem, the 'Jómsvíkingadrápa'. Magnus Olsen claims to have traced other examples of Norse poetry to Orkney and the Hebrides, whilst Sophus Bugge and Guðbrandur Vígfússon have stressed that the old Scandinavian colonies in Britain should not be excluded as a possible source of Eddic songs.

A few Scandinavian texts from both during and after the period of Norwegian and (later) Dano/Norwegian occupation have been attested from Orkney and Shetland. Our first example of a document written at the time when the islands were still in Norwegian hands is dated 'Kirkiuwaghe i Orknæyum [Kirkwall in Orkney], 4 April 1329', and its purpose is to explain that Catherine, Countess in Orkney and Caithness, has bought some property in the island of South Ronaldsay from Herr Erling Vidkunsson, a Dróttseti (or steward) of the King of Norway:

Ollum monnum þæim sem þetta bref sea æða hœyra sendir Katerin cunncteis j Orknœyium oc Katanese quediu guðs oc sina. Ver gerom ydr kunight at ver kœyptum af herra Siugurði Joðgeirs syni jarðer herra Erlings Vidkunnar sonar Noreghs konongs drotzseta þær sem hann atte j Rognaldzœy oc oss varo æighi aðr

dœmdar hans fullum vmboðs manne til þess at selia sem bref herra
Erlings þat sem ver hofum hia oss þar vm gort vattar oc swa heita
j Stufum xx skillinga kaup oc i Kuikobba xx skillinga kaup.

The language of this text is West Norse through and through –
identical in all essentials with that of the medieval Icelandic sagas.

Our next specimen dates from 1426, a mere forty years before the
islands were pledged to Scotland. The language of this, the last extant
Orkney document to be written in a Scandinavian tongue, is still
essentially West Norse in character. It shows, however, many of the
orthographic effects of fifteenth-century Danish, which may be
explained by the fact that, after Norway (together with its Atlantic
island colonies) had fallen to the Danish crown at Kalmar in 1397,
Danish scribal practices had begun to exert a profound influence upon
written Norwegian. This specimen is taken from a list of grievances
drawn up against one David Menzies of Weem, one of the 'Utlenders'
or Scots appointed by the Danish authorities to official positions in
the islands. Even at this early date, a few Scotticisms may be detected,
e.g. *thet* for *at* (as in 'for then sak thet') and *jærl* for *jarl*. The document
also contains a generous sprinkling of Scottish Christian names
(Dunkan, Malcum, Fergus, Sander, etc) and surnames (Brwn,
Sinklar, Yrwing, Fiif, Blare – note the Danish renditions) that were
already fairly widespread in the islands. Here is a short extract:

Jtem: Lagmansins hustru oc hans frændir kærdo thet han war
tyswa taghin oc sættir i torn then første sak war then, thet Jon af
Baddy lagmansins swen oc frænde thok ater sin hæst af Mikel
Magy for^de Dauids frænde thær han hafde takit fra honom oc
wilde haua ridit, for then sak tok han lagmannin oppa gatone
i Kærkewaw oc satte han swa i tornit. Æpter tha han war utkomin,
tha sænde han vtlænska mæn af Kattenæs til lagmansins gard
oc loot brytæ op hans kirkio oc thaka thær vt alt thet thær innan
war.

Jtem: For^de Dauid thok Willem Bres oc satte honom i stok oc
skattade honom af vij mark engelsche for vthan lagh oc dom,
oc for then sak thet han foor til Scotland tala med jærlen.

Jtem: Skipper Thomes Brwn kærde that for^de Dauid lot læggia
honom i tornit for then sak that han ey oppa stadhin gik til
honom i første ordh han sænde bud æpter honom.

Jtem: then tid for^{de} Dauid kom nw sidharst af Danmark tha tok han for^{de} schipper Thomas, oc hans schip ladit med gotz oc førde her af landit oc in til Schotland vthan hans wilia oc thok ther fra honom swa mykit hwetemiøl som løper oppa xxiiij nobla oc tha for^{de} schipper Thomas scholdo heem sighla tha miste han schip oc gotz oc en deels of mænnena oppa schipit waro for thy thet war swa langht oppa winteren.

(*Item:* The Lawman's wife and his kinsmen complained that he was twice taken and placed in the tower. The first charge was that John of Baddy, the Lawman's retainer and kinsman, took back his horse from Michael Magy, the aforenamed David's kinsman, which he had taken from him and would have ridden. For this reason he took the Lawman in the street in Kirkwall and threw him into the tower. After he [the Lawman] had come out, he [David Menzies] sent foreigners from Caithness to the Lawman's farm and had them break up his chapel and take out everything that was in it.

Item: The aforenamed David took William Brace and put him in the stocks and fined him seven English marks without law and without trial, because he had been to Scotland to speak with the Earl.

Item: Skipper Thomas Brown complained that the aforenamed David had him imprisoned because he [the skipper] did not report to him in the town at the first receipt of his summons.

Item: At the time when the aforenamed David last came from Denmark, he took the aforenamed Skipper Thomas and his ship, laden with goods, and left this land [i.e. Orkney], departed for Scotland without his consent and there took from him wheat meal to the value of 24 nobles and kept him there almost all the winter, and when the aforenamed Skipper Thomas wanted to sail home he lost his ship and property and some of his crew, for the winter was so far advanced.)

Our next example of North Island Norse is almost 200 years later than the above. This, the last extant specimen of a document written in a Scandinavian language in Shetland (and so, by the same token, in Britain), is an extract from a pledge. The language is Danish in every respect:

Thenne bekendis ieg Villem Monsøn uisted att ieg er Søerren Spens skøldig 9½ daller for en tl. smør och bepleghter ieg mig att betthale forne Søeren dee 9½ daller dette thiill kommendes sommer som er det oc thyll kommendes 1608. Thyll otter merre vinnes boerd. Setter ieg mynd sedvannelight merke iher vinden vnder som er gyffued paa Kocke B – den 18 daag deesember anno 1607.

Villem Monsøn
uisted egen hand.

(I, William Manson, confirm that I owe Søren Spence 9½ dalers for one portion of butter and promise to pay the abovenamed Søren the 9½ dalers by the coming summer, the summer of the coming year, 1608. With 8 men as witnesses, I set my customary mark hereunder, which is given at Kocke B – [?] the 18th day of December, 1607.

William Manson,
signed with his own hand.)

Slight though the linguistic interest of such a humble document may be, it does testify to the fact that, 150 years after Shetland had been ceded to Scotland, its inhabitants continued to conduct their day-to-day affairs in a Scandinavian language. Until the end of the sixteenth century, the bulk of the legal terms contained in North Island documents remained, even in Scots contexts, those established in Scandinavian times (e.g. *athmen* = oathmen (N: *eiðmenn*), *arvis skopt* = division of inheritance (N: *afskipti*), *mensvering* = perjury (N: *meinsværi*) and *ofhentit* = handed over (N: *afhenda* = to hand over). Indeed, a mere fourteen years before the above pledge was written, it had been necessary for a Shetland minister, one Magnus Manson, to go to Norway in order to learn Norwegian before taking up his incumbency on Unst, northernmost of the Shetlands. On account of this, his parishioners, many of whom would have been unable to understand him had he preached to them in English, nicknamed the minister 'Magnus Norsk'.

The transition from Norn to Scots in Orkney and Shetland was a very gradual affair, beginning, as we have seen, long before the transfer of the islands from Denmark/Norway to Scotland in the 1460s, although it was naturally *spoken*, rather than *written* Scots, that first made an impression on Shetland Norn. Indeed, David Murison tells us (in *Scots speech in Shetland*, 1954) that 'the earliest Scots document in Shetland, written of course by a Scots civil servant, dates from 1525' – 45 years after Scotland's acquisition of the islands. Of particular interest, as reflecting the possible main sources of Scottish immigration to Shetland and Orkney, is the fact that the form of spoken Scots destined to replace Norn in the islands appears to have been more closely akin to the speech of central Scotland than to that of Caithness or anywhere else in the extreme north-east.

As early as 1605, Sir Thomas Craig was observing that '... even in the Orkneys and Shetlands, where in the course of the present century nothing but Norse was spoken, the ministers of God's word now use English in Church, and are well enough understood'.

The contamination of Norn by Scots advanced steadily throughout the seventeenth century, during the second half of which another observer, the Aberdonian Mathew MacKaile, was able to declare, in his book *A Short Relation of the Most Considerable Things in Orkney*, that 'It is very probable that the inhabitants of the Orcades of old did only speak Noords or rude Danish; but there are only three or four parishes (especially on the Mainland or Pomona) wherein that language is spoken, and that chiefly when they are at their own houses; but all speak the Scots language, as the rest of the commons do'.

Maybe so, but even in Orkney isolated pockets of Scandinavian speech seem to have held out for at least another hundred years after MacKaile's visit. Martin, in his *Brief Description of the Isles of Orkney and Schetland* (1703), noted that 'They generally speak the English tongue, and many among them retain the ancient Danish language, especially in the more Northern isles', while the Rev George Barry, in his *History of Orkney* (1805) recounted the following anecdote: 'So late as 1756 or 1757, as a respectable native of this country was travelling from Kirkwall to Birsa, he heard two old men for an hour or more converse together in an unknown tongue; which, on enquiry, he found was the Norse language. For many years past it has been almost entirely forgotten, except in one parish in the heart of the Mainland (of Orkney), where the people are said, till of late, to have retained some acquaintance with it'. This confirms what Mackenzie had to say of the Orcadians in 1750: 'The customs of the inhabitants were all Norwegian; their language the Norse, or that dialect of the Gothic which is spoken in Norway and disused only within this present age, by means of English schools erected by the Society for Promoting Christian Knowledge, nor to this time is it quite disused, being still retained by old people, and in vulgar use among them at this day'.

It was, of course, in Orkney, the closer of the two archipelagoes to the Scottish mainland, that the old language succumbed soonest;

twenty-three years after Mackenzie, the Rev George Low (*Tour thro'*
Orkney and Shetland, 1774) remarked that 'The Language of these
Islands ... was here Norn ... but it is now so much worn out that I
believe there is scarce a single man in the country who can express
himself on the most ordinary occasion in that Language'.

In the remoter Shetlands, however, the old tongue proved more
resilient. Brand, writing in 1700, noted that 'English is the common
language among them, yet many of the people speak Norse, or corrupt
Danish, especially such as live in the more northern isles; yea, so
common is it in some places, that it is the first language that the
children speak. The Norse hath continued ever since the Norwegians
had these islands in possession, and in Orkney it is not quite extinct,
though there be by far more of it in Zetland, which many do commonly
use.' Eleven years later, Sir Robert Sibbald remarked of the parishioners of Cunningsburgh, on the south Mainland of Shetland: 'All the
inhabitants of the parish can speak the Gothick or Norvegian [sic]
language, which they call Norn, now much worn out, and seldom
speak other among themselves. Yet all of them speak the Scots tongue
more promptly and more readily than generally they do in Scotland'.

Even towards the end of the eighteenth century, there was still
plenty of Norn to be heard in the remoter corners of Shetland, and
it was in such outlying areas that the Rev George Low was able, during
his visit in 1774, to record several fairly extended specimens of the
old language – using as his informants crofters and fishermen of the
oldest generation.

On the island of Foula, which lies some twenty miles out in the
Atlantic west of Mainland Shetland, Low took down thirty-five
stanzas of a traditional 'veesick' (ballad, Dan: *vise*) from the mouth of
an illiterate old man, William Henry. In 1900, the Norwegian scholar,
Marius Hægstad, identified the ballad as a version of the *Hildinakvad*,
popular throughout Scandinavia in the Middle Ages. Although Low
himself knew little more Norse than his informant, who was ignorant
of the meaning of the words, his transcription of the veesick appears
to be phonetically accurate enough to permit a rough translation.
A typical verse runs:

> De vara Jarlin d'Orkneyar,
> For Frinda sin spir de Ro,
> Whirdi 'an skilde Menn
> Our glas buryan burtaga.

(It was the Earl of Orkney,
Of his kinsmen he asked advice,
Whether he should abduct
The maiden from the glass castle)

Whilst on Foula, Low also recorded the following Norn version of the Lord's Prayer:

Fy vor o er i Chimeri [Dan: *Himmerig*]. Halaght vara nam dit. La Konungdum din kumma. La vill din vera guerde, i Vrildin sinda er i Chimeri. Gav vus dagh u dagloght Brau. Forgive sindor wara sin vi forgiva dem ao sinda 'gainst wus. Lia wus eke o vera tempa, but delivra wus fra adlu idlu. For do i ir Konungdum, u Puri, u Glori, Amen.

A comparison may be made between this Shetland Lord's Prayer, as taken down by Low, and a version recorded in Orkney seventy-three years before by one James Wallace, in his *Account of the Islands of Orkney* (1700). 'Some of the common people amongst themselves', Wallace had noted, 'speak a Language they call Norns, which they have derived to them, either from the Pights [Picts], or some others, who first planted this country; for by the following Lord's Prayer in that Language, it has but little of the Danish or Norwegian Language, to which I thought it should have had more affinity, considering how long time they were possessors of this country'. In fact, of course, the language of this Lord's Prayer is even more truly Scandinavian than the version Low was to record in Shetland in 1774:

Favor i ir i Chimrie, helleur ir i nam thite. Gilla cosdum thite cumma, Veya thine mota vara gort o yurn sinna gort i Chimrie. Ga vus da on da dalight brow vora. Firgive vus sinna vora sin vee firgive sindara mutha vus. Lyv vus ye i tumtation, min delivra vus fra olt ilt. On sa meteth vera.

The Scandinavian prototype of this Lord's Prayer appears to have run something like this (English and Scots words italicised):

Far vor er ert í Himinríki. Heilagt verði namn þitt. Konungdómr þitt koma. Vili þinn *mot* ver gǫrt á jǫrðunni sem hann er í Himinríki. Gef oss dag um dag dagligt brauð vort. Fyrirgef oss syndir várar sem vér fyrirgefa syndar í móti oss. Leið oss eigi í *temptation* men *deliver* oss frá ǫllu illt. *And* svá má það vera.

During his visit to Shetland, Low was fortunate in obtaining two local versions of a veesick, the first from Cunningsburgh on the south Mainland:

> 'Myrk in e Liora,
> Luce in e Liunga,
> Timin e, Guestin e guengna'

and the second from the northern island of Yell:

> 'Mirka Lora,
> Lestra Linga,
> Tamra gestra gongera'
>
> (Dark in the smoke-hole [N: *ljóri*],
> Light on the heath,
> It is time that the guest was going)

Despite Low's somewhat inconsistent system of transliteration, there are obvious fundamental differences between these two versions, and it is clear from these and other specimens that, even at this late stage in its existence, Shetland Norn was still marked by radical dialect discrepancies. This diversity, especially of phonology, seems to have been carried over into the Scots that eventually submerged Norn in the islands, and the American/Norwegian investigator, G. T. Flom, for example, claims that as many as twelve clearly defined forms of Scots may be distinguished in Shetland. The fragmentation of Shetland Norn into a multiplicity of local dialects was paralleled in Faeroe; in both cases, the process was facilitated by the absence of a literary language – written Faeroese going back little further than 1854, when Venceslaus Ulricus Hammershaimb published his *Færøsk Sproglære*. The Icelanders have, by contrast, always had a standard written form of their language which has acted strongly against the splintering of the spoken tongue into regional varieties.

A hundred and twenty years were to elapse between the Rev George Low's visit to Shetland and that of the Danish scholar, Jakob Jakobsen, whose exhaustive examination into the last surviving relics of Norn in Shetland, conducted between 1893 and 1895, was to culminate in his doctoral thesis, *Det Norrøne Sprog paa Shetland* (Copenhagen, 1897).

We have already noted Low's remarks on the greatly deteriorated state of the Norn language in the islands during the 1770s, so it would be reasonable to assume that, after the lapse of a further half-dozen generations, there would be precious little left of the old tongue when Jakobsen landed in Lerwick in 1893. Many of Jakobsen's observations, however, reveal that Norn continued to hold out in certain sequestered corners of the islands until less than a hundred years ago – an astonishingly late date.

> In several parts of Shetland [he reported], especially Foula and the North Isles, the present generation of old people remember their grandparents speaking a language they could hardly understand, and which was called Norn or Norse ... As late as 1894, there were people in Foula who could repeat sentences in Norn, as I myself had the opportunity of hearing. The last man in Unst who is said to have been able to speak Norn, Walter Sutherland from Skaw, died about 1850. In Foula, on the other hand, men who were living very much later than the middle of the present century are said to have been able to speak Norn.

During his three-year sojourn in Shetland, Dr Jakobsen scoured the islands for information and amassed an impressive body of material in the Norn tongue, from fragments of verse and venerable adages to half-remembered stories and even snippets of conversation. Few of his informants – who were almost exclusively of the oldest generation – were able to offer reliable translations – but merely reiterated, as well as they could, the few shreds of the old tongue that they had heard from their grandparents' mouths.

One of the most illuminating of Dr Jakobsen's examples – illuminating in that it illustrates the attitude of the native speakers of Norn towards their own language as compared with the more prestigious Scots – is offered by the following lines, recorded by Jakobsen on Unst and believed by him to have been 'preserved from last century':

> De vaar e gooa tee,
> When sona min guid to Kaadanes;
> Haayn kaayn ca' Russa 'Mare',
> Haayn kaayn ca' Bigg 'Bere',
> Haayn kaayn ca' Eld 'Fire',
> Haayn kaayn ca' Klovandi 'Taings'.

> (It was a good time,
> When my son went to Caithness;
> He can call Russa 'Mare',
> He can call Bigg 'Bere' [Scots = barley],
> He can call Eld 'Fire',
> He can call Klovandi 'Taings' [Scots = tongs].)

This verse was clearly widespread in the islands at one time, and Jakobsen recorded a variant from Foula which ran:

> Hit was guid naer [Dan: *nær* = when],
> My son guid saer [Norw: *sør* = south],
> For he learned to ca' de Bugga de Bere,
> And de Russa de Mare.

These lines reflect, pathetically, the fact that the autochthonous Scandinavian language was, by the late eighteenth century, regarded by its speakers very much as an inferior tongue, and that the acquisition of the socially superior Scots was an accomplishment to be attained by all those who hoped to better themselves. This has so often been the fate of doomed, unwritten languages that are cut off from their main source of inspiration. It happened to Cornish at about the same time as to Shetland Norn, and a like fate is at this moment befalling the old Finnic language of the Livonians in northern Latvia; the Livonian language, long considered by its speakers as inferior to Latvian (and now, presumably, to Russian, too), has been relegated to the kitchen and the nursery, and is used today by none but the elderly, the women and the children. The situation must have been identical with regard to Shetland Norn in its final years.

Dr Jakobsen was struck by the resemblance between many of the Shetland Norn specimens he took down and their counterparts in his native Faeroese. Such convergences were especially noticeable in the numerous 'goadiks', or riddles (Dan: *gaader*), of which the following was typical:

> Flokkera flua fedderless,
> Sotsha goa benderless,
> Oot kom modera hengaless,
> An' drave awa' flokkera flua.
>
> (The bird flew featherless,
> Sat on the fence legless,
> Out came the man handless,
> And drove away 'Flokkera flua'.)

The answer is: a snowflake. It seems unlikely that Jakobsen's informant, who recited the goadik to him on the northern island of Yell, comprehended the words, or he would have realised that 'flokkera flua', in the last line, was not the name of the subject of the riddle, but merely a corruption of the opening words, which, in the original Norse, would have been *fuglinn flaug* = the bird flew.

The next little rhyme, noted by Jakobsen on Unst, also has an almost word-for-word counterpart in Faeroese:

> Buyn vil ikka teea,
> Buyn vil ikka teea,
> Tak an leggen,
> Slog an veggen,
> Buyn vil ikka tcca.

> (The child will not be quiet,
> The child will not be quiet,
> Take it by the leg,
> Hit it against the wall,
> The child will not be quiet.)

The Faeroese version – which is clearly identical in origin – runs:

> Vil ikki barnið tiga,
> So tak um legg,
> Og slá í vegg
> So skal barnið tiga.

On Foula, where, over a hundred years earlier, Low had taken down his Norn version of the Lord's Prayer, Jakobsen recorded this rather gruesome little rhyme:

> Skekla komina reena toona,
> Swarta hesta, bletta broona,
> Fomtina haala and fomtina bjadnis a kwaara haala.

(The skekill [a legendary monster] comes riding into town,
[on a] black horse [with a] brown blaze [on its forehead],
Fifteen tails and fifteen bairns on each tail.)

Faeroese mothers still warn their children with a very similar rhyme although in the Faeroes it is the *grýla* that will come and cut open the children's stomachs if they cry for meat during Lent.

Of the many Norn proverbs that Jakobsen collected in Shetland, the following are typical: 'Goit at taka gamla manna raw' ([It is] good to take an old man's advice); 'Up aboot de yora, goit fer a monga' (Up about the ear is good for the mouth – said of a cat); 'Marta de gorns teka de veps' (Much can be used for the woof that is useless for

the warp); and 'Day-a lengdi, mawgi swengdi' (As the days lengthen,
the stomachs grow hungrier – clearly identical in origin to the Norwegian: 'Dagarne lengjast, magarne svengjast').

The following are examples from Jakobsen of (i) a fragment of a
folk song, (ii) a nursery rhyme, (iii) a lullaby and (iv) a formula for
calling the cattle.

(i)   I have malet meldra min,
    I have supat 'usen,
    Enda ligger de søda min,
    And dayna komena lusa.

    (I have ground my flour,
    I have swept my house,
    My little ones are still lying asleep,
    And the day is breaking.)

(ii)   Clappa, clappa, søda,
    Bokshina skyolena bjøda.

(Recorded many years after Jakobsen by Jessie Saxby as:

    'Clapa, clapa, süda,
    Boochsina, schölina bjöda,
    Bauta deema kjota schin,
    Swala clovena vjenta in,
    Roompan pöman söda.'

Neither Jakobsen nor Mrs Saxby offers any translation of these
lines.)

(iii)   Vallilu, egga soer o a siggalin,
    Leka tu sa fru a mornin' a gibellin'?

    (Hushabye, the suckling does not sleep,
    Are you playing so gaily in the morning, waving your
       arms about?)

(iv)   Komme, komme, haste komme,
    So sal du ek skam
    Falalderalda kjøra, [Dan: *Talt er alle køerne*]
    Neppert, Nani, Lengsprali,
    Still kom øwer mi sholma,
    Falalderalda kjøra.

    (Come, come, hurry, come,
    Then you will not be scolded,
    All the cows are counted,

Neppert, Nani, Lengsprali [all names of cows],
Come quietly over, my helmeted one [ie a cow with a
'helmet' pattern on its face],
All the cows are counted.)

Among the most fascinating of all the Norn fragments gathered by Jakobsen in Shetland were the snippets of conversation – many of them still bearing the vestigial traces of Scandinavian inflections – that had evidently been passed down the generations from the time when the old language was the everyday vernacular. Typical examples were: *Skond dee* = hurry up; *Oba dona* = open the door; *Gyera so* = do so; *Faw me a duk* = get me a drink; *Ara du inya?* = are you in?; *Spongna ligger a gleggan* = the spoon is lying in the window; *Ølt i ryggen* = a pain in the back; and the greeting: *Goden dag til dora* = good day to you. A variant of this Norn greeting (cf: Icelandic: *Góðan dag til þér*) evidently survived in Orkney, too, although not for so long as in Shetland; Barry, in his *History of Orkney* (1867), quotes the sixteenth-century Scots writer, Jo Ben, who remarked of the Orcadians: 'Where we say: "Guid day, Guidman", they say: "Goand Da, Boundae"' [N: *bóndi* = farmer].

Dr Jakobsen was also able to interpret the following lines, which had first appeared in print in the *Shetland Times* in 1879, but had, until the Danish scholar subjected them to his expert scrutiny, defied translation. 'The formula', he commented, 'which is mainly Scoto-English, has Norn words sprinkled throughout, some of which show old grammatical endings that have lost their significance. Considering the fossilized Norn forms in it, the formula was probably first composed in that language'.

Da stuhl es scarp an fien,
Da schel es emer a snean,
Da vird es sicer an pura,
Da glimer i' mirk-as-dim hura,
La stuhl an vird ay gyrda,
An prof er an skylda, an svirda.

(The steel is sharp and fine,
The sickle is always sharp,
The word is certain and pure,
A glimpse of light in the darkest hour,
Let the steel and the word always guard her,
And appear to her as a shield, a sword.)

Although few of Jakobsen's examples referred to specific, identifiable Shetland localities, the following verse from a rowing song appears to mention two places whose names have survived to our own time:

Valafjel was tort o brotta,
Hafetu wis o hala,
Frem sokketu dafa voggedu noit,
An' rude kring de Yaala.

(Valafjeld [now known as Vall Field] was laborious and steep
There the damp seaweed was violent,
Seeking out the fishing ground at the Haaf [the open sea]
     by day,
They rowed round the [northern point of] Yell.)

Pathetically corrupt though the language of this example undeniably was, it was by no means the most intractable of the specimens collected by Dr Jakobsen in Shetland. Even he was completely baffled by the following verse, recited to him by a Mr R. Cogle, who believed the lines to be part of a charm used in olden times to drive out lung disease from cattle:

Enga bonga lora,
Bel skola reena,
Bel skola beti,
Andrew wistras,
Guid to bid to bretti,
Bitsha, gitsha gonga,
Bitsha, bitsha beti.

Jakobsen was able to offer a tentative translation only of the first three lines:

My own dear child sleep,
The evil shall stream out,
We shall chase (or subdue) the evil ...

One particular specimen obtained by Jakobsen from a North Yell man, Thomas Irvine, is remarkable for the fact that it is recognisably Danish rather than West Norse in character. It is a burial formula – apparently still used at Ness Kirk in North Yell until well into the eighteenth century – and evidently dates from the 1300s or early 1400s, a time when the ministers sent to the islands would more likely have

7

spoken Danish, as the official 'Kirkesprog', than the indigenous dialect. The formula runs:

> Yurden du art for af yurden du vis skav'd,
> Ok toa yurden nu ven død.
> Op fra yurden skal du opstaa
> Naar Herren laar syne Bastnan blaa.

> (Earth thou art for of the Earth thou wast created,
> And to the Earth now return dead.
> Up from the Earth shalt thou arise,
> When the Lord lets his trumpets blow.)

It was Yell, incidentally, that Dr Jakobsen believed would be 'the part of Shetland where the dialect with its intermixture of Norn will maintain itself longest' – although Norn itself, he believed, had probably survived intact on Foula longer than elsewhere in the islands.

Since Jakobsen's day, several more fragments of Norn have been recorded, and many of these have been published in the *Shetland Folk Book*. This boat song was recorded in Unst, and a tentative translation submitted by William W. Ratter, one of Jakobsen's Shetland helpers:

> Starka virna vestilie, obadeea, obadeea,
> Starka virna vestilie, obadeea monye!
> Stala stoita, stonga, raer, O whit says du, da bunshka baer;
> O whit says du, da bunshka baer; litra mae vee, drengie.
> Saina papa wara, obadeea, obadeea,
> Saina papa wara, obadeea moynie.

> (Strong weather from the west, danger, danger (Norw: *obyde*],
> Strong weather from the west, danger, lads,
> Brace up the shrouds, the mast, the yard, Oh, what do you say, that the boat will bear,
> Oh, what do you say, that the boat will bear; I'm pleased with that, boys.
> Bless us, our father, danger, danger,
> Bless us, our father, danger, lads.)

The following specimen, a fragment of the refrain of a ballad said to date from the seventeenth century, is, like Jakobsen's burial formula from Yell, interesting in that the language is Danish rather than strictly Norn:

> Skowan ørla grøn,
> Whaar gjorten han grøn oarlac

Two possible translations have been suggested:

> Early grows the wood,
> Where the garden grows green early

or

> Early grows the wood,
> Where the hart he goes yearly.

What can these tattered fragments tell us about the accidence and sound-system of the language of which they are such pathetic relics? Barely enough to permit the most tentative form of reconstruction, and just enough to enable us to identify a few affinities between North Island Norn and certain Norwegian and other Scandinavian dialects.

Correspondences between the vocabularies of Shetland Norn and those of the country dialects of south-west Norway – notably the West Agder area – convinced Jakobsen that the bulk of the Norse colonists of Shetland must have hailed from this corner of the Scandinavian mainland, whilst the same conclusion was reached, through similarities in phonology rather than lexis, by the Norwegian, Marius Hægstad. According to Hægstad, the vowels of Shetland Norn clearly mark it off from the Norwegian dialects of East Agder, whilst its consonantal sounds distinguish it from the dialects spoken north of Ryfylke. The same, Hægstad concluded, would seem to apply to the Orkney version of Norn (although specimens of Orkney Norn are much rarer than those of the Shetland form) – the only conspicuous differences between the sound-systems of the two varieties being that Orkney Norn appears to have made soundless consonants (such as P, T and K) sonant (as do the Sørlandske dialects of the 'soft-coast strip' in south-west Norway), whilst Shetlandic tended to compress the original diphthongs, AU, EI and EY – showing forms like *høs* for Norse *hauss* = skull.

Doubtless under the influence of an identical development that evidently took place in western Norway during the thirteenth century, the two dental fricatives, þ and ð, became stops in Shetland – though not in Orkney – Norn, and this trait was carried over from Norn to the existing Scots dialect of Shetland, which has *dis* for *this*, *tin* for *thin*.

Shetlandic seems to have had a number of features in common with Faeroese, which, like Norn, is basically a form of south-west Norwegian with a number of idiosyncrasies acquired through long isolation. The pronunciation of the consonant combination, *hj*, for example, became SH in both Shetlandic and Faeroese (e.g. *Shetland* for an earlier *Hjetland*), whilst both languages developed the old West Norse long *á* into a diphthong *ɔa* – e.g. ON: *álka* = auk, *álfr* = elf, becoming *ɔalka* and *ɔalvør* in Faeroese and *wolki* and *oalf* in Shetland Norn. Other similarities between Shetlandic and Faeroese phonology were the rendering of Norse *-rn-* as *-dn-* (e.g. *badn* for *barn*=child), and of Norse *-ll-* as *-dl-* (Shet: *idl*, Faer: *idlør*, for N: *illr* = ill), and the occluding of the original fricative *h* in the combination *hv* into *k*, yielding *kv* or *kw* (Shetl: *Kwalsay* for N: *Hvalsey* – the island of Whalsay), whilst the mutation of Norse *-fn-* to *-mn-* (as in the Shetland placenames: *Hamnavoe* and *Ramnaberg* for N: *Hafnavágr*, *Hrafnarberg*) also occurs throughout Sweden (*hamn*, *ramn* for N: *hǫfn*, *hrafn*) and in many of the West Norwegian dialects.

The grammatical structure of Shetland Norn, in so far as the fragmentary records of the language will permit us to adduce them, seems to have conformed in all essentials to that of West Norwegian and its Atlantic outliers – Icelandic and Faeroese – and fossilised vestiges of the morphology of the old language remained an integral part of many Shetlandic terms until long after their original function had been forgotten. They may thus be compared with English words, such as *scant* and *bask*, which, as we have remarked, preserve Scandinavian affixes. The Shetland term of endearment, *lammit* (literally 'my lamb'), in fact contains two characteristic Norse affixes, the neuter form of the possessive pronoun (ie *mitt* rather than *minn* for 'my', because *lamm* was a neuter noun in Norse) and its postposition after the noun it qualifies, *lamm mit* rather than *mitt lamm*. This latter trait is typical of the modern dialects of western Norway as well as of Icelandic and Faeroese. Other examples of Shetland Norn terms carrying the suffixed definite article in ossified form are: *sildin* = herring, *kusin* = cow, *knorrin* = boat, *hessin* = horse and *mostin* = mast.

The prosodic features of both Shetland and Orkney Norn appear to have been bequeathed to the varieties of Scots now spoken in the islands. As early as 1750, Murdoch Mackenzie was remarking that: 'The Language is English in the Scotch Dialect, with more of the Norwegian than any other accent; these Islands having formerly been a Province of Norway, of which they still retain a little of the Language, which they call Noren, much the same with what is presently spoken in Iceland and the Faro Islands'. The Rev George Low, in 1773, similarly observed that: '... they now altogether speak English, but with a great deal of the Norwegian accent'. Worsaae, too, was struck by the 'peculiarly sharp pronunciation' heard in Shetland, 'with a considerable rising and sinking of the voice, not unlike the vulgar pronunciation in the Faroe Isles'. Jakobsen noted that 'the common dialect' (ie the Scots) in Shetland 'has a distinctly Scandinavian accentuation and pronunciation', whilst Dr Marwick has pointed out that the Orkney cadence is

> quite different from that of any part of the mainland of Scotland, and there is not the slightest possibility of confusing it with that of our nearest neighbour – Caithness. But on the other hand, a Norwegian in Orkney, listening to Orcadians talking among themselves at such a distance that only their tones were audible, might well imagine he was at home in Norway. It is one of the most remarkable things about speech that people of the same stock, living out of touch with each other, may become mutually unintelligible so far as vocabulary is concerned, and yet retain 'the tune they speak to' practically unchanged through centuries. Such has been the case in regard to Orkney and its motherland Norway.

Apart from the patterns of intonation that still distinguish the speech of the Shetlanders and Orcadians from the mainland Scots, what other reminders are there in the dialects of the present-day islanders of the old Scandinavian language that was the daily idiom of their forebears? The answer must regrettably be – precious little. Aside from the placenames of both archipelagoes, over 90 per cent of which are wholly Norse, very few of the large number of Scandinavian words that were still remembered, and still in daily use, until a couple of generations ago, are now known. Although Dr Jakobsen, during his three-year stay in the islands in the mid-1890s, was able to record as many as 10,000 expressions of unambiguously Norse provenance, he ruefully confessed that: 'not more than half can be said to be in general use at the present time ... the number of obsolete words has steadily and uninterruptedly increased on account of the fact that from that time [the 1890s] a great many people of the older generation have passed away and a great part of their vocabulary has not been picked up by the next generation'.

It is clear that the Norn language in Orkney and Shetland is now irretrievably lost; it is, indeed, remarkable that it was able to withstand the erosion from Scots, to which it was subjected throughout the last five hundred years of its existence, for as long as it did. Only in those sections of the vocabulary covering familiar island concepts – crofting, fishing, weaving, turf-cutting, seabirds, weather conditions and the anatomy of small boats – plus a handful of well-loved terms of endearment and abuse (invariably the last wretched crumbs of a dying language to go under) may we still expect to find the few remaining sweepings of the Shetland and Orkney Norn. Even the rich repository of 'haaf' words – Scandinavian taboo terms once used by deep-sea fishermen for superstitious reasons in preference to dryland expressions (*husmor* for *wife*, *bønhus* = prayer house, for *kirk*, and *voaler* = wailer, for *cat*) has now been almost entirely depleted.

Ancient speech habits, however, can be astonishingly tenacious and may persist for generations after the disintegration of the structures and the dissipation of the lexicon of an expunged language. So it is not altogether surprising that, apart from the similarities between the prosodic patterns of North Island Scots and those of Norwegian and Faeroese noted above, other apparently Scandinavian features may still be detected in the English spoken in Orkney and Shetland.

Orcadian Scots, for example, makes use of a number of wholly un-English locutions that are clearly calqued on Scandinavian prototypes. The expression 'I'll have nothing with that to do' is a word-for-word rendition of the corresponding Norwegian: *Jeg vil ikke ha noe med det å gjøre* (or, in Nynorsk: *Eg vil ikkje ha noko med det å gjera*), whilst 'What for a lass is that?' – meaning 'Which girl is that?' – mirrors exactly the Norwegian pattern: *Hva for ei gjente er det*? Other Orcadian expressions that may initially bewilder an English speaker unfamiliar with Scandinavian usage include: 'At faa'in feet' (literally 'at falling feet') – used of a woman at the point of delivery, which reflects the identical Norwegian construction: *På fallande fot*; 'Oot apae the day' (near noon), which matches the Norwegian *Ute på dagen*; 'Right good' (very good), based on Norwegian *Ret god*; and 'In good ha'd' (in good condition), behind which surely lurks the Norwegian *I god hold*. The Orkney use of the term 'brigsteen' (bridge-stone) for 'flagstone' has confused many a Scot, who has failed to see the connection with bridges, although the meaning of the Orkney expression is transparent when we recall the sense of the Danish *brosten* – a paving stone. Similarly, 'bonieword' – in an expression like 'Be sure and say thee boniewords afore thoo goes tae bed' – which may perplex most English speakers, is clarified by reference to the Norse *bænarorð* = prayer word.

Some North Island expressions that have been singled out as being of Scandinavian inspiration, however, may equally well be Scots. The Orkney 'Half seeven' for half past six is, for example, as likely to reflect the Lowland Scots 'Hauf seeven' as the Norwegian *Halv sju*.

Both Orkney and Shetland Scots display some peculiar uses of gender that have no counterparts in the mainland dialects and may be carry-overs from Norn usage. Masculine personal pronouns are used when, for example, speaking of time or the weather, just as in collo-quial Icelandic and in certain Norwegian dialects, so that we hear: 'What time o' day is he?', 'He's a caald day' and 'He'll be snaa (snow) afore long', etc. The island dialects have also preserved a distinction between formal and familiar personal pronouns when used as terms of address – *ye* or *you* inferring respect or deference, *thou* (Orkney: *thoo*, Shetland: *du*) inferring familiarity. The latter form is, just as in Scandinavia, used among intimate friends, by grown-ups to children and by anyone speaking to an animal or to an inanimate object. In the following verse from James Stout Angus' Shetland dialect poem 'Voar' (Spring), the familiar term occurs both in its nominative form (*du*) and in the inflected forms *dee* and *dy* (*thee* and *thy*):

> Boy, skut i da door an tell's da time,
> As lang's du taks dy smok;
> If da møn be's ower da Burgataing
> He's efter aucht a'clock.
> So, well I wat du's tired da nicht,
> Efter da day't du's hed;
> An du'll jøst hae sic anidder da moarn,
> Sae gae dee wis ta dy bcd.

Apart from such minor traits as these, however, and the occasional fossilized idiom (such as 'Tara gott', meaning, roughly, 'That's finished, then' – a probable reflection of the Norwegian *Det er godt* = that's good), there are few features peculiar to present-day Orkney and Shetland Scots to remind us of the salty Norn tongue – the last wholly Scandinavian vernacular to be spoken in the British Isles.

In the last few years, there has been a revival of interest among the Shetlanders and Orcadians in their Scandinavian connections. Al-though this interest has been primarily political – and exemplified by

Orkney's 'Back to Denmark' movement and the 'Republic of Shet-land' movement – it has been accompanied by an active desire to restore a Scandinavian language to the islands. In Shetland, Scandin-avian names are being used more frequently than for hundreds of years, although the main sources are not the old autochthonous island Norn but rather the modern Scandinavian languages – particularly Norwegian. There is, inevitably, something a little recherché about these attempts at synthetic renordicisation; recently, for example, when a new guesthouse, bearing the Norwegian name 'Kveldsro', was opened in Lerwick, the *Shetland Times* found it necessary to explain to its readers that 'the name can be roughly translated as "Evening Quiet".' One wonders how many of the great-great-grand-parents of today's Lervíkings would have required such a translation!

The Channel Islands

From Orkney and Shetland we move south on our quest for Scandin-avian linguistic relics in Britain, south almost 700 miles to the Channel Islands, which lie in the great right-angled bight of north-west France between Normandy and Brittany.

These islands, which have been an integral part of Britain for over a thousand years, were occupied in about 300 BC by a Keltic (Gaulish)-speaking people, the Unelli. During the fourth century AD, the islands were under Roman occupation, and the resulting Latinised speech of their inhabitants continued until it was overlain in turn, during the tenth century AD, by Norman French. Norman dialects, closely akin to those spoken on the neighbouring Cotentin peninsula, are still spoken on Jersey, Guernsey and Sark, although French is now extinct on Alderney.

The Norman dialects ancestral to the present 'Jèrriais', 'Djernésiais' and other island patois were implanted here in 933, when the islands were captured from their Breton overlords by William Longsword, son of the Danish chieftain, Rolf the Ganger (see p. 52 above). Although it is known that the Norse language spoken by Rolf's henchmen was soon abandoned in Normandy in favour of French, many Scandinavian expressions – particularly those having to do with navigation and ship-building – found their way into Norman French, where a number of them remain to this day.

It was, therefore, largely through the agency of Norman French that most of the Scandinavian terms still heard in the indigenous Channel

Island patois first arrived in the islands, although it is not impossible that speakers of Norse itself were still to be found in the islands until as late as the eleventh century. Certainly the Vikings were very active in the waters off the north of France, and there is little doubt that, as well as using the Channel Isles as bases for wider-ranging piratical excursions, many Scandinavians made their homes on them.

Of the sizeable vocabulary of Norse terms still used in the Channel Islands, almost fifty are common both to the island patois and to standard literary French. Pre-eminently maritime and nautical expressions, these include such terms as *vague* = wave (N: *vágr*), *tillac* = planking (N: *þilja*), *hune* = the knob at the top of the masthead (N: *hunn*), *étrave* = the stem of a ship (N: *stafn*), *guindas* = windlass (N: *vindáss*), *guinder* = to hoist (N: *vinda*), *hommard* = lobster (N: *humarr*) and *marsouin* = porpoise (N: *marsvín*).

Seafaring terms also predominate among the thirty-odd Scandinavian terms heard in the Channel Islands but *not* in standard French, although topographical and agricultural expressions are also fairly frequent. Typical examples are: *chel* = keel (N: *kjǫlr*), *écoute* = sheet (of a sail) (N: *skaut*), *dal* = the opening in front of a pigsty through which food can be placed in the eating trough (N: *dola* = a groove, trough or trench), *gamer* = to amuse oneself (N: *gama*), *grei* = harness (N: *greið*), *hav* = a shrimp net (via a hypothetical intermediate form: **havenet* from N: *hafr* = sea + *net* = net), *haugar* = stackyard for corn (N: *haustgarðr* = harvest yard), *hougue* = a Neolithic dolmen (N: *haugr* = a burial mound), *merchi* = to mark (N: *merka*), *regaumi* = to vomit (N: *gómr* = the roof of the mouth), *meuque* = rancid (of butter) (N: *mjúkr* = soft), and *stegrin* = mean, avaricious (N: *styggr* = peevish).

Four

Scandinavian placenames in Britain

Although the many hundreds of Norse loanwords in English and Gaelic testify to a strong Scandinavian influence on the earlier forms of these two languages, they have, in common with all words in general circulation, been bandied back and forth across the land for a thousand years and more, and most of them have found their way to districts far from those where they were first picked up. *Hit, die, they, cast, both* and *till*, for example, were once peculiar to the dialects of the north and east, but are now common currency throughout the English-speaking world. Consequently, they can hardly be used to pinpoint with any degree of precision the exact areas where direct Norse influence was most acutely experienced. For information concerning the geographical distribution and approximate density of the primary and subsequent Scandinavian settlements, it is necessary to turn from the examination of Norse lexical constituents, both living and dead, in the spoken languages of Britain, to an investigation of placenames.

'Northumberland was mostly settled by Northmen after the sons of Hairybreaks won the land', wrote the great thirteenth-century Icelandic chronicler, Snorri Sturluson, 'and many of the places there have been given names in the Norse tongue – *Grímsbær* and *Hauksfljót*'.

Grímsbær, of course, is still with us – as Grimsby – although its one-time Humberside neighbour, Hawksfleet, has, like so many of our old Scandinavian placenames, completely vanished from the map; either the site itself has disappeared, or, more likely, its name has been supplanted by an alternative.

Naturally, very few placenames, Scandinavian or otherwise, have come down to us in anything approaching mint condition. All have been subjected over the centuries to a constant and relentless process of erosion and distortion, so that their existing forms seldom give much, if any, indication of their underlying meanings. Who could possibly guess that, for example, a Norse *Sigurðarhaugr* (Sigurd's mound) lies behind the Sutherland placename Cyderhall? That Hackensall is a corruption of the Norse *Hákonshaugr* (Hákon's mound)? That Orkney's Cairstone is really *Kjarreksstǫðum* (at Kjarrek's place)? That Sutherland's Oldshore hides an original *Ásleifarvík* (Ásleifr's inlet)? Or that the Inverness Arisaig began life as the Norse *Árisvágr* (Ári's inlet)? It is only by referring to medieval documents, in which the earlier forms of such names are recorded, that we can begin to recognise their undistorted elements and from these attempt to elucidate their underlying meanings. Although most of the surviving Scandinavian placenames in Britain have been satisfactorily deciphered in this way, there are many that are, even in their earliest accessible forms, already so disfigured that no reasonable interpretation is possible.

It was Worsaae who first recognised the significance of Scandinavian placenames in Britain; a study of their distribution would, he asserted, be a reliable means of locating fairly accurately the chief areas of Danish and Norwegian settlement.

Worsaae regarded the 1,400 Scandinavian placenames already identified on British soil in his day as reflecting the ejection of the former inhabitants by the Vikings, who had appropriated existing villages and given them new names in their own language. Such a view, which is still adhered to by a minority of scholars, is today regarded by most as basically unsound. Investigations conducted since Worsaae's day have shown convincingly not only that the Northmen, far from displacing the native population, tended to establish themselves in hitherto unworked areas, but that many – perhaps the majority – of British placenames containing Scandinavian elements date from after – sometimes a considerable time after – the various initial landnams of the Vikings. This is largely due to the fact that a comprehensive lexicon of Scandinavian toponymic terms, incorporated into both English and Gaelic a thousand and more years ago, has continued to yield productive placename ingredients right up to the present day. The meanings of such originally Norse terms as *scow* (wood), *beck* (brook), *gate* (road), *slack* (hollow), *carr* (swamp), and *ing* (meadow) are still familiar to the speakers of certain provincial forms of English, as are those of *òb* (creek), *mal* (shingly beach), *ùig* (cove) and *cuidh* (pen, enclosure) to the speakers of Scots Gaelic.

Nevertheless, even with these reservations in mind, there is still a striking conformity between the distribution of Norse placenames in Britain and the areas known from historical evidence to have been occupied by the Scandinavians. This is particularly true of the east Midlands, where all but about a score of the Danish or partly-Danish placenames lie east of the boundary fixed by Alfred and Guthrum to mark the western limit of the Danish settlement area – the later Danelaw. Within this area, the greatest concentrations of Scandinavian parish names occur in the North and East Ridings of Yorkshire, where they attain a maximum density just south of the Tees, in Lincolnshire (notably in Lindsey and Kesteven, but with very few examples in the fens of Holland, which were not completely reclaimed from the sea until the later Middle Ages), in Nottingham, in Rutland and in Leicester (especially along the valley of the river Wreak).

Norse placenames are only slightly less ubiquitous in Norfolk and Suffolk (where they cluster especially tightly along the river Waveney, a favoured Danish port of entry into East Anglia), in Northampton, Derby, the West Riding of Yorkshire, Cheshire (whose Wirral peninsula, between the Mersey and the Dee, has a particularly dense crop of them), and in Lancashire, where they are densest in Furness.

The maximum west-coast concentration is attained in Westmorland and Cumberland, an area known to have been intensively settled by Norwegians – the bulk of them from Ireland – during the tenth century. In the southern reaches of the Danelaw – Cambridge, Huntingdon, Bedford, Hertford and Essex – Norse placenames are thin on the ground, and there are few north of the Tees in either Durham or Northumberland, an area believed to have been largely vacated by its once substantial Scandinavian-speaking population after William's 'Harrying of the North', and not resettled until a later date. The south-eastern counties of Scotland – Roxburgh, Berwick and the Lothians – an area to which these Northumbrian expatriates fled in substantial numbers, contain an appreciably richer assemblage of Scandinavian placenames than is found anywhere between the Tweed and the Tees.

In south-west Scotland, Norse placenames are plentiful in the counties facing Cumberland across the Solway Firth – Wigtown, Kirkudbright and Dumfries. They thin out perceptibly towards the north until the Hebrides are reached; here, they occur again, sparsely

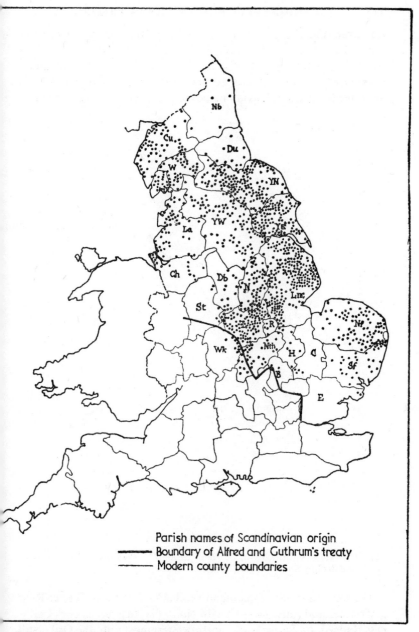

FIG. 9. Scandinavian parish names in England (based on the map in *The Age of the Vikings* by P. H. Sawyer, 1962, p. 157).

on Arran and Kintyre, more profusely on Islay and Colonsay, and
most abundantly of all on Skye, Barra, North Uist and on Lewis,
where they outnumber Gaelic names by four to one. The maximum
concentration on Lewis itself occurs in the parish of Ùig, where there
are some thirty Scandinavian names to every one of Gaelic origin.

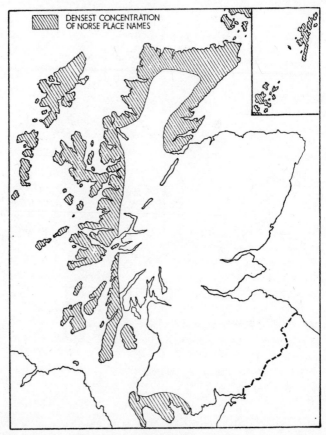

FIG. 10.   Norse settlements in Scotland (from *The Prehistoric Settlements of
Scotland* edited by Stuart Piggott, 1962).

The western fringe of mainland Scotland – Inverness, Wester Ross
and Sutherland – also swarms with Norse placenames, as does Caithness. Indeed, on Sutherland's north-westernmost nub, the Ord – still
known in Gaelic as *Gall-Aobh*, 'the headland of the strangers' (i.e.

Northmen) – three out of four placenames are Scandinavian. Down the entire east coast of Scotland south of Beauly Firth, however, there is scarcely a Scandinavian name in sight; for some reason, still unaccounted for, the Northmen appear to have shunned this part of Scotland lying closest to their own homeland.

The placenames of Orkney and Shetland are almost exclusively Scandinavian, whilst Norse names also abound on Man, notably in the southern and eastern Sheadings (N: *skeiðarþing* – place of assembly for warship-crews). Only a few – perhaps less than a dozen – have survived in Ireland, whilst apart from a small cluster on the south-western extremity of Pembroke, they are scarce in Wales. Early records, however, suggest that they were once much more numerous in the Principality, particularly in Glamorgan. Certain of the small islands off Wales and in the Bristol Channel still carry their Norse names, although the majority have long since been replaced by English or Welsh alternatives.

The Scandinavian element in English placenames is recognisable by the same parameters as those employed in identifying the Norse influences in other sections of our language: many English placenames are made up of one or more terms unattested in Old English but known to have existed in Norse; others carry vestigial traces of Norse grammatical inflections; and others contain sounds or sound combinations that are suspected to have been characteristic of Norse but probably not of early English.

A large number of English placenames, especially in the north and east, reflect the substitution of original English by Scandinavian sounds and sound combinations, and it is clear that Danish speech habits were strong enough in certain districts to cause the pronunciation not only of native colloquial words but also of long-established placenames to be refashioned to conform with the locally prevailing, Nordicised norm. A classical example is that of York, whose present form is the end-product of a series of remodellings that have repeatedly altered the phonic shape of the name over the last 2,000 years. York began life as *Eborakon*, a Keltic name containing the element *Eburos*, meaning a yew tree, and the town was mentioned by this name by the Greek geographer, Ptolemy, in AD 150. The Romans latinised the name to *Eboracum*, and the Anglians in their turn corrupted it to *Eoforwic*, in which their own word, *eofor*, a boar, was substituted for the quite incomprehensible first element. It is, however – as with so many placenames in the north of England and in Scotland – the Scandinavian form (*Jórvík* – which rapidly contracted to *Jórk*) that lies behind the city's present name.

In some areas, Scandinavian traits in the local pronunciation of English persisted until an astonishingly late date, and certain north-country placenames appear not to have acquired their present Nordic-ised forms until well into the Middle Ages. To judge from their earlier renditions, Yorkshire's *Bradewell*, Leicesterhire's *Cyningestun* and Durham's *Ciningesclif*, for example, acquired their present, Scandinavianised forms, Braithwell, Congerston and Coniscliffe, as recently as the thirteenth century.

Scandinavian speech habits are also responsible for the present forms of many originally Gaelic placenames in Scotland. The existing names of four of the large Hebridean islands, for example, result from the Norse pronunciation (perhaps 'mispronunciation' would be more apt) of Keltic originals. Neither the English names of these islands – Harris, Lewis, Uist and Skye – nor their modern Gaelic equivalents – Hearradh, Leodhas, Uibhist and Sgidh – make any sense as placenames, and the same can be said of the Norse prototypes upon which they are based. Harris is named, in the Icelandic sagas, as *Herað* (a *herað* was a minor administrative district in Denmark and parts of Sweden). Lewis was referred to as *Ljóðhús* (literally = 'people house'), Uist was *Ívist* (a dwelling), whilst Skye's Scandinavian name was *Skíð* – a billet of wood (the same word as the Norwegian *ski*). As placenames these are all nonsensical, and are almost certainly Scandinavian garblings of Keltic originals that were incomprehensible to the North-men. Orkney's name, on the other hand, reflects an attempt on the part of the Northmen to rationalise the old Keltic *Innse Orc* – Islands of the Boars (the name of a Pictish tribe) – by making it their own *Orkneyjar* – Islands of the Young Seals.

It is by no means always easy to distinguish between the native forms of English placenames and those whose pronunciation has been remodelled as a result of the influence of Scandinavian speech habits. Such doublets as English: *dæl*/Norse: *dalr* (valley), E: *fleot*/N: *fljót* (stream), E: *hlīp*/N: *hlíð* (slope), E: *hrīs*/N: *hrís* (brushwood), E: *hwamm*/N: *hvammr* (hollow), E: *stīg*/N: *stíg* (path), and E: *stofn*/N: *stofn* (treestump), for example, represent a range of place-name elements which, because of their evidently very similar pro-nunciation in both languages, would invariably have yielded identical modern forms. If, however, names containing such elements as these occur in areas where the place nomenclature is already overwhelmingly Scandinavian, they are naturally as likely to be of Norse as of native inspiration, especially if they are found in conjunction with other Norse elements. This applies, for example, to the numerous placenames in the north and east in which -*thorp*, a word common to Old English and Old Norse, is compounded with a Scandinavian personal name. Similarly, the suffix -*acre* in Stainsacre, Yorks, coupled, as it is, with a Norse personal name, Steinn, and located in an area of intense Scandinavian influence, is more likely to reflect an original Norse *ákr* (field) than its native equivalent, *æcer*.

In a very few instances, we are fortunate to have documentary evidence that can assist us in determining a placename ingredient as native or Norse. Were it not, for example, for the following extract from a medieval Icelandic text, the second constituent in the Yorkshire placename, Scarborough, might as easily have been accepted as containing the English *beorg* = a fortified place, as the corresponding (and almost homophonous) Norse, *borg*.

> The brothers, Thorgils Harelip and Kormak, harried in Ireland, Wales, England and Scotland, and were considered the doughtiest of men. They first built the stronghold that is named 'Skarðaborg' [after Thorgils' nickname, Skarði = Harelip].

Unfortunately, contemporary documentary evidence of this sort is extremely rare, and in most of the many cases in which English placenames contain an element that would have been identical, both in sound and meaning, in Old English and Old Norse, it is impossible to divine which of the two languages contributed the element.

Aside from these uncertain cases, however, there are many examples of placenames in England in which elements evidently common to Old English and Old Norse bear the unmistakable imprint of Scandinavian phonology. In some cases, the element itself may be an original Norse contribution, although it is just as frequently a remodelling of an earlier English form.

In areas where the local form of English was heavily Nordicised in pronunciation, the palatal consonants of Old English have frequently been usurped by the corresponding Scandinavian 'hard' K, SK, and G, in positions where the native form would more likely have been CH, SH and Y. Placenames are, of course, much more resistant to

8

change than are words in colloquial idiom – especially when these are constantly subjected to normative pressure from the standard language – and those placenames featuring Scandinavian sounds that have clearly displaced earlier English ones give a much clearer indication of the areas where the influence of Scandinavian phonology was formerly at work than do the lingering Nordic articulatory habits in surviving dialects.

FIG. 11.   'Caster' placenames in England (based on the map in *Modern Linguistics* by Simeon Potter, 1957, p. 137).

Thus, while many speakers of northern English dialects have long since forsaken such traditional Nordicised pronunciations as 'kist' for *chest*, 'skaft' for *shaft*, 'garn' for *yarn*, 'hame' for *home* and 'rowk' for *reek*, hundreds of Lowland Scottish and northern and eastern English placenames have retained the Scandinavian sounds they acquired in the Middle Ages.

In this way, the familiar Charlton (farm of the *ceorls* or peasants), Chiswick (cheese farm) and Chester (from Latin *castra* = camp) which, in the old Scandinavian areas, acquired at some stage in their development a 'hard' K in place of their former English palatal CH, remain Carlton, Keswick and Caster (or Caister – see map for distribution of 'Caster' forms).

Similarly, although many Scottish and north-country placenames have inherited the Scandinavian 'kirk' in place of their original English 'church' (e.g. Kirton, Kirkstead, Kirkland, Kirklees), few of their inhabitants will nowadays use the form 'kirk' for 'church' in their daily speech.

In identical fashion, the native palatal SH – as in such south-country placenames as Shirley, Shillington, Shelton, Shipton and Shalford – are matched in the old areas of Scandinavian influence by forms with the Norse SK, e.g. Skirlaugh, Skillington, Skelton, Skipton and Scalford, although equivalent pronunciations in the dialects spoken in and around these northern towns – such as 'skift' for *shift* and 'skudder' for *shudder* – are archaic, if not completely obsolete.

Placenames in which the native Y before front vowels has been replaced by the Norse 'hard' G are somewhat scarcer – and toponymic equivalents to the Scandinavianised 'give', 'girl' and 'guess' in spoken English are more difficult to locate than those showing Norse K and SK for native CH and SH. Gilling in Yorkshire may be an example of this particular sound substitution; it appears to be a Nordic reshaping of a native prototype that might otherwise have survived as Yilling or Yelling.

In a few rare cases, placenames reveal the one-time existence of Scandinavian speech mannerisms in local English dialects from which such features have long since died out. Danelaw placenames such as Goathland, Mythop, Tathwell and Louth, for example, contain the fricative sounds, Þ and Ð in positions where the native English forms would have had the corresponding stop, D. Early spellings of these four names confirm that they began life as the perfectly 'regular' English Goodland, Midhope, Tadwell and Loud before acquiring their present fricatives from local, Scandinavianised peasant speech.

Native English vowels, too, were frequently replaced by their Scandinavian counterparts. In the north country, the Norse diphthong EI often worked its way into placenames that had formerly contained the corresponding English vowel, Ā. Norse *breiðr* (broad) has thus

replaced Old English *brād* in Braithwell (note also the medial fricative
– Braithwell's southern counterpart is Bradwell), whilst Norse *steinn*
(stone) has ousted Old English *stān* from Stanton, Stanley and Stan-
field (all of which survive intact in the south) to produce the Danelaw
Staintons, Stainleys and Stainfields. Again, it is the Norse *eik* (oak),
rather than the native *āc*, that is the first part of the Lincolnshire
placename Eagle, which would, had it escaped Norse recasting, have
survived as Oakley. Many placenames containing Norse EI for
English Ā are located in parts of the Danelaw from which such
pronunciations as 'stain' for *stone* and 'hame' for *home* were long ago
discarded; indeed, this particular pronunciation is now restricted to a
gradually diminishing area in Scotland and the extreme north of
England (see the map on p. 22 above). The evidence of placenames,
however, shows clearly that the distribution of EI for Ā was at one
time much more widespread – occurring as far south in the Danelaw
as Leicestershire. Earlier spellings indicate that the substitution for
English Ā of Norse EI extended in former times to many placenames
that have long since reverted to their original English form. Leicestershire's Humberstone, for example, was recorded as 'Humbersteyne'
until as recently as the fifteenth century, while Waddingham and
Alvingham in Lincolnshire were formerly written and so, presumably,
pronounced, 'Wadingeheim' and 'Alvingeheim', with Norse *heim*
for Old English *hām*.

Examples of the substitution of native ĒA by Norse AU are not
quite so common as those showing EI for Ā. They include Owstwick
(for Eastwick), Rawcliffe (for Redcliffe), and the lost Noutegang (N:
naut = cattle, answering OE: *nēat*). Many others that formerly carried
the Scandinavian diphthong have long since been re-anglicised, Oust
Cal (recorded thus in 1118) becoming East Keal and Oust Mersc
reverting to East Marsh. The form 'oust' (N: *austr*) for 'east' seems,
incidentally, to have been characteristic of peasant speech in many
parts of the old Danelaw until a relatively late date. In a Lincolnshire
charter from the time of Henry II (1154–89), a place named 'Oust in
wra' (N: *austr í vrá* = east in (the) nook) is mentioned, the East Riding
of Yorkshire is recorded in the Domesday Book as 'Oust Redinc',
whilst there were formerly many others of the type Oustscow (Dan:
Østskov = east wood) and Austerby (Dan: *Østerby*) that have
vanished from the map. Sometimes, a name appears in early documents in both its native and its Scandinavian form, as did Eastbec/

Oustbec, in which the original Norse *austr* was probably in the process of yielding to the English *east* – the older generation preserving the Norse form, the younger generation using the native form.

Instances of the substitution of native elements beginning with the English *Wu-* by Norse *U-*, as at Ulverston in Lancashire, which appears to be a remodelling of an original Wulfherestun, are much rarer. Slightly more widespread are examples of the substitution of SH – derived from the Norse *hj* – for the English clusters *hea* and *heo*. By this process, an original Heoptun (hip farm) became Shipton and early Heap (heap) became Shap. The rendering of Norse *hj* as SH seems to have been characteristic of the variety of Norse spoken in much of Britain – Shetland having begun life as Hjetland or Hjaltland, Orkney's island of Shapinsay as Hjalpandisey, Shoulthwaite as Hjólþveit (N: *hjól* = wheel) and Shawm Rigg as *hjálm* + *hryggr* (helm ridge – or ridge shaped like a helmet). This pronunciation of *hj* as SH is typical of the modern Norwegian dialects spoken in the Gudbrandsdal, where *hjerne* (brain) and *hjå* (at) sound like *sjerne* and *sjå* and the placename Hjerdkinn becomes 'Sjerkinn'. In Faeroese, *hj* becomes CH, as, for example, in the man's name Hjálmar, which is pronounced 'Tjåalmar'.

It should be clear, from all this, that Scandinavian speech habits have exerted a much more intense influence on English placenames than on our standard spoken language.

The recognition of Scandinavian phonological features is of course only one – albeit an important – method of identifying Norse influences in English placenames; there are also innumerable lexical criteria that we may apply to a name in order to determine whether it is of native English or Scandinavian derivation.

In many instances, it was not merely an English sound, but an entire native element, that was replaced by its Scandinavian equivalent. In Conington, Coniscliffe, Conisbrough, Coniston and several other north-country and Danelaw placenames, the Norse *konungr* = king, has ousted the original English *cyning*; at Askham, native *æsc* (*ash*) has yielded to Norse *askr*; at Howden, Norse *hǫfuð* (head) has eclipsed English *heafod*; whilst English *middel* (middle) gave way to Norse *meðal* at Melton (compare native Middleton). In a few cases, the process was reversed, with earlier Scandinavian names being anglicised. An original Norse Fagherwald (N: *fagr* = fair), for example, became Fairwood, Elptarvatn (swan water) became Elterwater and *Nybøle (new homestead) became Newball.

Instances of the complete usurpation of former native names by new alternatives of Scandinavian coinage are rare, two notable examples being Derby, which replaced an earlier English Northworthy, and Whitby, which eclipsed both an earlier Norse Prestebi and an even earlier English Streonæshalch. Despite the apparent infrequency of such transformations, however, it is likely that many others took place during and after the period of the Scandinavian settlements, but were not recorded.

Of particular interest, in that they indicate the often surprisingly late survival of Scandinavian expressions and personal names in certain districts, are those placenames compounded of a native and a Norse element. These hybrid names fall naturally into two categories, the first comprising names in which the Scandinavian element refers to some natural feature, as at Aikhead (N: *eik* = oak), Beanthwaite (N: *þveit* = clearing), Ryeholms (N: *holmr* = a piece of dry land surrounded by *moister* terrain) and Wetwang (N: *vangr* = a field). That such terms are found in conjunction with native elements, and that names of this type are often demonstrably recent formations, shows clearly that such Scandinavian words as those contained in the above examples still flourished in the rural vocabulary of certain areas until well into the Middle Ages.

The second class of mixed Anglo-Norse placenames, those compounded of a Scandinavian personal name plus a native suffix, which usually refers to some topographical feature, are known as 'Grimston hybrids', Grímr being an unambiguously Norse name, *-ton* being the common native suffix signifying a village or hamlet. Apart from Grimston itself, which occurs no less than a dozen times on English soil, other typical representatives of this category of hybrids are Caxton (N: *Kakkr*), Branston (N: *Brandr*), Gamston (N: *Gamal*), Thelveton (N: *Þjalfi*), Thurgarton (N: *Þórgeirr*) and Thurlaston (N: *Þórleifr*). Berkshire's East Garston was named after a Dane called Esger Stallere, mentioned in *Domesday Book* as a tenant in Lambourne. The village was still known as 'Esgareston' in the first half of the thirteenth century, although later generations forgot the old Scandinavian name that it enshrined, substituting for it the native East.

In contrast to the first type of Anglo-Norse compound, most Grimston hybrids date from early in the Danish landnam and are characteristically found around the margins of areas of intense Scandinavian settlement. They are therefore much commoner in East Anglia than in the more central Danelaw Shires, such as Lincolnshire. Although it is generally believed that Grimston hybrids were either coined by Anglian speakers to designate existing villages that had been appropriated by Danes or result from an early adoption of Danish personal names by Anglians, there is a possibility – so far unhinted at – that they may have been entirely Danish (some of them, at any rate). *-tun* had been a productive placename element in Scandinavia (notably in Middle Sweden, cf Sigtuna, Eskilstuna, etc) prior to the Viking Age and there is no reason why such a term, like so many other archaisms, should not have continued in use among the Danish settlers in England long after it had fallen out of favour in the mother country. Grimston hybrids occurring far from the old Scandinavian settlement area (like Swainston on the Isle of Wight, Thurloxton (ODan: *Thurlakr*) in Somerset and Thruxton (N: *Þórkil*) in Hereford) may well have been named after Danish Thingmen (members of the *þingmannalið* (bodyguard) of Canute the Great or Edward the Confessor) who received manors in various parts of the country outside the Danelaw. This type of hybrid is also characteristic of those parts of the Scottish Lowlands settled by families of part-Scandinavian extraction displaced by William's pogroms in Northumbria; typical examples are Dolphinston (N: *Dolgfinnr*) in Peebles and Ormiston in East Lothian.

A number of English placenames have preserved vestigial, but nonetheless unmistakable, traces of Norse morphological inflections. Placenames embodying the unreduced genitive affix, *-ar*, typical of West Norse, are significantly more frequent in those parts of the country known to have been settled predominantly by Norwegians rather than by Danes. Characteristic examples are: Beckermet (N: *bekkjarmót*=the junction of two streams), Amounderness (N: *Qgmundarnes* = Qgmundr's ness), Borrowdale (N: *borgardalr* = valley of the fortress), Aismunderby (Ásmundr's village), Amotherby (Eymundr's village), Helperthorpe (Hjalp's village), Litherskew (N: *hlíðarskógr* = wood on the slope), Fouldray (N: *Fuðarey* = the island of Fuð) and the vanished Wymundergil (Vígmundr's valley). In prevailingly Danish settlement areas, on the other hand, the reduced form of the inflection, *-a*, is more in evidence in placenames; vanished Danelaw examples like Aslocahou (Áslak's mound),

Osgotabi (Ásgaut's village), and Esbernebi (Ásbjǫrn's village), and
surviving locations like Hawerby (Hávarð's village), correspond to
such medieval village names as Signbiornatorp and Gutmundatorp in
Denmark itself. This East Scandinavian genitive inflection was even,
on occasions, extended to Danelaw placenames containing English
personal names, as at Atterby (Ēadrēd's village) and Audleby
(Aldwulf's village).

An alternative Norse genitive ending was -s (corresponding to the
Old English -es), which, being voiceless itself, also made a preceding
consonant voiceless, if it was not so already. V, for example, became
F, and D or Ð became T. Although the voiceless consonant preceding
S was often lost from placenames, the -s itself remained, yielding
examples like Braceby (Breiðr's village), Laceby (Leif's village),
Ulceby (Ulfr's village) and Faceby (Feitr's village) which would,
if pronounced in the native English manner, with voiced S, [Z],
have come down to us as Brazeby, Lazeby, Ulzeby and Fazeby.

Another Norse inflection that occurs, in fossilised form, in a
number of English placenames, is the dative plural suffix -um, which is
met at Ayrsome (N: *Árhúsum* = at the buildings by the riverside),
Hoon (N: *haugum* = at the mounds), Kelham (N: *kjǫlum* = at the
keels, ie ridges), Botham (N: *búðum* = at the booths), Arram (N:
ergum = at the shielings), Lathom (N: *hlaðum* = at the barns),
Lytham (N: *hlíðum* = at the slopes) and Crookham (N: *krókum* = at
the bends).

The distinction between English placenames of East Scandinavian
– specifically Old Danish – and those of West Scandinavian or Norwegian inspiration is seldom easy to determine. The toponymic
evidence permits no hard-and-fast line to be drawn anywhere in
Britain to separate those areas settled predominantly by Danes from
those more favoured by Norwegians. There is little doubt that Norwegians were present in substantial numbers throughout the Danelaw – especially in its northern reaches – whilst Danish and Norwegian
settlement areas appear to have overlapped along a broad front
running from the North Riding south into Derby.

There is, however, no denying the fact that certain Scandinavian
placename elements have a discordant distribution on English soil;
many are much more characteristic of the Danelaw than of Cumberland, Westmorland and Furness, whilst a whole range of elements
found abundantly in the fell country of the north and west – the area

of Hiberno-Norwegian colonisation – are entirely lacking from the old Danish districts.

A survey (by regions) of Scandinavian placenames in Britain

This rapid survey of Britain's enormous legacy of Scandinavian place-names begins in the shires of old East Mercia and southern North-umberland – the Danelaw proper – crosses the Pennines into north-western England and pays a fleeting visit to the Isle of Man before heading north through the Scottish Lowlands to the Western Isles. The western and northern mainland of Scotland are considered next and the survey returns south again, after a fairly detailed investigation of the Scandinavian placenames in Orkney and Shetland, to Ireland and Wales. Last to be dealt with are the Scandinavian place-names that are found in such abundance all around the coasts of the British Isles, and the correspondingly rare Norse influence on inland hydronymics.

The Danelaw

Placename-conscious visitors to England from Denmark or southern Sweden are often impressed by the fact that, although many of the placename elements familiar to them from their own countries occur profusely between the Welland and the Tees, there are other elements – equally typical of Denmark and much of Sweden – that are nowhere to be found on English soil. Why, the visiting Dane might ask, are *by, thorp, toft, carr, ing, beck* and *holm* (which he will doubtless recognise after a little reflection as being none other than his own *by, torp, toft, kær, eng, bæk* and *holm*) so well represented in England, whereas *-lev, -løse, -vin, -sted* and *-inge* are entirely absent?

The reason is that the five last-named elements are representative, in Denmark itself, of a stratum of placename constituents that had become obsolete by the time of the Danish settlements in England.

Where, then, the persistent Dane may continue, are the *-røds, -holts* and *-købings* of his native land? Surely there is nothing ante-diluvian about *these* elements, for they are still living words in the vocabulary of modern colloquial Danish? Precisely. *-rød* (a clearing), *-holt* (a wood) and *-købing* (a market town) are historically recent Danish placename elements; they did not become widespread in Denmark itself until well after the Viking Age, and so can hardly be expected to have been carried to England by the crews of the longships.

Obviously, the most recurrent Danish placename ingredients in England must be those, such as *by*, *torp*, *toft*, *bæk*, etc. – that were the most productive in the mother country during the ninth, tenth and eleventh centuries, the period of the Danish settlements in England.

-by   Far and away the most recurrent of the Norse placename elements in the Scandinavian settlement areas in England is the suffix *-by* (ON: *býr* = a village – although in England it seems to have referred to farmsteads or, at most, isolated hamlets). It occurs more than 700 times on English soil and is particularly abundant in the Old Danelaw shires, where no fewer than 543 villages whose names ended in *-by* already existed at the times of William's Domesday survey in 1085: 217 in Lincolnshire alone, 203 in Yorkshire, 55 in Leicester, 22 in Nottingham, 21 in Norfolk, 13 in Northampton, 9 in Derby and 3 in Suffolk.

Approximately two out of every three English placenames ending in *-by* are compounded with personal names, the bulk of which are Scandinavian – e.g. Swainby (Sveinn), Gunnby (Gunnarr), Haconby (Hákon), Laceby (Leifr), Stakesby (Staki), Scratby (Skrauti, a nickname meaning 'boastful'), Ormsby (Ormr), Ulceby (Ulfr), Grimsby (Grímr), Thirkleby (Þórkell) and Throxenby (Þórsteinn). From Danish sources, we learn that *-by* names compounded in this fashion with personal names are by no means typical of Denmark as a whole, being confined for the most part to the southern islands of Lolland, Langeland and, especially, to south-east Jutland – although it would be rash to infer from this that the majority of the Danish colonists in England hailed from the southern part of the old country. *-by* appears to have enjoyed a long life as an independent word in many of the northern and Danelaw dialects; not only did men continue to speak, long after the Danish period, of 'Going to the By', they also used the compound form, complete with genitive suffix *-ar*, 'Bierlaw' (from the Norse *Býjarlǫg*, whence also the synonymous Scots: Burlie, Burley, Burlaw, Byrlaw, Birley, etc) which meant both the laws of a *by* or township and the district over which such bylaws held good (whence such placenames as Ecclesall Bierlaw in Yorkshire). The fact that *-by* continued in common use until at least the twelfth century in certain districts is attested by such late formations as Flimby in Cumberland – named from a community of Flemings who settled there during the 1100s – and Aglionby, in which *-by* is combined with the name of a Norman, Agyllun, who held land in Cumberland in the twelfth century. Occasionally, -by even replaced the native suffix -byrig, meaning 'fortified place'; Greasby in Cheshire, for example, appeared in *Domesday Book* as Gravesberie, Naseby as Navesberie, and Rugby as Rocheberie; later forms of these names, with -by, date from the twelfth century and testify to the enduring vigour of the Scandinavian term.

Certain English family names containing -by, such as Sotheby, Easterby and Dunnaby, also testify to the protracted use of the term in provincial English; they refer to men who lived, respectively, 'south', 'east' and 'down' in the By. The surname Easterby was still circulating in such Scandinavian forms as Oustinby and Austebi as late as the thirteenth century.

Other -by names refer to the provenance of settlers in areas where men of their nationality were in a minority; the occurrence in certain districts of places named Denby and Denaby (village of the Dane or Danes) suggests that Danes were something of a rarity in the neighbourhood, whilst Ingleby (village of the English) implies that there were some areas where the native Anglians were in the minority. Other names of this type include Irby (farm of the Irishman), Scotby, Birkby (1163: Brettebi = farm of the Briton), Frisby (farm of the Frisian), Normanby (farm of the Norwegian), and even Ferrensby, named from a Faering or man from the Faeroe islands. Romanby has, of course, nothing whatever to do with a Roman; it takes its name from a Scandinavian called *Hrómundr*.

A minority of English -by names contain as their first element a term relating to some topographical feature and in this way conform much more closely to the Danish norm; the English Aby (N: *ár* = river), Dalby, Beckby, Borrowby (N: *berg* = hill), Lumby (N: *lundr* = grove), Mickleby (N: *mikill* = large), Sinderby (Southby), Raby (N: *rá* = boundary mark), Keadby (originally Hedeby = Heathby), and Utterby (Outerby), are matched in Denmark by Aaby, Dalby, Bækby, Borreby, Lumby, Møgleby, Sønderby, Raaby, Hedeby and Yderby.

-thorp The suffix -thorp is almost as common in parts of the old Danelaw as -by. Indeed, there are sections of east Yorkshire and Norfolk where -thorp names outnumber -by names appreciably. In Denmark and Sweden, where the word has always been more productive as a placename element than in Norway and its Atlantic outposts, including the English north-west and Scotland, -*thorp* (nowadays reduced to -*drup*, -*rup*, -*arp*, etc) was originally applied to a secondary settlement or outlying farm (Dan: Udflytterbebyggelse) and this appears to have been its primary meaning in the Scandinavian districts of England. Even today, few of the surviving English- *thorps* are large parishes or towns (Lincolnshire's Scunthorpe, Cleethorpes and Mablethorpe have only comparatively recently attained their present size), and the majority of those that have not disappeared from the map are either small and insignificant places or daughter communities dependent on larger settlements (Dan: *Adelbyer*) – as at Burnham Thorpe, near Burnham in Norfolk, and Ixworth Thorpe near Ixworth in Suffolk. *Thorp*, like *by*, survived as a much-used lexical item in the Scandinavianised dialects of the Danelaw – Tennyson used it in Maud: 'I hurry down ... By twenty thorps, a little town, and half a hundred bridges' – and many English *thorps* are of comparatively late origin, as is suggested by the fact that they are typically situated on very low-lying, recently-reclaimed land. Characteristic English *thorp* names, containing, as do the bulk of the *thorp* names in Denmark, Norse personal names, are: Sculthorpe (Skúli's thorp), Knostrop (Knútr's thorp), Scagglethorpe (Skakil), Gribthorpe (Grípr), Ugthorpe (Uggi), Cawthorpe (Kali), Owsthorpe (Úfi), Hawthorpe (Hávarðr), and the lost Colestainthorpe (Kolsteinn), Grinklethorp (Grímkell), and Swaynesthorpe. Others contain Scandinavian renditions of native English personal names (e.g. Yaddlethorpe: Jadulfr for Éadwulf), whilst even later examples contain Norman personal names, as does Baconthorpe (Norman: *bacon* = 'pig's body', a typical nickname). A few, such as Copmanthorpe (N: *Kaupmannaþorp* = merchant's village), contain occupational names. *Torp* also survived as a productive placename element in Denmark until well into the Middle Ages, as evidenced by the occurrence of late examples containing foreign names such as Mikkelstrup, Abrahamstrup, Bendstrup and Ibstrup (Bent = Benedict, Ib = Jacob).

Toft   According to the Swedish linguist, Bengt Holmberg, the Old Norse word *topt* or *tupt* was originally applied to a plot of land marked out for a house (a building site is still known as a *byggnadstomt* in Swedish). Later, however, it came to mean a homestead (N: *Hann byggvir toptir fǫðir* = he lives in his father's house) and it is in this sense that the word, in its Danish form, *toft*, occurs in English placenames. Names ending in *toft* are typical of the eastern Danelaw, with examples scattered from Suffolk to the North Riding, although the suffix occurs neither in the old Norwegian districts in the north-west nor in the most southerly Danelaw shires. *Toft* is still used in the sense of a homestead in some of our rural dialects, notably in Lincolnshire, where the owner of such a *toft* is known as a *tofter* or a *toftman*. The word can also mean a low eminence or 'tump', and it was used in this sense by Langland in his prologue to *The Vision of Piers the Plowman*: 'I saw a tower on a *toft;* a deep dale beneath'.

In Denmark, where *toft* survives as *towt* in the Jutland dialect in the sense of 'the part of a farm lying nearest the house' (Feilberg), most placenames containing the word feature it in its plural form, *tofte*, and it is commonly compounded with a personal name – presumably that of the original owner of the site, as at Terkelstofte, Ormstofte and Ravnstofte (identical with a vanished English Rafenestoft). The majority of English *tofts*, too, contain as their first element a Scandinavian personal name – as at Sibbertoft (Sígbjǫrn), Lowestoft (1212: Lothewistoft – Hloðver's toft) and the lost Aslactoft and Ulvestoft, while certain vanished examples occurred, Danish style, in plural form, as at Eyrichtoftis and Hafketelstofta. Other *tofts* are compounded with an adjective describing the site, as at Bratoft (N: *breiðr* = broad) and Langtoft (N: *langr* = long), or with the name of some nearby topographical feature, as at Wigtoft (N: *vík* = an inlet or creek). Quite frequently, *toft* occurs on its own, either in the singular or in the plural: *tofts*.

Minor features Less densely distributed than *-by*, *-thorpe* and *-toft*, yet equally characteristic of the old Danelaw, are the elements *beck* (N: *bekkr* = a stream), *how* or *hoe* (N: *haugr* = a mound – more specifically a tumulus), and *gate* (N: *gata* = a street). *Beck* occurs throughout the Scandinavian settlement area as far south as Nottingham, Lincoln and Derby, and typical Danelaw examples are: Holbeck (a Danish rendition of an earlier English *on holan broc* = 'at the hollow (i.e. deep) brook') and Skirbeck (N: *skíri* = bright), which are the exact counterparts of Holbæk and Skærbæk in Denmark. Starbeck in Yorkshire equals Starbæk in Denmark (N: *stǫrr* = coarse grass used for thatching) whilst Skirpenbeck in the East Riding contains the Norse *skerping* = barren land, identical with the common Norwegian placename element, Skjerping.

Haugr, a mound, is also widely, though thinly, distributed throughout the north and east of England. It frequently contains as its first element a Scandinavian personal name – presumably that of the occupant of the mound – as do the two Lincolnshire wapentake names Aslacoe (Áslakr) and Haverstoe (Hávarðr), and the Lancashire Hackensall, which was first recorded as Hacunesho = Hákon's howe. Hoby (village at the mound) and Thingoe (N: *þinghaugr* = mound where the district Thing, or moot, assembled) match the several villages named Hoby (or Højby) and Tinghøj in Denmark, whilst there was formerly a place named Huttoft (toft at the *haugr* or mound) in Norfolk. Dringhoe in Yorkshire refers, as does Droiton in Stafford, to a *drengr*, a title which originally meant 'a bold, valiant daring man' (Cleasby) but came, in Danish Northumbria, to be applied more specifically to a freeman holding a tenure ('Drengage tenure') that was partly military and partly servile.

In many of the older towns in the north and east, street-names are still to be found bearing the suffix *-gate*. This does not refer to the original 'gates' of the town, but is merely the Old Norse word for a street, *gata*. *Gate* is still used in Scotland and the north of England, in the sense of 'road', 'way' or 'street', in such expressions as 'to take the gate' (to be on one's way), 'to get things agate' (to get things moving), and 'I'll get you the length of the gate' (I'll walk to the end of the road with you). Streets bearing the name *-gate* are found from Norwich, which has a Pottergate, to Edinburgh, with its Cowgate and Netherkirkgate. York has a large number, including Fishergate (formerly found in its pure Scandinavian form: Fiskergate), Goodramgate (containing the man's name Gúðþormr), Coppergate (N: *koppari* = a joiner), Skeldergate (N: *skjaldari* = a shield maker), Staingate, Walmgate, Monkgate and Fossgate. Early examples from York which have long since been renamed included the wholly Danish Plouswayngate (Ploughmangate, now Blossomgate!), Ketmangergate (Fleshmonger or Butcher street, N: *Kjǫtmangaragata*, synonymous with Copenhagen's famous Købmangergade – originally Kødmangergade), and Haymangergate (N: *heymangari* = hay merchant). Other Danelaw examples are Sheffield's Fargate, Derby's Bridge Gate, Leicester's Abbey Gate, Leeds' Briggate, Lincoln's Danesgate, Winterton's Yarlesgate (N: *Jarl*) and Newcastle's Gallowgate, whilst the East Riding town of Hedon has its Souttergate (N: *sutari* = a shoemaker), identical with Sudergade in Hamlet's town of Elsinore in Denmark. Many road-names containing *gate* are compounded with the names of the place to or from which they led – and in some cases villages along the route have acquired the name of the *gate* itself, as has Harrogate, 'the road to Harlow', Harlow being the name of a hill in the neighbourhood.

That so many *-gate* names have managed to survive until the present day is largely, if not solely, due to the fact that the Scandinavian meaning of the word *gate* is still retained in the living northern and eastern dialects. The same, however, is no longer true of such other Danish 'minor' elements as *-busk* (literally = bush, used of a small coppice), *-lundr* (grove), *-skógr* (wood), *-teigr* (a narrow strip of land), *-geiri* (a triangular piece of land), *-holm* (water-meadow), *-eng* and *-vang* (both meaning a meadow), and hundreds of placenames containing these terms have long since vanished from the map. Examination of medieval documents however, reveals that these words and their meanings were still remembered, and much used, by the peasantry in many parts of the old Danelaw until the fourteenth century and even later. For example, a document from the Leicestershire parish of Hoby, dating from 1322, lists many dozens of localities whose names contain some of the above elements, *-holm* occurring at Swinholm, Thacholm (holm where reeds were gathered for thatching) and Scrapholm (containing the Old Danish man's name, Skrapi), *-eng* at Oustrenges (N: *austrengjar* = eastern meadows) and *-vang* at Mikelwonges (large meadows) and Thurbernewonges (N: Þórbjarnarvangar = Þórbjǫrn's meadows), whilst *-busk* occurs in the lost Norfolk placename Aslakebusk (Áslak's copse). Streatfield cites as examples of *teigr* and *geiri* the two Lincolnshire placenames Tyger Holt and Bradley Geers, a part of Bradley Wood near Grimsby.

Despite the disappearance of so many minor names of this type, however, there are still plenty of *-holms*, *-ings* and *-wongs* in the old Danelaw – as, for example, at Haverholme, Bloxholm and Wong Farm, all within the same Lincolnshire parish. One of the few Norse terms referring to smaller topographical features that has managed to survive in provincial English speech is *fit* = a meadow bordering a lake or lying alongside the sea. This word persists, as 'fittie', among the farmers and graziers of south-east Lincolnshire, whilst its plural form, *fitjar*, occurs, as 'fidge', as a placename element in Orkney.

Other Scandinavian names of topographical minutiae in the Danelaw are much scarcer than the above. The rare Danish term *lá*, a creek or water alongside the sea (the first element in the Danish island name Lolland) occurs apparently but twice on English soil, at Goxhill (one in Yorkshire, one in Lincoln) which look suspiciously like corruptions of 'Gauk's (or Gaut's) Lā', as suggested by such earlier spellings as 'Gousla'. Intack, on the coast of the East Riding (and elsewhere), also reflects a rare Norse term seldom testified from Scandinavia itself, *inntak* = a piece of land (taken in), or enclosed, whilst Baysdale in the North Riding contains the Norse *báss* = a cowshed (Dan: *bås*).

North-west England

The most conspicuous difference between the Scandinavian place-names of the old Danish areas and those in the parts of England settled chiefly by Norwegians is the much richer variety of elements encountered in the Norwegian districts. Whilst only about ten Norse placename ingredients occur repeatedly in the Danelaw, upwards of a hundred have been noted in those parts of the country settled by Norwegians. This is not to imply that the vocabulary of West Scandinavian was any more copious than that of Old Danish, but merely that the topography of north-western England, the centre of Norwegian colonisation, is considerably more variegated – with its forests, large lakes, extensive tracts of swamp, upcountry moors, fells, long valleys, precipitous ravines and deeply indented coastline – than is most of the old Danelaw. It is probably more than coincidental that the Danes chose to settle in the flatter, more open parts of eastern England that most resembled their homeland, whilst the Norwegians tended to favour the more rugged, mountainous and fjord-bitten north-west.

The Scandinavian colonisation of the English north-west was no-where as intense as it appears to have been in parts of the Danelaw, and the pattern of settlement was also different. Whilst many of the villages founded by Danes in East Mercia rapidly grew, thanks to the commercial enterprise of their inhabitants, into sizeable townships, the Norwegian settlers were sparsely scattered, often occupying sites in isolated dales, on fell-sides and on remote islands or promontories.

The topography of the English north-west was ideally suited to the shifting system of stock-breeding (transhumance) practised by the Norwegian settlers. This involved the seasonal moving of livestock between regions of different climate, and is a method of husbandry still widely practised by fell farmers in the more mountainous parts of Norway.

Although settlement names such as -*by* and -*thorpe* do occur in the north and west (as at Thursby, Gutterby (contains the name Guðþormr), Fockerby (Folkvarðr), Netherby and Overby (identical with the many Danish Nederbys and Overbys), Scosthrop (Skotti), and Crackenthorpe (Krakandi)), they nowhere – except on the Wirral peninsula which has a tight cluster of names ending in -*by* – approach the density attained in the old Danish parts of Lincoln, Leicester or the East Riding.

Much more characteristic of the Norwegian areas are elements such as *garth* (N: *garðr* = a farm), *thwaite* (N: *þveit* – literally, a piece cut off, in placenames = 'a homestead in a forest clearing'), *scale* (N: *skáli* = a temporary dwelling-place), *side* (a corruption of *sætr* = a shieling or small upland farm) and *erg* (also meaning a shieling, from the Gaelic *airghe*, a term adopted by the Northmen in Ireland and transplanted, along with many other expressions of Keltic inspiration, to north-west England).

The word *garth* is still used of a farm in the dialects of the English north-west, as is *gard* in Norway, *garður* in Faeroe and Iceland and *gård* in Denmark and Sweden. The word was adopted by the Slavs from the Varangians in eastern Europe, where it occurs, as *grad* (in the sense of 'town'), in such placenames as Leningrad and Beograd (Belgrade). Typical English *garth* names are Applegarth, Stainsgarth (N personal name: Steinn), Arkengarth (Arnkell's farm) and Kalegarth (N: *kálgarðr* = cabbage farm). Danelaw *garths*, such as Lincolnshire's Baysgart and the East Riding's Hawsker (Haukr's garth), are rare.

Thwaite is one of the most recurrent placename suffixes in the old Scandinavian settlement areas in England, although it is now much scarcer in the old Danelaw than it was formerly. It occurs only seven times in Nottingham and three times in the East Riding – although it is common in field names, as opposed to settlement names, in both counties. Medieval Lincolnshire also had plenty of *thwaites* (such as Scrapthwaite and Strathwaite = straw thwaite), but here, as throughout the east Midlands, original *thwaites* have usually been distorted to -*thwick*, -*twick*, -*twight*, -*wick* and even -*field*, -*wood* and -*worth*. Lincolnshire's Stainthwaite, for example, which was recorded as recently as 1268 as 'Steynthweyt', is now Stainfield.

The situation is, however, very different in the north-west. Some 200 placenames containing the element *thwaite* have been recorded in the old Norwegian districts of Cumberland, Westmorland, Lancashire

9

and the western reaches of Yorkshire, typical examples being Smaithwaite (N: *smár* = narrow), Thistlethwaite, Swinithwaite (N: *sviðningr* = a place cleared by burning), Seathwaite (N: *sef* = a sedge), Haythwaite (N: *hey* = hay), Gristhwaite (N: *gríss* = pig), Ickenthwaite (N: *ikorni* = squirrel), whilst Birkerthwaite (N: *bjǫrk* = birch), Applethwaite, Mickelthwaite (N: *mikill* = large) and Braithwaite (N: *breiðr* = broad) are the exact counterparts of Birketveit, Epletveit, Mykkeltveit and Breitveit in Norway. Further examples are: Storthwaite (N: *storr* = large), Thackthwaite (N: *þak* = straw used for thatching), Fusethwaite (N: *fors* = waterfall), Ruthwaite (N: *rug* = rye), Rounthwaite (N: *raunn* = rowan or mountain ash) and the lost Haverthwaite (N: *hafri* = oats) and Austhwaite (N: *austr* = east). Less than a tenth of the English *thwaite* names contain personal names as their first element, but those that do are almost exclusively Scandinavian, e.g. Allithwaite (Eilifr), Gunnerthwaite (Gunnarr), Inglethwaite (Ingólfr) and Gunthwaite (Gunnhildr). *Tved* occurs as a placename element in Denmark, e.g. Næstved and Bregentved (which corresponds to Cumberland's Brackenthwaite), and was transplanted to Normandy, where it usually appears as 'Tuit'.

An alternative Norse name for a clearing, *ryð*, which is much more productive than *þveit* as a placename element in Scandinavia itself (e.g. Hillerød in Denmark, Långaröd in Sweden, Skogsrud in Norway) occurs but rarely on English soil; a notable example from the north-west is Ormerod (Ormr's clearing), which matches Ormaryd in Sweden. In Scandinavia, it appears to have come into use later than *þveit*, which probably accounts for its rarity in England.

Skáli, a Norse word applied to the type of temporary hut (commonly constructed with log walls and roofed with turf) still used by Norwegian shepherds and goatherds, occurs in the English north-west at Scaleby, Scawton, Scholes, Windscales, and Scawdale, whilst Selkirk in the Scottish border country was originally Scalekirk (N: *skálakirkja* = church built of timber after the manner of a *skáli*). A stretch of road running through the Westmorland fells still bears the fine Scandinavian compound name Scalthwaiterigg gate – road (*gata*) to the ridge (*hryggr*) of the hut (*skáli*) in the clearing (*þveit*).

Sætr, a shieling, or small mountain farm commonly used only during the summer months by shepherds grazing their flocks on the fell slopes, has been corrupted both to -*side*, as at Kettleside (Ketill's shielding), Arnside (Arni's shieling) and Ambleside (N: *á melr sætr* = shieling by the sandbank in the river), and to -*head*, as at Hawkshead (Haukr's shieling).

Erg, a Keltic term synonymous with the Norse: *sætr*, occurs in the English north-west at Grimsargh (Grímr's), Kellamergh (Kelgrímr's) and Torver (N: *torf* = peat).

Apart from the settlement names proper, other Scandinavian placename ingredients in the English north-west referring to man-made topographical features include: *haugr* (burial mound – often altered in post-Norse times to the English 'barrow') as at Torpenhow (Þórfinn's mound), Gunnershow, Scoat How (Skúti's mound), Burnbarrow (Bjǫrn's mound) and Buckbarrow (Bukkr's); *varði* and *hreysi* (both applied to cairns or piles of stones raised either as landmarks or over the dead) as at Warthall and Dunmail Raise; *stíga* (path), as at Bransty (Brand's path) and Swansty (Sveinn's); *stǫðr* (a landing place) as at Burton on Stather; and *skeið* (a racing-track) as at Hesketh (N: *hestr* = horse) and Wickham Skeith.

Turning from the names of man-made features to the natural geographical aspects of the landscape, we find that a wealth of Scandinavian terms has survived as placename elements in the northwest of England. These fall into four categories: names of elevations (mountains, hills and prominent rocks), of depressions (clefts, valleys, passes and ravines), of bodies of water (including marshland), and of forest.

Hill names   *Fjall* (fell) occurs at Cam Fell (N: *kam* = comb – here a reference to a 'comb'-shaped crest), Hest Fell (N: *hestr* = horse), Sca Fell (N: *skáli* = hut), and Mickle Fell (N: *mikill* = large), whilst *berg*, identical in meaning, appears in such names as Wiberg (N: *ví* = a place consecrated to one or other of the heathen deities) which is synonymous with Viborg (formerly Vibjerg) in Denmark, and Legberthwaite (N: *Lǫgberg* = 'Law hill' or hill on which legal assemblies were convoked).

Other recurrent names, describing minuter details of fell topography, are: *brekka* (slope) as at Caldbreak and Larbrick (N: *leir* = clay), *hjálmr* (a conical, 'helmet'-shaped rock) as at Helm Crag, *hlað* (a pile of rocks) as at Lad Crag, *hlíð* (slope) as at Lyth, *hnípr* (sharp ridge) as at Knipe Scar, *hnúkr* ('knuckle'-shaped ridge of knolls) as at Knock Pike, *hvall* (rounded hill) as at Whale, *kleif* (steep slope) as at Claife, *knappr* (knobby outcrop of rock) as at Knab Scar, *knottr* (rounded hill) as at Scald Knot (N: *skǫllóttr* = bald) and *toddi* (blunted mountain peak) as at Dodd Fell.

Valley names   Dropping from the hills to the valleys, we find that, of the many Norse names given to various types of depression, *dalr* (dale) is far and away the most ubiquitous in the English north-west, well-known examples being Swaledale, Kendal, Lonsdale, Birkdale, Mossdale, Widdale and Langdale. Grisedale is the valley of the pigs, Codale of the cows, Uldale of the wolves (N: *ulfar*) and Rosedal of the stallions (N: *hrossar*), whilst Thrixendale began life as Sígsteinn's Dale.

The innermost recess of a valley (or of an arm of the sea) was often referred to in Norse as a *botn* (bottom), the most prominent Scandinavian example being the Bothnian Gulf (Swedish: Bottenviken) which separates Sweden from Finland; in Viking times, this gulf was known as Helsingjabotn (from the province of Helsingjaland), whilst the Gulf of Finland was Kirjalabotn, 'the Karelian gulf'. English examples of the term in its dryland sense are Bottom and Starbotton (N: *stafr* = stave).

The Norse term *gill* is still used in the Lake District to describe a ravine or narrow glen, as at Gaisgill (N: *gás* = goose), Swarthgill (N: *svartr* = black), and Gatesgill (N: *geit* = goat). A close variant, *geil*, a narrow ravine, occurs at Thursgayle, Feltergayle and Hugill (N: *haugr* = mound).

A shallow dell is still referred to in parts of the English north-west by its Scandinavian name *slack* (N: *slakki*), which occurs in such placenames as Witherslack (N: *viðarslakki* = wooded dell).

Skarð, a mountain pass, is found suffixed to Ulsgarth (Ulfr's pass), Baldersgarth and Scordale – identical with Skordal in Norway – whilst *vrá*, literally 'nook' and referring in placenames to out-of-the-way valleys and similar secluded sites, occurs at Wray, Rowrah (N: *rug* = rye), Thackray (N: *þakkr*, literally 'thatch', here = 'rushes used for thatching') and such lost examples as Bigwra (N: *bygg* = barley), Heywra (N: *hey* = hay), Osmundwra (N: Ásmundarvrá = Ásmund's nook), Stodfaldwra (cattle-fold nook), Swindalewra, Scalewra (N: *skáli* = hut) and Koupemoneswra (N: *kaupmannavrá* = merchant's nook).

Flat, open country was often referred to in the north by the name *sletta* (according to legend, Dan, eponymous ancestor of the Danes, named his kingdom *Withæslæt* or 'wide plain'), which occurs in the

English north-west at Sleights and Sleightholme, whilst low-lying marshland could be described both as *mósi* (as at Holme Moss and Mozergh – for *erg* see above) and as *kjarr*, which referred more specifically to a swamp overgrown with alder scrub. This latter term occurs at Ellerker (N: *elri* = alders), Bicker (the swamp near the *býr* or village), and Lucker (N: *ló* = plover). All three survive, as "sleet", "moss" and "carr", in northern English dialect.

Water names Scandinavian terms still serve as productive elements in the names of lakes, pools, streams and waterfalls in the north-west of England. *Beck* (N: *bekkr* = a brook or burn) is universal throughout the old Norwegian settlement area, as at Scalebeck (N: *skáli* = hut), Troutbeck, Mossbeck, Gillerbeck (N: *gildri* = a fish trap), Roe Beck (N: *rá* = boundary), and Ged Beck (N: *gedda* = a pike fish – still known as a 'ged' in parts of the north country and the Scottish Lowlands). *Sike* (N: *sík* or *síki* = a small water-course) occurs at Calf Sike, Blind Sike, Foul Sike and Sandy Sike (and, of course, in the well-known family name, 'Sykes'; the native equivalent 'Sitch', is also used as a surname). *Dike* (N: *dík* – the word is still pronounced 'deek', in Scandinavian fashion, in parts of the north-west) occurs at Grindle Dike, Basco Dike and Whas Dike (N: *hvall* = a knob or hillock). *Pot* (N: *pottr* = a deep place in a river) occurs at Kettle Pot ('Ketill's Pot'), Spear Pot (N: Spǫrr's) and Honey Pot (N: Hǫgni's). *Wath* (N: *vað* = a ford) occurs at Winderwath and Stockdale Wath. *Keld* (N: *kelda* = a spring) occurs at Keldholm, Hallikeld and Kelsick. *Fors*, a waterfall, lives on in its Scandinavian sense throughout the Lake District.

A large body of water was often referred to in Norse as a *vatn* (water), and most of the larger lakes in the English north-west still carry the suffix *-water*, as, for example, do Ullswater (N: Ulfr's lake), Hawswater (Harfi's), and Skeggleswater (Skǫgul's). An earlier name for Coniston Water was Thurstaineswater.

A *tjǫrn* was smaller than a *vatn*, and the term occurs in English placenames as *tarn* – e.g. Stickle Tarn (N: *stikill* = a sharp rock), Loughrigg Tarn (N: *laukr* = wild onion + *hryggr* = ridge) and Blea Tarn (N: *blár* = dark blue, as in the identical Swedish tarn name, Blåtjärn). A much rarer term for a lake or fen, unattested in Old Icelandic but recorded in Old Swedish as *Thraesk*, occurs but once on English soil, at Thirsk in Yorkshire (*Domesday Book*: Tresc). The term is familiar, as Träsk, in the far north of Sweden.

Forest names The two most recurrent Norse terms for woodland in English placenames – *skógr* (related to the English *shaw* = a copse, and to the adjective *shaggy*) and *viðr* (akin to Old English *wudu*) are still heard in Lakeland dialect as 'scow' and 'with'. *Skógr* occurs as *scoe* in Thurnscoe (N: *þyrniskógr* = thorny wood), Swinscoe (swine wood), Briscoe (*birkiskógr* = birch wood) and Haddiscoe (Haddr's wood), as *skew* in Aiskew (N: *eikiskógr* = oak wood), and as *scough* in Myerscough (N: *mýrrskógr* = marshy wood). Scowgarth (forest farm) is identical with the many Skovgaards in Denmark.

Viðr is found both in pure Scandinavian placenames, such as Askwith (N: *askviðr* = ashwood) and Blawith (N: *bláviðr* = black wood), and in others, such as Tockwith, Skipwith and Bubwith, from which it has ousted an original English *wīc* (farm). The Scandinavian word has led such a vigorous life in north-western English dialect that it has even elbowed, at quite a recent date, the native *wood* out of such placenames as Beckwith, Skirwith (originally Sherwood) and Yanwith (N: *jafnviðr* = even wood, originally Evenwood).

Gaelic influence It is an established fact that the bulk of the Scandinavians who settled in the north-west of England during and after the tenth century had come, not directly from Norway, but from Ireland, where both they, their customs and, to a large extent, their speech, had become hibernicised, and a strong Irish influence is reflected in many of the Norse placenames in Cumberland, Westmorland and Lancashire, which contain not only Irish personal names but also examples of Goidelic grammatical structure. One of the most conspicuous differences between Scandinavian and Irish name formation was the Irish habit of placing any personal name which the placename might contain *after* the term describing the natural feature itself. Gilcambon (Kamban's gill), Kirkoswald (Ásvaldr's church), and Brigsteer (Styr's bridge) are typical examples of this wholly un-Norse construction, as were the lost Brigge Thorfin (Þórfinn's bridge), Set Forn (Forni's shieling) and Beck Troyte (Troit's beck – now Trout Beck). Similar Hiberno-Norse placenames, such as Torthorwald (Þórvaldr's tor) and Corstorphine (Þórfinnr's cross) are also fairly ubiquitous across the Solway in the Scottish Lowlands.

The Isle of Man

Crossing from north-west England to the Isle of Man, the visitor is struck by the similarity of the Scandinavian placenames in this former

Norwegian colony to those in Cumberland and Westmorland – although the Gaelic element is understandably even more in evidence here and the majority of the Norse placenames are appreciably more distorted than in the English north-west through accommodation to Gaelic phonology.

Although there are no signs of -*thorp* on Man, there are plenty of villages with names ending in -*by*, as at Dalby, Jurby (either N: *dyr* = deer, or Ívarr, the man's name), Sleckby (N: *slakki* = a dell), Raby (N: *vrá* = a nook), Crosby, Grenaby (N: *greinn* = the branch of a stream), Surby (N: *saurr* = mud), Scolaby (N: *skáli* = a hut) and Colby (containing the man's name, *Kol*), whilst another settlement name familiar from the English north-west, -*garðr* = farm, is also present, usually in the form *gary*, as at Amogary (Ásmundr's farm).

One Norse settlement name found on Man that is absent from the English north-west but common in western Scotland is *staðr* = place, usually clipped on Man to -*st*, as at Aust (N: Ottar's farm), Ulist (Ulfr's), Shonest (N: *skaunn* = meadowland) and Braust (N: *braut* = road cut through a forest).

As on the mainland, there are plenty of valleys bearing the Norse termination *dalr* (dale) on Man; typical examples are Orrisdale (N: *orri* = a blackcock, here, possibly a nickname), Ravensdale (*Hrafn's* valley), Baldwin (N: *bóldalr* = farm valley), Scarsdale (N: *skarð* = mountain pass), Brundale (N: *brunnr* = a spring or well) and Skerrisdale (N: *skári* = a young gull – also used as a nickname). *Haugr*, a mound, is here, too, and is usually, as in England, rendered *how* – as at Swart How (N: *svartr* = black), and Croit-ny-How (croft on the mound), whilst *vað*, a ford, appears as *wath* (as at Oxwath), *vat* (as at Sandvat), or *way* (as at Ronaldsway – Rǫgnvaldr's ford).

A few Scandinavian elements otherwise absent from British placenames occur on Man. Such are *slók* = a water course, as at Sloggel (N: *slókuhóll* = stream hill), *traðkr* = a well-trodden place, as at Howstrake (N: *hǫfuðstraðkr* = traðkr at the headland), *tá*, identical in meaning (and occurring as the second element in the Danish *fortov* = pavement) as at Thaa, and *lǫgr* = water (*ljoag* was an old taboo word in Shetland for the sea), which occurs on Man in its dative form with suffixed definite article at Billown (N: *við lǫginn* = by the water).

Those of the Manx mountains that are not called by the Gaelic name, Slieau, are known as fells, as are Roze Fell (N: *hrossa* =

stallion), Sart Fell (N: *svartr* = black), Ward Fell (N: *varði* = cairn) and Snae Fell (snow mountain), the last two examples echoing Vöröfell and Snæfell in Iceland.

Skógr, forest, survives intact at Mirescog (N: *mýrr* = bog) but has been distorted to *Skye* at Skyehill (N: *skógarfell* = wood mountain). Norse names for smaller topographic features, especially those found in rough upland country, are abundant on Man, characteristic examples being: *kluft* (cleft) as at Scarlet, *grefja* (ravine) as at Garff, *hryggr* (ridge) as at Brerick (N: *brú* = bridge), *klettr* (rock) as at the Clytt, *brekka* (slope) as at Corbreck and Injebreck (Inga's slope), *skor* (rim) as at Skinscoe, *gnípa* (overhanging rock) as at Kneebe, and *hlíð* (slope) as at Ormsly.

Western and Northern Scotland

The same assortment of Scandinavian placename elements, both of settlement sites and of topographical features, that we have already met on Man and in north-west England, occur again in western Scotland, where they are especially abundant on some of the Hebridean islands. Here, as a result of the radically dissimilar sound systems of Norse and Gaelic, Scandinavian names are in general much more distorted than in England, although reference to earlier forms of their spelling invariably yields fairly reliable clues to their interpretation.

Of the settlement names, *býr* is conspicuously rare, examples such as Sorbie (N: *saurr* = mud) being thinly scattered. *Sætr* (shieling) becomes *shader*, as at Grimshader and Carishader (Kári's shieling), whilst *erg*, itself a Norse borrowing from Gaelic, becomes *ary*, as at Ormsary, Langary, and Aulasary (Óláfr's). Two Norse settlement names unattested in England but ubiquitous in western Scotland are *ból* (a familiar placename suffix in Denmark, e.g. Skovbøl), as at Arnaboll, Thorboll, and Ullapool (Ulfr's farm) and the compound form *bólstaðr*, which occurs, usually in the clipped form -*bost*, at Colbost (Kol's farm), Swanibost (Sveinn's) and Kirkibost.

Most of the familiar Scandinavian topographical names occur in western Scotland: *fjall* (mountain) is usually rendered *val* or *bhal*, as at Roineval (N: *hraun* = rugged ground), Hestavall (N: *hestr* = horse), Arnavall (Arni's fell) and Soavall (N: *sauðr* = sheep); *gil* (small valley) occurs at Vidigill (N: *viðr* = wide), Galtrigill (N: *galti* = pig), and Urigill (N: *orri* = black cock); *skógr* (wood) at Birkiscoe, Scourie (Gaelic: *sgoghairigh*, reflecting N: *skógarerg* = forest shieling),

Grasco (N: *grár* = grey), Scone, and Loch Scoin (both of which preserve the Norse suffixed definite article *-inn*, ie *skógrinn* = the wood). *Dalr* (dale), on the other hand, seems not to have been universally understood by the Gaels, and many western Scottish placenames containing the Norse term also carry the native synonym *glen* as an explanatory prefix, as at Glen Arnisdale, Glen Scamadale (N: *skammr* = short), Glen Ollisdale (N: *Óli*, familiar form of the man's name Óláfr), Glen Alladale and Glen Stockdale (N: *stokkr* = log).

Wester Ross – which, as Professor Brøgger remarks, 'is shot through with Norse names' – has, like Argyll and the Hebrides, a goodly number of *-dale* names, as have its northern and eastern neighbours, Sutherland (N: Suðrland = south land – presumably named by Orcadians) and Caithness (N: Katanes). In this part of Scotland, the relatively late survival of the Norse language seems to have made the addition of the explanatory Gaelic term *glen* unnecessary, typical examples from hereabouts being: Ospisdale (N: Óspi, a diminutive form of the man's name Óspakr), Ullipsdale (Ulfr), Navidale (N: *nefr* = birchbark), Trantle (Þrøndr's dale), Sletdale (N: *slettr* = plain), Osdale (N: *austr* = east), and Halladale (N: *heilagr* = holy). At Helmsdale (N: Hjálmundr's dale) the Norse name has replaced an earlier Gaelic Strath-Ilidh. Elsewhere in the north-west mainland of Scotland, the Norse *dalr* has survived in place-names as *dal* – just as in Scandinavia – typical examples being Dibidal (N: *djúpr* = deep), Tungadal, Eskidal, Screapdal, Holmisdal, Caradal and Tusdal, the last five containing the Scandinavian men's names Eskil, Skrappi, Holmi, Kari, and Þórr.

The Norse settlement names *garðr*, *ból*, *bólstaðr*, *skáli* (hut) and *sætr* (shieling) all occur in Sutherland and Caithness; *garðr* at Rogart (N: *rauði* = the red one (nickname)), and *bólstaðr* at Ulbster (Ulfr's) and Scrabster (N: *Skáraból staðr*, a name actually recorded in the Orkneyinga Saga; Skári was a nickname, literally meaning 'young gull', and the word *scorie* still survives in this sense in the Caithness dialect). *Skáli* occurs at Skail, whilst *sætr* is found at Falside (N: *fjall* = mountain), Linside (N: *lín* = flax), Clayside (N: *kleif* = cliff), Sandside and Conesaid (N: *kónasætr* = woman's farm). Grimshader and Helshetter (N: *hellr* = flat rock) reflect the Gaelic form of the Norse word, i.e. Seadair.

Of the topographical names (apart from *dalr*), *kjarr* (low-lying land overgrown with alders) and *vǫllr* (field) are common in this northernmost part of Scotland, both occurring at Carroll (: *kjarrvǫllr* = carr-field) and *vǫllr* at Rossall (N: *hross* = horse), Langwell and Musal (N: *mós* = bog). *Vǫllr* also occurs at Dingwall on the Cromarty Firth, and marks the site of an important *þingvǫllr*, or place of assembly. The name is thus synonymous with those of the two Tingwalls in Orkney and Shetland and with the 'Tynwald' – the Manx parliament. A notable Sutherland example of N: *haugr* = a burial mound, is Cyderhall (formerly Sytheraw, Siwardhoch, etc), reputed to be the tumulus beneath which Sigurðr, the first of the Orkney jarls, was interred. The jarl's fatal wound was inflicted by one of the monstrous fangs of Melbrig Bigtooth, a Scottish chieftain whom Sigurðr had slain. After the killing of Melbrig, Sigurðr hung the Highlander's severed head as a trophy from the pommel of his saddle; as Sigurðr rode, one of Melbrig's teeth punctured the jarl's thigh and Sigurðr soon afterwards died of blood-poisoning.

Many of the lakes of Sutherland and Caithness still carry their old Scandinavian names – commonly affixed with the Gaelic *loch*, as at Loch Assynt (N: *áss – endi* = end of ridge), Loch Staing (N: *stǫng* = a pole) Loch Stack (N: *stakkr* = a high rock, here, the mountain Ben Stack), and Sandwood Loch (still known locally as 'Sandwat' – N: *Sandvatn* – until the seventeenth century), whilst Loch Watten in Caithness is simply the Norse *vatn* = water.

Orkney and Shetland

The placenames of the northernmost Scottish islands, the Orkneys and Shetlands, are almost without exception of unambiguously Scandinavian inspiration. As F. T. Wainwright has observed:

'Without long lists of place-names, or at least of elements, it would be quite impossible to indicate the thoroughly Scandinavian character [of the Orkney and Shetland place-names]. Scandinavian names – of hamlets, hills, ravines, rocks, nesses and voes, farms, fields, streams and mounds, banks and enclosures – run into thousands, and they wrap the islands in a thick and distinctively Scandinavian blanket. Even if we did not know that a Scandinavian language was spoken in the Northern Isles until about two hundred years ago, we could account for such an overwhelming linguistic influence only by assuming the occurrence at some date of an immigration sufficient to wipe out almost every linguistic trace of earlier peoples .... We are entitled to assume, on the evidence of placenames growing and developing over a thousand years, that the settlement which took place early in the ninth century had the force of a mass-migration'.

Elsewhere, Wainwright says: 'So strongly Scandinavian is the place-nomenclature of the Northern Isles, that in it the stranger from the south at once feels the impact of another world and the stranger from Scandinavia feels oddly at home.' Of Shetland, Jakobsen wrote: 'Every fairly small mound, point, cliff, valley, crevice, stream, piece of ploughed land and field has its own name, and these names with comparatively few exceptions have been handed down in Norse dialect. The tiny island of Fetlar, the area of which is not one square mile, has about two thousand placenames', whilst Brøgger estimates that perhaps as many as 100,000 placenames of Scandinavian inspiration have survived in Shetland.

It would, of course, be unreasonable to expect any of the North Island placenames to have survived in mint condition, especially in view of the fact that, in passing from Scandinavian into Scottish hands, the islanders had a foreign language – English – superimposed over their traditional tongue. North Island Norn was not a literary language, so that, even before the transfer of the islands to Scotland, there were no fixed, standard forms for any of the indigenous placenames. The distortion of the original Scandinavian forms of North Island placenames was greatly accelerated from the moment the Scots took the islands in possession. To the Scots, North Island Norn was an outlandish tongue, an incomprehensible gibberish, and they subjected the local Scandinavian placenames to a refashioning every bit as drastic as that undergone by the Danish placenames in Slesvig under the Prussians, who twisted Svedenmose (burnt bog), for example, into Schweinemoor (pig moor), Rævemose (fox bog) into Roimus and Tykskov (thick wood) into Tückschau. Many of the existing forms of Orkney and Shetland placenames reflect the orthographic habits of Scottish cartographers and scribes, and some are so abysmally warped and disfigured that it takes more than guesswork – no matter how enlightened – to discern the underlying Norn originals which they so thoroughly blanket. Perhaps the most pathetic North Island equivalent to the Prussianised placenames of Slesvig is Willamina Hoga, as one location on the Shetland island of Yell now appears on the Ordnance Survey map. This grotesque and utterly meaningless name began life in Norn times as Almenning Haga, meaning the public pasture-land where cattle were grazed during the warm months – a name transparently clear to any Scandinavian.

The multitudinous Scandinavian placenames of Orkney and Shetland have been subjected to close scrutiny by many scholars, notably Hugh Marwick, A. W. Brøgger, Jakob Jakobsen, Magnus Olsen and F. T. Wainwright, and their investigations reveal that these placenames are capable of yielding much valuable information concerning the Norse colonisation of these northernmost British isles. At least three chronological layers of early Scandinavian settlement names have been differentiated in Orkney and Shetland – the deepest, i.e. the oldest, stratum being represented by names containing the elements *-vín*, *-sætr*, *-land*, *-garðr* and *bólstaðr*.

The suffix *-vín*, which occurs repeatedly in Norway (where, for example, Bjǫrgvín was the old name of Bergen) and parts of western Sweden, is clearly one of the most archaic of Scandinavian farm-name elements, although it dropped out of the Norse language too early to be either recorded in the written language or transplanted to Faeroe and Iceland. It was clearly identical in meaning to cognate forms in Gothic (*vinja*), Old High German (*winne*) and Old English (*winn* – likewise unattested in Anglo-Saxon literature but found as a placename element in, for example, Winton, Wimborne and Winnersh) in all of which languages it referred to natural, uncultivated grazing land. Despite its early disappearance from spoken Norse, it is just possible that *vín* is contained in the two early Orkney farm names Lyking (N: *leikvín* = sports field) and Greeny (1492: Grynning, N: *Græn-vín* ? = green pasture) and it is almost certainly the first element in such later Orkney names as Vinbreck, Vinquin and Vinikelday (N: *vínkelda* = pasture – spring).

The Norse *-sætr*, which, as we have seen, refers in northern English and Scottish placenames to a temporary shieling, seems to have been applied in the Northern Isles to a more permanent dwelling site. It occurs frequently in Orkney, as at Grimsetter and Melsetter, and is even more ubiquitous in Shetland, where an estimated 40 per cent of the oldest-established farms have names ending in *-sætr*, as at Dalsetter (valley farm) and Bakkasetter (slope farm). The bulk of the Northern Isle *sætrs* contain as their first element a Scandinavian personal name – often, no doubt, that of a man who took part in the early colonisation of the islands – as at Barfennsetter (Bergfinn) and Hestinsetter (Eysteinn) and with the suffix reduced to *-ster*, at Ketelster

Krukster (Krókr), Levister (Løifr), Tronister (Þrǫndr), Swinister (Sveinn), Ukinster (Hákonr), and Okister (Hǫskuldr). Some of these -*ster* names may, however, contain another familiar suffix, -*staðr* (place), rather than -*sætr*.

While -*sætr* names may be reckoned among the oldest stratum of Scandinavian elements in Orkney and Shetland, there is ample evidence to prove that the suffix continued to be used productively in the formation of new farm names until as recently as the thirteenth century, and later examples include Yoknister (N: *yxni* = oxen) and Kolvister (N: *kalfr* = calf). A minority of Shetland -*sætr* names contain as their first element a reference to some natural feature, as at Gjoster (*sætr* by the chasm or inlet), Kulster (N: *kollr* = knoll) and Bruster (N: *brú* = bridge).

In Norway itself, the 900-odd names containing the element -*sætr* are largely confined in distribution to the coastal districts between Møre and Nordland, and they have been fairly precisely dated to between the sixth and eighth centuries AD, a time when the north-western coastal fringe of Norway was being pioneered for colonisation. As a result of the meagre soil in which they were planted, these -*sætr* farms were, in the main, very extensive; moreover, their original occupants were in large measure drawn from the established land-owning aristocracy (*adelstand*) of southern and south-western Norway who had retained the traditional *Odel* system, whereby each family had the prior and unchallengeable right to purchase or redeem land that had been sold out of its possession. It is easy to imagine that both the restricted nature of available farmland and the practice of *Odel* rights were two factors that may well have induced the younger members of these families to seek their fortune elsewhere, the only two directions in which they could turn being back into the forbidding Norwegian hinterland, or 'West over Sea' to the sparsely inhabited islands of the north Atlantic. To the young, landless peasantry of north-west Norway, Shetland and Orkney thus became a land of opportunity and it is doubtless for this reason that the -*sætr* names characteristic of Møre and Trøndelag are found so abundantly among the oldest layer of Shetland and Orkney farm names.

Even more venerable than the -*sætr* names in Orkney and Shetland, the majority of which appear to date from the early tenth century or shortly before, are those containing the Norse elements -*bólstaðr*,

-land, -garðr and *-bær* (or *býr*), all of which refer to farms, and *-skáli*, which in the Northern Isles refers to a hall.

The majority of names in which these elements appear date from around the year 900. *-bólstaðr* is usually compressed to *-bister*, as at Kirkbister and Walbister in Orkney and Braebister and Fladdabister in Shetland; *-land* (typical of 'secondary settlement' names in the extreme south-west of Norway – Jæren and West Agder) occurs in such Orkney farm names as Bigland (N: *bygg* = barley) and Mousland (N: *mósi* = bog). *-garðr* is either *-garth*, as at Vatnagarth (N: *vatn* = a loch) and Kurkigarth, *-gord*, as at Gamlagord (N: *gamal* = old) and Sodragord (south farm, identical with the many farms called Sørgard in Norway and Søndergaard in Denmark), or *-gert*, as at Fogrigert (N: *fagr* = fair) and Toptigert (N: *topt* = homestead). *-bær* appears in Orkney as *-bay* at Housebay, as *-by* at Everby (N: Ívarr), or simply as Bea, and in Shetland as *-bi* at Norbi, Melbi and Voksterbi (N: *vágsætrbýr* = farm at the *sætr* near the inlet), or as *bø*, (compare Faer: *bøur*) at Exnabø (N: *yxni* = oxen).

Skáli, which elsewhere in Scandinavian Britain refers to a hut, was exalted in Orkney to the status of a hall, and several of the '*gødings*' or chieftains under the old Norse jarls – men such as Sveinn Ásleifsson and Sigurðr of Westness – resided at *skálar*. In Orkney, the usual pronunciation is 'skail', 'skeel' or 'skel', as at Langskaill and Skelwick, whilst the typical Shetland form is closer to the original Norse, as at Grindiscol, Netherscoule and Skolla.

Farm names containing the Norse suffix *-stað* = a farmstead – usually in its dative plural form, *stǫðum* – occur some twenty times in Orkney, and Hugh Marwick regards them as evidence of a secondary settlement from Norway 'considerably later than the original settlement'. The Orkney names in *-stǫðum* invariably have a Scandinavian personal name as their first element, and almost all appear with the 'anglicised' ending *-ston*, as at Germiston (N: *Geirmundarstǫðum* = at Geirmund's places), Grimeston and Clouston. In Shetland, the form is more often *-sta* (reflecting the Norse singular: *stað*), as at Grimista and Gunnista (N: *Gunnhildr*).

Marwick regards the element *kví* = an enclosure for animals, as one of the youngest of those established in Norse times and he suggests that the common siting on the outskirts of early tunships or farms whose names contain *kví* may be due to the appropriation of previous animal folds, with their rich layer of manure, by the occupants of the parent farm for the setting up of subsidiary farms. *Kví*, or 'quoy' as it is usually rendered, was a productive name for new farms for many generations after the original settlements – whence such examples as Angusquoy, Chalmersquoy and Coupersquoy, which contain Scots or English rather than Norse names. Typical Orkney examples from the Scandinavian period are Cumlaquoy (N: *kuml* = burial mound), and Stenaquoy (N: *Steinarkví* = Steinn's quoy), whilst from Shetland come Okraquoy (N: *ákr* = field) and Lerquoy (N: *leir* = clay). Orkney's Queenamugly and Queenaneo contain the term as their first element and are corruptions of the Norse *kvíin mikla* and *kvíin nýa* – the large quoy and the new quoy. (This construction – noun followed by adjective – occurs repeatedly in old North Island names, and suggests the participation of Gaelic speakers in the settlement of Orkney and Shetland.) Alternative Shetland renditions of *kví* include: *whee*, as at Grøtwhee (N: *grjót* = gravel); *hwi*, as at Vatshwi (N: *vatn* = loch); *whaei*, as at Nordrahwaei; *waei*, as at Sondrewaei; *kwaei*, *quie* and *quhey*, as at the Quheys of Catfirth.

Among the many Norse terms applied to the smaller features of the farm and retained in Northern Isle placenames we may cite: *kru* = a sheep-fold – a term borrowed from Gaelic: *cro*, as at Cruar (N: *kruar* = sheep folds) and Cruannie (new sheep fold) in Orkney, and Krooster (Krusætr) and Stoori Kroo (big kru) in Shetland; *topt* = a house-site, as at Howatoft (N: *haugr* = mound) and Greentoft in Orkney, and Colbinstoft (N: *Kolbeinn*) and Tuptaby in Shetland; *stofa* = a house, as at Midstove and Netherstove in Orkney, and Uppistova (N: *uppi í stofu* = in the upper house) and da Bastivvategs (the bath house tegs) in Shetland – 'teg' being the Norse *teigr* = a (cultivated) plot of land. Shetland also retains examples of the Norse *rett* = a sheep fold, as at Tararet (N: *þari* = seaweed) and Søret (N: *sauðr* = sheep); *-ból*, a resting place for animals, as at Koobel and Bola Hill; *hagi* = a hill pasture, as at Hogan, Lambhoga and Buynhoga (N: *Barnhagi*, literally 'child-pasture' – here: 'place of birth' or 'old place of residence'); and *stilli* = an enclosure for trapping animals in, as at 'de Stilli o' Nibon'.

A profusion of Norse terms designating every kind of natural feature has been retained in Shetland and Orkney placenames – indeed, many of the original meanings of such terms are still understood and used by the islanders. The following are but a small representative selection of the many hundreds of Scandinavian topographical terms fossilised in North Island placenames, and although few, if any, have managed to retain much semblance of their original form through centuries of distortion, erosion and finally anglicisation, early records often reveal them for what they are.

1. Names of inland elevations:
   Áss = a ridge; *bakki* = a slope; *bjǫrg* = a crag; *brekka* = a slope; *brun* = a rise in the ground; *dys* = a knoll or pile of rocks; *fjall* = a mountain or hill; *gnípa* = steep rock; *hals* = a slack (lit. neck) in a hill; *hamarr* = projecting rocks on the side of a hill; *haugr* = a mound; *hlíð* = a slope; *hóll* = a hillock; *hraun* = a rocky place; *kambr* = a ridge of hills rising like a crest; *kleif* = a steep track up a hillside; *knukr* = a high knoll; *kollr* = a hill with a rounded top; *kula* = a rounded lump; *kuml* = a grave mound; *mor* = moorland; *skarð* = pass; *tind* = a conical peak; *þúfa* = mound; *varði* and *viti* = a beacon; *ǫxl* = a shoulder-like formation.

2. Names of inland depressions:
   Botn = a deep, rounded valley; *dalr* = a valley; *gil* = a ravine; *gljúfr* = a chasm; *hvammr* = a ravine; *hvarf* = a deep-lying place; *slakki* = a hollow.

3. Names of inland bodies of water:
   Á = a burn; *brunnr* = a well; *dý* = a marshy place; *fors* = a waterfall; *kelda* = a spring; *lækr* = a patch of green turf through which a streamlet runs; *mýrr* = miry ground; *tjǫrn* = a tarn or small loch; *vatn* = a loch.

The frequent occurrence of the Norse *skógr* (wood, forest) in such North Island placenames as Skooan (N: *skógrinn* = the forest) in Orkney and Scooin Brenda (the burnt forest) in Shetland testifies to the presence of woodlands on the islands during the period when Norse was spoken there, although *skógr* hereabouts possibly referred to nothing more than the stunted tree-growth still typical of Orkney and Shetland.

We are fortunate that many Orkney and Shetland localities are named in such medieval Icelandic texts as the *Heimskringla*, *Orkney-inga Saga*, *Egil's Saga*, *Njál's Saga*, *Hákon's Saga*, *Flotsdœl Saga* and the *Landnámabók*. Dunross, for example, appears as Dynrǫst (N: *dynr* = noise + *rǫst* = a roost), Girlsta as Geirhildarvatn (Geir-hild's Loch), Gulberwick as Gullberuvík (Gullbera's creek), Burra

Firth as Borgarfjǫrðr (firth of the 'broch' (Pictish fortification)), and Mousa as Mósey (N: bog island). The numerous saga renditions of Unst (Aumstr, Anst, Onst, Jennst, etc.), of Yell (Ála, Jala, Iaale, etc.) and of Fetlar (Fetilár, Faetilǫr, etc.) are, however, no clearer in meaning than their surviving forms. They are almost certainly corruptions of pre-Norse, possibly Pictish, prototypes.

The Scandinavian placenames of Orkney and Shetland contain a treasurehouse of information concerning both the Norse settlements and the social conditions and folklore of the Islands during the period between the original landnam and the time when the Norn language finally disintegrated during the seventeenth, eighteenth and early nineteenth centuries. Not only do many North Island placenames mirror exactly their counterparts in Scandinavia, some are clearly transplants of specific names that still exist in the Norwegian motherland. Voss, Moster and Visdal in Shetland were evidently named by Norse settlers after places in their own country, whilst Fluravag, Godal and Troswick appear to have been inspired by Florevåg, Gydal and Trossevigen in western Norway.

Other placenames speak of the Picts (N: *Pettir*) who occupied the islands before the coming of the Scandinavians; these original inhabitants are remembered not only in the famous Pentland Firth (N: Pettlandsfjǫrðr = Pictland's Firth) but in such names as Pettawater, Pettafjell, Pettidale, Pettigarth and Pettasmog (N: *smoga* = a hiding place). This latter example comes from a part of the Unst coast which, according to local tradition, was a place of refuge used by the Picts at the time of the Norse settlements. Other North Island placenames refer to the Irish anchorites (N: *Papar*) who appear to have still been present in Orkney and Shetland at the time of the Norse landnam; examples are Papa Stour and Papa Litla (Large and Small Island of the Priests respectively), Papyl, Papilwater, Papilsgio, and Papa Skerry.

The name 'Fivla' (N: *fifill* = a fool or clown), used by the Shetlanders as the name of a 'troll's child', is also preserved in certain localities, as at the 'Hellyer' (cave) and the 'Ayre' (beach) of Fivlagord. The legend of the 'Trows (Trolls) of Fivlagord' spoke unequivocally, Dr Jakobsen believed, of the descendants of the Picts who, after the Norwegian landnam, may well have continued to hold out in isolated areas, especially in the remoter islands. The tale tells of one Bjørn, an old Fetlar crofter, who, whilst riding past a knoll on his grey horse with a red horse in tow, heard a voice pipe out in broken Norn: 'Du, at

10

rides da grey and rins da red, tell Tona Tivla at Fona Fivla is fa'en i da vjelna vatna'. When Bjørn reached home, he shouted these words into the byre, where a troll-woman sat milking one of his cows. On hearing his message she dropped her pan and fled, crying: 'Oh, dat's my bairn fa'en idda kirnin' (churning) water!' Bjørn picked up the pan, took it indoors and 'caused his house to prosper ever afterwards'.

Placenames like Finnigord and Finnister Hadds, many of which have traditional associations with occult practices of one description or another, were believed by Jakobsen to perpetuate the memory of the Lappish thralls who may have been brought to Shetland by wealthy Norwegian colonists, and the Lapps certainly have a deep-rooted reputation in Scandinavia for magic and witchcraft. It seems more likely, however, that such names merely incorporate the familiar Scandinavian man's name, Finnr. Other denizens of Shetland and Orkney folklore, including the trolls themselves and the 'njuggles', or water-sprites (N: *nykrar*) are remembered in placenames, the former at Trølliwater and the latter at Njuggle's Water. Elves (N: *álfir*) are recalled at Wulvershool and Wulhool – now known as 'Da Fairy Know' (knoll) – whilst giants are associated with the Yetna-Steen (N: *jǫtnarsteinn* = giant's stone) in Orkney.

References to the old Scandinavian administrative system have been preserved in several Orkney and Shetland placenames. The term *þing*, a place of assembly, occurs frequently, as at Tingwall in both Orkney (1307: Tingvold) and Shetland, and Dingishowe (N: *haugr* = mound) in Orkney. The suffixes to both these names, -*wall* and -*howe*, refer to the most favoured sites for Thingsteads or district moots (N: *vǫllr* = field and *haugr* = mound). Near the site of the Thingstead, usually on an eminence, stood the gallows, whose Norse name, *galgi*, is preserved at several places called Galga in Shetland. Six Shetland districts still carry the name of the Thing from which they were administered in Norse times: Westing, Sandsting, Delting (N: *dalr* = valley), Aithsting (N: *eið* = isthmus), Nesting (N: *nes*= headland), and Lunnasting (N: *lundeið* = grove-isthmus). Two others, Thveita-thing and Raudarthing, have long since vanished from the map.

Three districts known as 'da Herra' survive in Shetland (on Yell and Fetlar and at Lunnasting) to remind us of another old Scandinavian administrative district, the *herað*, which was the subdivision of a county (*syssel*) in Denmark and south Sweden (Danish: *herred*, Swedish: *härad*).

Although the bulk of Shetland's and Orkney's earliest Scandinavian colonists came to the islands direct from Norway, the occurrence of such Gaelic placename elements as *cro*, *erg* and *cnocc* (hill), plus such 'inversion compounds' as Quoybernardis (Bernard's paddock), suggest that, at any rate later in the settlement, others came from the Norse roots in Ireland, Man and the Hebrides, whilst early Danish settlement is implied by such names as Dainaberg in Shetland. A further placename reminder of the presence of Danes in the islands is offered by Guttorm's Cave on Unst – where none other than Guthrum, leader of the *mycel here*, is said to have been hidden by a local girl after a shipwreck.

Ireland

Considering that Norse was spoken in various parts of Ireland from the 820s until the occupation of the 'Ostman' towns by the Normans in the twelfth century, it is astonishing that so few recognisably Scandinavian placenames have survived in Ireland. Apart from a few obscure references to the 'Strangers' (i.e. the Vikings), as at Donegal (Gael: *Dúinne-na-nGáill* = stronghold of the strangers), the only certain Norse names in Ireland are Leixlip (N: *laxhlaup* = salmon leap) and possibly the second element in Carnsore (N: *eyrr* = sandbank). Dublin and Limerick were rendered *Dýflin* and *Hlymrekr* in the Sagas, but both are clearly Scandinavian renditions of underlying Gaelic names – as, in all likelihood, was Wicklow's Norse name, *Víkingaló*. Wexford, Strangford, Waterford and Carlingford may possibly contain the Norse *fjǫrðr*, a firth, as their second element, although even this is doubtful, as is the identification of the suffix *-ster* in the three province names, Ulster, Munster and Leinster, as a corruption of the Norse *staðr* = place. The paucity of identifiable Scandinavian names in Ireland has been attributed both to the great dissimilarity between the Norse and Gaelic languages and to the fact that, unlike the Scandinavian settlements in England, which were spread liberally over a wide area, those in Ireland were concentrated at specific points around the coast. There is no doubt, however, that Norse placenames were formerly much more widespread in Ireland, the majority having been either subjected to drastic erosion in the mouths of Gaelic speakers or translated (very often re-translated) into Irish.

Wales

Wales, rather surprisingly, has retained more Scandinavian names than has Ireland. Pembroke's Tenby is evidently 'Daneby', or village of the Danes, Milford Haven reflects an original Norse *melfjarðarhǫfn* = harbour in the firth of the sandbank (*melr*), the bay known as Angle is probably N: *ǫngull* = hook, whilst Hasguard, Fishguard, Freysthrop (Dan: Frøstrup) and Skrinkle (Swedish: *skrynkla* = wrinkle?) certainly have a Scandinavian aspect, as does Landshipping (N: *landsskipti* = a division of land – a term recorded in the Grágás, one of the medieval Icelandic Lawbooks). Further east, as Dr Patterson points out in *Archaeologia Cambrensis* (1922), Swansea (recorded as late as 1210 as Sueinsei) is surely *Sveinnsey*, Sveinn's island, whilst the lost Laleston and Crokeston contained – as revealed by their early spellings–the Norse nicknames *Lǫglauss* (lawless) and *Krókr* (crooked, bent). Homri and Lamby near Cardiff were formerly Hornby and Langby, whilst the street in Cardiff now called Womanby began life as the Scandinavian Hundemanby (N: *Hundmaðr* = dog keeper, which occurs again in the Yorkshire village name, Hunmanby).

Placenames with religious associations

Scandinavian placenames alluding to heathen practices and beliefs are rare in Britain, their paucity being no doubt due to the fact that the broad mass of the Scandinavian settlers were, once established on British soil, quick to forsake their old religion and embrace Christianity. We have already noted Wiberg as a possible contender, and its first element, *vé*, a hallowed place, occurs again in the Hebridean island name, Wiay. Two Scandinavian hill-names in Yorkshire, Solberge and Sulber, may, like so many of their counterparts in Denmark, Norway and Sweden, enshrine the memory of some heathen sun cult (N: *sól* = sun), whilst Roseberry Topping near Cleveland was known as Othenesberg (Odin's hill) until as late as the twelfth century. Its present form results from the assimilation of the final -*r* of the preposition *under* by the abbreviated 'Oseberry' (compare Onsbjerg in Denmark). Pagan practices are also intimated at Hoff (N: *hof* = a temple or sanctuary) and Harras (N: *hǫrgr* = place of worship + *hreysi* = cairn), and superstitious beliefs may be implicit in Thrushgill and Thursgayle (N: *þurs* = monster), Trowburn and

Troughburn (N: *troll*), Sculler Wood (N: *skullr* = fox, used figuratively of an evil spirit), Gander Hill (N: *gandr* = magic staff) and Scrimthorp (N: *skrípindi* = monster, goblin). Even in the Northern Isles, the Norse landnamsmen appear to have given up their old religion fairly rapidly, and placenames with heathen associations are no commoner hereabouts than further south. *Hof* appears in Hovland, *hǫrgr* was featured in its plural form, *Hargar*, in a lost Orkney location, whilst Shetland's Heglibister seems to reflect an original Norse *Heilagr bólstaðr* = sacred dwelling place.

Names of coastal features

A rich variety of Scandinavian toponymics is to be found around the coasts of Britain from Shetland in the north to the Channel Islands in the south. The Northmen, as seafarers, developed an extensive terminology to specify every conceivable type of coastal feature from river mouths and sand bars to headlands, crags, islands, broken rocks, isthmuses, skerry clusters, inlets and cliff formations of every shape and size imaginable. Unlike many of the dryland names discussed above, few of the Norse terms describing coastal features are restricted in distribution to any particular part of the country – although the Northern and Western Isles contain a more comprehensive selection than is found elsewhere around the shores of Britain.

Taking island names first, we find that by far the most recurrent Norse term is *ey*, a derivative, via Primitive Norse *auiu* (recorded in the Swedish Rök inscription from *c* AD 800), of the common Gothonic: **auio* (the second element in Scandin*avia* – first recorded as 'Scadinauia' by Pliny). The Gothonic prototype is preserved in almost pristine form in Lappish placenames calqued on early Norse originals, as at Makkaraujo for Norwegian Mågerøy, and from it stem such later Scandinavian forms as Faeroese *oy* (or *oyggj*), Norwegian *øy*, Swedish *ö*, Gutnish *oy* and Danish *ø*. Ultimately, the word is connected with the Indo-European root: **ahua* = water (cf Latin *aqua*). Of the Gothonic languages, only the varieties spoken in Scandinavia have retained the term in its original sense, although High German has *Aue*, meaning a water meadow or river island. The corresponding Old English form *eg* (or *ig*) survives only in placenames (e.g. Sheppey = sheep island). British placenames containing the Norse form, *ey*, include: from Shetland – Whalsay (N: *hvalr* = whale –

identical with Valasay in the Hebrides), Foula (N: *fugl* = bird), Mousa (N: *mósi* = bog), and Uyea (pronounced as in Norwegian, Øya, and meaning 'the island' – N: *eyinn*); from Orkney (which itself contains the Norse *orkn* = a young seal) – Egilsay, Risa (N: *hrís* = brushwood), Ronaldsay (*Rǫgnvaldr's* island – spelt Rognaldsœy in a manuscript from 1329), Swona (N: *svín* = pig), Flotta (N: *flatr* = flat), and Hoy (N: *háey* = high island); from the Hebrides – Colonsay (Kolbeinn's island, the Kolbeinn in question being very likely one Kolbeinn Áslaksson, who accompanied King Harald Fairhair to the Western Isles), Grimsa, Rothesay (N: *Rauði* = 'the red one', a popular nickname), Eriska (Eiríkr), Torsay (N: Þórr), Soay (N: *sauðr* = sheep), Staffa (N: *stafr* = stave), Rona (N: *hraun* = rough ground – compare Raunøy in Norway) and Jura (N: *dyr* = deer). The Hebrides themselves were known collectively to the Scandinavians as Suðreyjar – the 'southern isles' – to distinguish them from Norðreyjar – the 'northern isles' of Orkney and Shetland – and it is a Latin corruption of this Norse name, 'Sodorensis', that is preserved in the title of the Bishop of Sodor and Man.

Off the Isle of Man we have Gandsay (N: *gandr* = a monster); Lambay, off Dublin, contains N: *lamb* = lamb, whilst the Copeland Islands, off the north-east coast of Ireland, were evidently known to the Vikings as 'Kaupmannaeyjar' – Merchants' Islands. According to Worsaae, they may have been so named on account of their use by Scandinavian traders as an entrepot – 'a sort of rendezvous for the ships of Scandinavian merchants. The Icelandic and Norwegian ships brought fish, hides and valuable furs to the English and Irish coasts; whence, again, they carried home costly stuffs and cloths, corn, honey, wine and other products of the south.' (Worsaae, p 336). Foulney and Walney off Lancashire contain N: *fugl* = bird and *vǫgn* = the killer whale, respectively; Anglesey (whose Welsh name is *Môr*) contains N: *ǫngull* = hook, whilst other Welsh *ey* names include Bardsay (N: Barðr), Caldy (N: *kaldr* = cold), Sulley (N: *súla* = gannet) and Skomer (formerly Scalmey, from N: *skalm* = a cleft or inlet). An outlier off North Devon is Lundy (N: *lundi* = puffin), whilst even further to the south are the Channel Islands of Jersey, Guernsey and Alderney off Normandy – all three of which are likely to be Scandinavian renditions of non-Norse, presumably Keltic, originals. It is interesting to note in this connection that the Northmen, wherever they travelled, appended their suffix -*ey* to existing island names, Sicily and Sardinia, for example, being rendered Sikiley and Sandanarey in the Sagas.

Another Scandinavian island name common around British coasts is *hólmr*, which was generally applied by the Northmen to an island smaller than an *ey*. The term occurs in the expression *hólmganga*, the well-known trial of strength of Viking times, wherein the two combatants were belted together, provided with weapons and left alone on a holm to fight until one or the other was slain – the winner being automatically deemed the victor of the lawsuit that had occasioned the duel. In Danish, *holmgang* is still used as a figurative expression for 'single combat', e.g. '*De to ordførere tog sig en vældig holmgang*' = the two speakers entered into a heated debate. The word *hólmr*, borrowed from the Varangians by the Russians, who render it *kholm* = hill, is akin to the Greek *kholmnos* = a peak and to the Latin *collis* = a hill, and goes back to an Indo-European root **kel* = to project. Shetland and Orkney abound in placenames containing this term, as at Swine Holm, Rusk Holm (N: *rusk* = old, wizened grass), Lamb Holm, Glimsholm (N: Glumr), and the Holm of Scockness – and, although there are few *holms* in the Hebrides, the term has found a place in the Manx vocabulary. Wales has several *holms* – Priestholm, Grassholm, Gateholm (N: *geit* = goat), Skokholm (N: *stokk* = log, cf Sweden's capital, Stockholm), Flat Holm and Steep Holm. Midland Isle was formerly Middleholm whilst a Trellesholm, recorded in the 1300s, has still to be located. When the term occurs inland, as at Wragholm, Axholm, Keldholm and Stockholm, it refers to an area of dry land – ordinarily elevated – in otherwise fenny country.

Even smaller than a *hólmr* was a *sker* (skerry), whilst a *stakkr* (stack) was smaller still. Orkney and Shetland swarm with skerries – Seal Skerry, Fugla Skerry, Outskerries (N: *útsker* = an outlying skerry), Nakkaskerry (N: *hnakki* = the nape of the neck), Auskerry (N: *austr* = east), and Carling Skerry (N: *kerling*, an old woman), the old name for the skerry in Scapa Flow now known as the Barrel of Butter. There are a scattering of skerries down the west coast of Scotland and among the Hebrides, as at Erisgeir (N: Eiríkr), Sulisgeir (N: *súla* = gannet), Sgeir nan Sgarbh (N: *skarfr* = cormorant, cf the identical Scarfskerry in Caithness), Masgeir (N: *már* = seagull), and Sgeir na nGall (skerry of the strangers, possibly a former Viking roost). Off the coast of Aberdeen lie the Skares, and off Portrush in Northern

Ireland the Skerries. There are also Skerries off Anglesey and off Withernsea in the East Riding, a Sker Point at Porthcawl in Glamorgan, a Black Scar and a Green Scar in St Bride's Bay, a Tusker Rock (N: *þurs* = a giant or monster) off Glamorgan, Ravenscar in the East Riding and two lost Welsh skerries, Blackescerre and Emsger. *Sker*, derived from the Gothonic root **skarja*, something cut off, survives in Scandinavia (Icel. and Faer: *sker*; Norw: *skjer*; Swe: *skär*; Dan: *skær*) and was adopted, not only by all the English- and Kelticspeaking Britons, but also by the Germans (*Schär*), the Russians (*shkery* = cliffs), the Finns (*kari*), the Estonians (*skäär*), and the Lapps (*skaerre*). The Norman placename, Le Sceret, is a French rendition of the word.

The term *stakkr* was frequently applied by the Northmen to a tall, isolated rock that had been broken or eroded away from its parent cliff and now stood some way out to sea. Rocks named Stack are found all round the British coasts, from Shetland and Orkney through the Hebrides to Man, Anglesey, South Wales and the Channel Isles – where the form is 'Étaque'

Two Norse terms for particular types of coastal rock formation, *fles*, a flat skerry, and *boði*, a submerged rock, are somewhat less widespread in their British distribution. *Fles* occurs at several places in Shetland and Orkney (e.g. Flashes, Less, Lashy, etc) and at Fleshwick in the Isle of Man, whilst *boði* appears in the Northern Isles as *baa*, *bee*, *boo*, etc, in the Hebrides as *bo*, and in Man as *bowe*.

The shapes of islands, unusual rock configurations and the profiles of cliffs as seen from the sea frequently suggested to the Scandinavians associations with all kinds of familiar objects and implements. Shetland's name seems to have been inspired by the resemblance of some natural feature to the hilt (N: *hjalt*) of a sword, whilst both the English and the Gaelic names of the St Kilda group – remotest of the Hebrides – appear to be of Scandinavian derivation. St Kilda itself has nothing to do with any saint (let alone with N: *kelda* = spring); sixteenthcentury spellings, such as Skilda and Skildar, point to an underlying N: *skildir* = shields, whilst the islands' Gaelic name, Hirt or Hirta, may be another allusion to some distinctive landmark (N: *hirtir* = stags – perhaps referring to an 'antler'-shaped rock formation?).

The figurative use of *kalfr* (calf) by the Northmen to describe a small island lying near a larger one (as at Strynø and Strynø Kalv in Denmark) has been retained in Britain at, among other places, the

Calves of Eday and Flotta in Orkney, the Calf of Man and Scotland's Calf of Mull (N: Mylarkalfr).

The term *drengr*, which, in later Norse, acquired the meaning of a warrior and then, more specifically, that of a 'boy' in the modern Scandinavian languages, has preserved its early topographical significance of an isolated, vertical offshore rock in such celebrated North Island placenames as the 'Drengs' in St Magnus' Bay, Shetland.

Of the many Norse terms for a headland or promontory, *nes* (derived from the Gothonic root **naso* = that which protrudes – and thus a cousin of the word *nose*), was by far the commonest, and headlands whose names contain this term as their second element are found all round the coasts of Britain. Typical Shetland examples are Hestaness and Fuglaness, whilst Stromness and Stenness are but two of the many to be found in Orkney. Scotland's Caithness – called Katanes by the Northmen – was known simply as 'The Ness' to the Orcadians – its inhabitants being referred to as nesþjóð – the 'Ness folk'. Sutherland's northernmost tip, Cape Wrath, was *Hvarfnes* to the Norsemen. The Western Isles offer scores of examples – Ullinish, Brattanish, Arnish (N: *ǫrn* = eagle) being typical. The four natural divisions of Skye are all named from Nesses (Trotternish – Þrǫndr's ness; Waternish; Duirinish – deer ness; and Minginish – N: *meginn* = main), whilst the northern part of the island of Mull is likewise divided into three Nesses – Mornish, Quinish and Mishnish. Many of these west Scottish *-ness* names also carry the explanatory Gaelic prefix *ard-* (headland), as at Ardtornish (N: *Þórsnes* = Thor's ness). Man, too, has its Nesses – as at Cregneish, Agneish and Langness – as does Wales with its Newton Ness. In the east of England are Skegness and Holderness, and over in the west are Widness and Furness – the latter from N: *fuð* = rump.

Although the various 'Nazes' and 'Nesses' of southern England, such as Dungeness and Orford Ness, are more likely to have been inspired by the corresponding English term *næss*, Norman examples such as Cap Gris Nez are almost certainly of Scandinavian derivation.

Less ubiquitous than *nes* is *oddi*, from *oddr* = the point of a weapon (Dan: *od*). Around the coasts of Britain, *oddi* is found at, for instance, Oddasta in Shetland, Greenodd in Lancashire, Ravenser Odd in Yorkshire and Tromode (Þrumm's *odd*) in Man.

Múli, literally the snout or muzzle of an animal (whence the Scots *mool*) was often applied figuratively to a jutting cape or crag, as at Mull Head in Orkney, the Mool of Aeswick in Shetland, the Hebridean island of Mull and the Mulls of Galloway and Kintyre.

Both the English and the Scandinavians made use of the word *head* (N: *hǫfuð*) when naming promontories – e.g. Durlston Head in England, Fyns Hoved in Denmark, etc, and, whilst most of the British 'Heads' are obviously of native coinage, a few contain the imprint of the corresponding Norse form. Three Cumberland placenames, Whitehaven, Swarta Brow and the bizarre Glaramara, all contained at an earlier stage in their evolution the Scandinavian *hǫfuð*. Whitehaven reflects the Norse prototype *Hvítahǫfuðhǫfn* = white head harbour, Swarta Brow was still known locally as 'Suart Houed' (Black Head) in the early 1300s (a vanished Irish 'Sortadbud' may have been identical), whilst Glaramara was recorded in 1210 as 'Houed Gleuermerhe' – Glaramara Head. This is yet another example of the habit of 'inversion', practised by the Hibernicised Northmen who settled the English north-west, although the actual elements themselves appear to be Scandinavian, *Glaram* being the Norse *gljúfr* = a chasm or ravine, *ara* being, possibly, the Norse *erg* = a shieling. The Scandinavian *hǫfuð* also lurks behind Lancashire's Preesall, which was recorded in *Domesday Book* as 'Pressouede' (*Press* – Welsh: *pres* = brushwood), and the word occurs again at Howstrake and Bradda (N: *breiðhǫfuð* = broad head) in Man, at the Orkney farm of Howth, and in the earlier forms of Hawshead and Ramshead in England – Houkeshowth and Ramshouth. An alternative form, *Hǫfði* (cf Trøllhøvdi in Faeroe) has inspired the numerous Hevdis of Shetland. Two Welsh heads, Orme's Head at Llandudno and Worm's Head on Gower, although not Scandinavian, are believed to preserve the memory of the Danish Viking Chieftain, Gorm (or Ormr), who, driven out of Ireland by Olaf the White in 855, harried in Wales until his slaying at the hands of Rhodri Mawr, Prince of Gwynedd.

Among the more fanciful Norse names for headlands, those most in favour alluded to parts of the human physiognomy. Typical examples from Shetland are *kjálki* = a jaw (the Scots *chowk*) as at Kjolka; *kinn* = a chin, as at 'da Keen o'Haamar'; *hauss* = a skull, as at 'da Høs'; *snyta* and *rani*, both meaning a snout, as at Snooti and Rana; and *enni*, a forehead, as at Ennisfirth. *Koddi*, a pillow, was figuratively used of a small, rounded headland, as at Tøvakudda (N: *þœfa* = to shrink cloth, here an allusion to the shrinking of wadmal (coarse Shetland cloth) in the sea in order to make it thicker and denser), whilst *barði*, the prow of a ship, was applied topographically to a headland whose top projected beyond its base, as at Da Bard o' Bressay. Other names for headlands included *bringa*, a breast, as at Brunga in Shetland; *grandi*, a low point projecting far into the sea, as at the Graand in Egilsay, Orkney and at Gransh (N: Grandanes) on Man; and *gnúpa* and *gnípa*, both referring to peak-shaped projections, as at da Noop in Shetland and Knoop in Orkney and at da Neep in Shetland and Greeba (formerly Gnebe) on Man.

Tangi, a tongue of land, occurs frequently as *teeng* in Orkney, and in Shetland as *tonga* (e.g. Longatonga) or *taing*, as at Skjotaing – a skjo (Norw: *skjá*) being a small stone hut with slits to admit the wind for the purpose of drying unsalted fish or mutton. *Blað*, literally a blade or leaf, occurs at da Blade o' Hellyer and Ørablaa (beach-point) in Shetland; whilst *nǫf*, literally the 'nave' of a wheel (whence Norw: *nov* = the projecting end of a beam) refers to a headland in such Shetland placenames as da Niv or da Nov, as does the identical Faeroese term *nøv*.

A whole range of terms was also employed by the Northmen to describe other coastal features such as spits, sandbanks, isthmuses, reefs and bars.

A gravelly spit or sandbank – either in a river or off the coast – was commonly termed an *eyrr* (whence Øresund, the Sound separating the Danish island of Sealand from Sweden and Elsinore (Dan: *Helsingør*) – the *eyrr* at the neck (*hals*) of the Sound). In Shetland placenames it is still pronounced 'ør', in the Norn fashion, as at Ørafirth, whilst the usual Orkney form is the uncontracted 'ayre' (as in the Ayre at Kirkwall). Two Hebridean placenames containing the word are Earrabhig and Eorrbhaidh (N: *vík*, *vágr*, both meaning an inlet). The northern point of the Isle of Man is called the Ayre, whilst the lost Eirewere in Wales also contained the word.

Melr, a sandbank, occurs for example at Milford Haven (N: *Melfjarðarhǫfn*) in Wales, Meal in Orkney and at such localities as Cartmell, Eskmeals and Ingoldmeals in England. The word has found its way into the Gaelic, where *Melilearach* refers to sand-grass.

Eið, an isthmus or narrow neck of land, is contained in the Orkney placenames Sanday and Eday (N: *eiðey* = isthmus island) and in the 'Eye' on the Isle of Man. It is also embedded in the Shetland Brae

(N: *breiðeið* = broad isthmus), Mavis Grind (N: *maev – eiðs – grind* = gate of the narrow isthmus) and Northmavin (earlier: Northmavid = N: (Fyrir) *Norðan Maev – Eið* = north of the narrow isthmus. In a deed dated 26 August 1403, the latter name appears as *Firer nordhan Moefeid*.) The word appears, in several Gaelic guises – e.g. *eie, huy, ui, aoi, uidh* – in many Hebridean placenames.

At least a dozen of the rich fund of terms used by the Northmen to describe various types of creek or inlet have survived in British placenames. Of these, *fjǫrðr* (whence Icelandic *fjörður*, Faeroese *fjørður*, Norwegian and Danish *fjord*, Swedish *fjord, fjärd*, Lappish *fir'da*, and English *firth*) is the most widespread. No fewer than eight of the larger inlets along the east coast of Scotland carry the word in its anglicised form: Pentland, Dornock, Moray, Tay, Forth, etc. Across on the west coast, several names containing the Scandinavian word – commonly clipped to -*art*, -*ard* or -*ort* hereabouts – have survived, as at Snizort (Snei's Firth), Suianeart (Sveinn's firth), Gruinard (N: *Grunnfjǫrðr* = shallow firth) and Knoydart (Knútr's firth). Many of these west Scottish firths also carry the explanatory Gaelic prefix, *loch-*, as at Loch Inchard (N: *Engifjǫrðr* = meadow firth). Two important British waterways that were known as 'fjords' in Viking times have shed their Norse appendage, and have long since been known by alternative names: the Little Minch, separating Harris from Skye, was known to the Northmen as Skotlandsfjǫrðr, whilst the southern approach to the Irish Sea was Veðrafjǫrðr = the firth of the 'wether' or ram. *Fjǫrðr* has become -*ford* in Sutherland, as at Laxford (corresponding to the Norwegian: Laksefjord = Salmon firth), as it has in Wales (e.g. Haverford = N: Hafrarfjǫrðr = Goat firth) and may have in Ireland (Wexford, Waterford, etc). English firth-names are rare, although the Solway Firth, which Cumberland shares with Scotland, has an interesting name – a corruption of the Norse Súlavað fjǫrðr – firth at the ford (*vað*) of the gannet (*súla*). The Northern Isles, of course, abound in firths – as at Westray Firth, Stronsay Firth and the Bay of Firth (originally N: Aurriðafjǫrðr = trout firth) in Orkney, whilst the old Shetland name for the Bight of Conningsburgh was 'da Fjørd', pronounced in true Norse fashion.

A *vík* was generally smaller than a *fjǫrðr* (although Víkinn – Norway's '*vík*' par excellence – referred to the whole of the Oslo Fjord). Shetland, too, had its Víkinn – with typical Scandinavian suffixed definite article; the name is now 'Veegen'. Whilst *víks* are scarce in

England (Blowick and Lowick are two of the few examples) the word is common in Scottish placenames from Lerwick in Shetland (identical with Leirvik in Norway and Leirabhig in the Hebrides and containing N: *leir* = clay), to Selwick in Orkney, Wick in Caithness, Ùig on Lewis, Sandbhig in the Inner Hebrides (identical with Sandvig in Denmark) and Prestwick in Ayrshire. Soderick on the Isle of Man reflects, as does Søndervig in Denmark, N: Suðrvík = southern wick, whilst other Manx examples are Garwick and Little Wick.

Another term for an inlet, *vágr* (Icel: *vógur*, Faer: *vágur*, Norw: *våg*), survives in Shetland and Orkney dialect as *voe*, and in such North Island placenames as Scalloway in Shetland (N: *Skálavágr* = inlet where the *skálar*, or booths, were set up to accommodate the Thing-bønder on their way to the assembly at the nearby Tingwall Loch) and the Orkney capital of Kirkwall (N: Kirkjuvágr = church inlet – a name recorded in this form in the *Orkneyinga Saga*). It has been suggested that 'Scallewaag' – an early form of Shetland's Scalloway – lies behind the term 'scallawag' or 'scallywag', which may once have been applied either to the Shetland ponies or to the diminutive island cattle. Confusion between N: *vágr* and Scots: *waa* (wall), is reflected in the Shetland 'Walls' (from an original name: *Vágar* = inlets). The same confusion gave rise to such early spellings of the name of the Orkney capital as Kyrkewa (1274), Kirkwaw (1422) and Kærkewaw (1425) alongside such comparatively uneroded forms as Kirkiu-vaghe, Kirkiuwaghe and Kirkiuuaghe (all from 1329). Although *vágr* has become -*way* in the Lewis placenames Stornoway (N: Stjórnuvágr = steering bay), it is Gaelicised elsewhere in the Western Isles to -*bhaidh* (*vaig*) or -*aig*, as at Hamnabhaidh (N: *hafnarvágr* = harbour inlet, identical with Shetland's Hamnavoe – also the old name for Stromness harbour in Orkney), Alcaig (N: *álkr* = auk), Ostaig (N: *austr* = east), Fiskavaig, Tokavaig (N: Tóki), Tarskavaig (N: *þorskr* = cod) Aulavaig (N: Óli), Bearraraig (N: Bjǫrn), Arisaig (N: Ari), Dibaig (N: *djúpr* = deep), Shieldaig (N: *sild* = herring) and Smiùthaig (N: *smúga* = cave).

Gjá (Icel: *gjá*, Faer: *gjógv*, Norw: *gjå* – the word is a distant cousin of our *yawn*) lives on as *gio*, or *geo* in Shetland and Orkney, as *goe* in Sutherland and Caithness, as *geodha* in the Hebrides and as *giau* and *ghaw* on Man. In all these districts, *gjá* is a recurrent placename element, referring to short, generally steep-sided inlets.

Ǫgr, a small creek or inlet, is a rare placename ingredient in Britain, occurring only at such Manx localities as Ooig Voar and Ooig Veg (large and small *ǫgr* respectively), where it refers to cliff caves rather than inlets.

The Norse *flói* had two meanings. The first, preserved by the Norwegian *floe*, the provincial Danish *flo*, and the Scots and northern English dialect term *flow*, referred to waterlogged marshland (this was also the sense of the taboo word *flo*, used by the Shetland fishermen of the deep sea). The second meaning, retained in Icelandic *flói* and Faeroese *flógvi*, referred to the broad mouth of an estuary or a firth, and it is in this sense that the term occurs in such British placenames as Scapa Flow (N: Skalpaflói – *skalpr* = something hollowed out) which is ringed by the islands of Hoy, South Ronaldsay, Flatta, Hunda, Burray, Cava and the Orkney mainland.

The opening of a firth, or of an estuary, was often referred to by the Northmen as a *mynni* (mouth), and this term is fossilised in the Shetland place-names Vog Minn (mouth of the voe) and Swarback's Minn (N: *svartbakr* = greater black-backed gull), and at Airmyn – mouth of the river Aire, in England.

The specific term for an estuary, however, was *óss*, which survives in Orkney as Oyce (pronounced 'Øs') and in the Hebrides as Oss. Mull's Aros (N: *árós* = river's mouth) is identical with Denmark's Aarhus. Other names for inlets were: *hópr*, as at Openham and Obbenin in Sutherland, Obe on Harris, Oban in Argyle, da Hoobins in Shetland, Loghope and Hubbit (N: *hópit* = the inlet) in Orkney and the lost Goultrop and Loudeshope in Wales; *pollr* = literally a pool, as at Saltapøl in Shetland; *glupr* = literally throat, as at Gloop, also in Shetland; and *effja* = a bay with a swampy margin, as at Evie in Orkney. *Naust*, a stance for boats dragged up on the beach, occurs at such North Island sites as Nouster (plural) and Noustigar (N: *garðr* = farm); *vaðill*, a shallow, fordable place in an estuary, at Vaddle in Shetland; and *hellir*, a coastal cave, at innumerable placenames containing the word Hellyer in the Northern Isles. The Norse *hǫfn* = harbour, survives in its two Norn forms at Hamnadale in Shetland and Ham in Orkney, whilst *stǫð*, a landing place, is found in Orkney at Stuian (pronounced 'Støen' = the *stǫð*) and Toxteth (Tóki's *stǫð*) in England. Yet another term for an inlet, *kíll* – familiar from such Swedish placenames as Lysekil and retained in Danish dialect in the sense of 'a hollow between two sandbanks' – occurs at the Kyles of Lochalsh and of Bute in Scotland. *Kill* is also found at Kyleakin, where it is believed to refer to none other than King Hákon Hákonsson of Norway, who passed this way before and after the skirmish at Largs in 1263 that brought an end to Norse overlordship in the Western Isles.

River names

In contrast to the rich variety of apparently original Scandinavian toponymics around the coasts of Britain, river names of primary Norse inspiration are rare, although surviving dialect terms of Scandinavian origin, such as *beck*, *sike*, *wath* and *keld* are, as noted on page 111 above, still productive constituents in the minor inland hydronymics of the English north-west.

Of the many British river names mentioned in the sagas – Ekkjal (Oykell), Skjalg (Shallog), Spæ (Spey), Þǫll (Thuil), Njǫrn (Nairn), Tvedda (Tweed), Þyn (Tyne), Svǫl (Swale), Úsa (Ouse), Humra, Tems, etc – almost all are merely Scandinavian renderings of existing British prototypes.

A few English river and stream names may reflect the influence of a Scandinavianised pronunciation of English or Keltic originals. The Skerne in Durham, and its Yorkshire namesake, Skerne Beck, seem to be Nordicised versions of an underlying English name, which could have been something like 'Shern', whilst the present forms of the river names Wharfe and Ure are said to be examples of British (ie Keltic) prototypes that have undergone anglicisation and later been remodelled to conform with local Scandinavian habits of pronunciation. In the case of Wharfe, there was even a Scandinavian adjective (*hverfr* = winding) which happened to fit the requirements of both pronunciation and natural description, and there are a few other stream names in England that appear to be based on substantivised adjectives in the Norse language. Such are Bain (N: *beinn* = handy, direct), Brennand (burning, foaming), Seph (OSwe: *sæver* = calm, slow – as in the Swedish stream name, Säveån), Skell (N: *skjall* = resounding), Winster (N: *vinstri* = left, ie the left stream) and Gaunless (ME: *gaghenles* = useless, from N: *gagnlauss*).

A further category comprises stream names coined directly from Norse substantives. Representative of this group are: Skirth (N: *skurð* = a cutting or canal – the word *skirth* survives in this

hydronymic sense in Lincolnshire dialect), Bleng (N: *blæingr, an unattested noun derived from blár = dark, blue, livid), and Wreak
(doubtless inspired by N: vreiðr, reiðr = wrathful, originally 'twisting').
The Wreak, incidentally, winds its way through a part of Leicestershire that was, judging by placename evidence, exceptionally heavily
colonised by Scandinavians.

Occasionally, Scandinavian stream names have been inherited, not
by the watercourse which they originally described, but by a village
lying on the stream. Lincolnshire's village of Skinnand may be an
echo of the old Danish name (N: skínandi = shining) of the river
Brant, while the first element in the Yorkshire placename Skutterskelf
is the Norse skvaðrá = chattering brook.

The last example carries the suffix -á, which was the primary Norse
term for a watercourse. Unlike beck and sike, á is no longer a living
word in provincial English and has probably not been a productive
placename ingredient in Britain since the time when Norse was still
spoken 'West over Sea'. In England, its distribution is largely restricted
to the north-west, where we find Rawthay (N: rauðr = red, here,
perhaps, an allusion to the trout), Brathay (N: breiðá = broad stream),
Greta and Liza – the latter two identical with Iceland's Grjótá =
gravel stream and Ljósá = light stream.

In mainland Scotland, the term occurs as a suffix in Thurso, which
may be either N: Þórsá = Thor's stream, or N: þjórsá = bull's stream,
Calda (N: kaldá = cold stream) and Forsay (N: forsá = waterfall
stream). It occurs as the first element in Arscaig (N: árskiki = strip
of land along a burn side) and Amat (N: ámot = place where two
rivers converge).

In Shetland, a number of burn names still carry the -á suffix, e.g.
Laxo and Bretto (N: laxá = salmon stream and brattá = steep stream,
respectively). In Orkney, however, most original -á names now carry
the explanatory prefix burn, as at the Burn of Suso. Hugh Marwick
suggests that the medial -a- in such Orkney dale names as Durkadale
and Eskadale may also represent an original Norse -á. Apart from an
occasional -á name, only two significant river names on the Scottish
mainland appear to be of unbroken, primary Scandinavian derivation:
Naver, which is probably the Norse næfr = birch bark, and Forss,
which looks like N: fors = waterfall.

Five

Scandinavian personal names in Britain

One of the commonest and most convenient methods of personal appellation in former times was to name a man after his place of origin. In Britain, this practice persisted longest in the Northern Isles. In fifteenth-century Orkney, men known by the name of their birthplace – Sighurdr af Pappley, Cristen af Sanday, Adam af Næstagard, etc. – were still familiar enough, whilst others with names like Olaw in Flattabustare, Rasmus in Ocraquoy and Magnus in Howkenasetter (now Ukinster) were still typical of Shetland in the sixteenth century. Elsewhere in the British Isles, however, surnames had long since become fixed, and many thousand placenames had been inherited by families who had quite forgotten their original connection with the places whose names they bore. Among the British placenames of Scandinavian derivation that are in use today as family names are Askwith (or Asquith), Isbister, Clouston, Ormerod, Thackeray, Gaitskell, Summerskill, Wintersgill, Boothby, Sykes, Storr, Scales (or Scholes), Copeland (N: *kaupland* = bought land), and a few, such as Wisby, which, while still in circulation as family names, have long since disappeared from the map.

Apart from those enshrining placenames compounded of Scandinavian elements, many British surnames perpetuate personal names that were carried west by the crews of the longships or east across the Irish Sea from the Viking roosts in Ireland. Some 530 Scandinavian names have been recorded from English sources – names embedded in placenames, scratched on bone and metal implements, inscribed on coins, and included in monastic registers, parish rent-rolls and other inventories. It is hardly surprising that many of these names, which

11

continued to circulate widely in certain parts of the country until long after the grammatical disintegration of the Norse language West over Sea, have been passed down the generations as British family names. So far, 177 British surnames of wholly Norse derivation have been identified – although the number would certainly be brought up to a total of 200 and above if the many examples that have fallen out of use over the past few hundred years were also taken into account.

British surnames of Scandinavian inspiration are recognisable by the same earmarks that are used to identify Norse loanwords and placenames. Some, such as Clack, Scowle, Skeat, Stain and Goke, contain characteristic Scandinavian sound combinations, whilst the majority are renditions of familiar northern names that were completely unknown to the British before the coming of the Vikings.

England

Many of the earliest Scandinavian personal names in English texts appear in extremely archaic form: the spellings Vnlaf and Inwaer, for instance, indicate that the medial -n- that was destined to be dropped from unstressed positions in later Norse (these two names had become Óláfr and Ívarr by the literary Old Icelandic period) were still a feature of the language spoken by the Danish landnamsmen in the ninth and early tenth centuries. Some Scandinavian names are anglicised beyond recognition – as is that of Bagsecg, a Danish chieftain mentioned in the *Anglo-Saxon Chronicle* as a participant in Halfdan's ill-fated campaign in Wessex. In others, the distortion is less drastic, Sveinn, for example, occurring as Swegen, Ubbi as Hubba and Ásketill as Oscytel, whilst the Danish names of such churchmen as Ulfcytel, Thurfearth, Wither and Fræna (N: Ulfketill, Þorfrøðr, Víðarr, Fráni) – listed in the long charter granted to Eynsham Abbey in 1005 – are unmistakable.

After the Viking invasions had ended and the Danes had been settled for some time in the north and east, Scandinavian names, those of Danelaw jarls and later of merchants, lawmen, ecclesiastics and other dignitaries, began to flood the chronicles in forms which were usually fairly accurate renditions of the Norse originals.

These Scandinavian names, although appearing most often in records and on coins from the north and east, were by no means confined to the original areas of Danish settlement; to judge from the wide distribution of Norse names throughout England, Scandinavian 'copemen' or merchants seem to have been active in commercial centres as far from the Danelaw as Devon and the west Midlands. As long ago as 1846, Hildebrand listed some fifty unmistakable Scandinavian names from British coins found in Sweden. Although the bulk of these coins were struck at Lincoln, Stamford and York, many came from as far afield as Chester, London, Norwich and even Exeter. Typical examples from Hildebrand's inventory – all of them dating from between 979 and 1066 – are Arngrim, Arnkil, Arnthor, Auti, Beorn, Cetel, Colgrim, Eilaf, Escer, Grim, Grimcytel, Iric, Jelmer (Hjálmarr), Othgrim, Ræfn, Scula, Swarti, Thor, Thorcetel, Thorstan, Thorulf, Ulfcetel and Widfara.

As Anglo-Danish marriages became more common, the offspring of such unions were as likely to be given Scandinavian as English names. Earl Godwin of Wessex and his Danish wife, Gyða, for example, called their three sons Tostig, Harald and Sveinn, all good Danish names, and other Scandinavian names, such as Ulf, Orm and Toke, remained popular in the old Danish areas and beyond for many generations after the Norman Conquest. *Domesday Book* lists one Lincolnshire family in which two of the brothers have Danish names – Oune (Auðun?) and Ingemund – and two English names – Edric and Eculf. Also from Lincolnshire came such examples as Turued, son of Vlued, in which the father has an English name – here, Wulfferð – and the son a Danish – here, Þorfrøðr. As Sir Frank Stenton has observed:

> Something more than the settlement of a few ships' companies must have lain behind the survival of northern habits of nomenclature in the Danelaw through three centuries of virtual isolation from the Scandinavian mainland. No doubt the isolation was incomplete. There was direct intercourse between Lincolnshire and Norway in the twelfth century. Earlier and unrecorded intercourse may well have helped to keep alive ancient traditions in this as in other matters. But their origin must be sought in a Scandinavian colonisation of northern and eastern England at least comparable in scale to the later movement from which the Duchy of Normandy arose.

In 1086, when William initiated the compilation of the great statistical survey of his English domains, later known as *Domesday Book*, the returns showed that, in the shires of the northern Danelaw, well over half the population had Scandinavian or partly-Scandinavian names; although this does not, of course, mean that the bearers of these 550 or so names were necessarily of unbroken Danish descent. Whilst the bulk of these names were found throughout the old areas of Scandinavian settlement and beyond, some were more restricted in distribution: 56, for example, were peculiar to Yorkshire, 34 to Lincolnshire, and 41 to the north-west. Most of the Scandinavian names recorded in *Domesday Book* are instantly recognisable, despite the fact that the scribes who made the compilation were for the most part Frenchmen, to whom English, let alone Norse, was an outlandish tongue. Many of these Normans themselves, not surprisingly, bore Scandinavian names, although these had long since been adapted to conform to the sound system of northern French.

Many of the Scandinavian names in *Domesday Book* were distorted by Norman scribes who tended to substitute sounds and sound combinations from their own language for troublesome Scandinavian sound clusters. The Norse *kn-* for example, was wholly alien to French (*knífr* = knife, becoming *canif*), so that Knútr frequently appears in *Domesday Book* as Canut, Chanut, etc. Initial *Sn-* was equally foreign to the French scribes, who prefixed an epenthetic *e-* to Norse names beginning with this combination; Snæbjǫrn, for instance, appears in *Domesday Book* as Esnebern. French also lacked the dental fricative sounds – þ and ð – of Norse, and the scribes rendered these phonemes either as T (e.g. Toroldus and Torgis for Þórvaldr and Þórgisl) or as D (e.g. Drondus and Durilda for Þróndr and Þórhildr). Again, the absence of an initial H- in French led to such *Domesday Book* versions of Scandinavian names as Acon for Hákon.

Many Scandinavian names were further disguised by the appending of a gratuitous Latin nominative suffix, *-us*, as in Algodus for Álfgautr, Anschillus for Áskell, Torphinus for Þórfinnr and Scalpinus for Skálpi, whilst the ending *-i* to many familiar Scandinavian names was frequently altered to *-o* or *-a* – Bósi becoming Boso and Gauti becoming Gouta.

In some cases, the French scribes grafted their own diminutive suffixes, such as *-et* and *-el*, on to Norse names, e.g. Touet for Tófi and Dringhel for Drengr, whilst the native Scandinavian ending *-ill* to names like Hrafnketill was often lopped off by the Normans, who evidently confused it with their own diminutive suffix – shaving Hrafnketill to Ravechet.

Certain of the Scandinavian names that survive as English surnames do so in a Normanised form; Gamlin, for example, represents the Norse Gamall with a Norman diminutive suffix, whilst Ankin, Antell and Haskins are inspired by French corruptions of the familiar Þórketill.

The Scandinavian names in *Domesday Book* fall into five main categories:

1. Mono- or disyllabic names, such as Acon (Hákon), Ailof (Eilafr), Ainar (Einarr), Baret (Barðr), Gunnerus (Gunnarr), Raven (Hrafn), Roulf (Hrólfr) and Suinus (Sveinn).
2. Names compounded in characteristic Scandinavian fashion from two smaller elements, such as Agemund (Qgmundr), Bergulver (Bergulfr), Dolfin (Dolgfinnr), Oudgrim (Auðgrímr), Sitricus (Sigtrygg) and Turstinus (Þórsteinn).
3. Diminutives or affectionate names, such as Aschi (Aski, short for Ásketill), Balchi (Balki), Ote (Otti), Toue (Tófi – short for Þjóðvaldr, and whence the family names Tovey and Toovey) and Tochi (Tóki – short form of Þórketill, and surviving in the English surname, Tuck).
4. Names describing a man's occupation, such as Batsuen (N: *bátsveinn* = a boatswain), Dring (N: *drengr* = a warrior), and Wiching (N: *Víkingr* = viking).
5. Nicknames, of which the Vikings were inordinately fond, such as: Wacra (N: *Vakr* = alert), Feg (N: *feigr* = cowardly), Langabein (N: = long leg), Let (N: *ljótr* = ugly), Escelf (N: *skelfr* = trembling), Roc (N: *hrókr* = cormorant), Nabe (N: *nabbi* = warty) and Waih (N: *veikr* = weak). A number of these Scandinavian nicknames have been bequeathed as English family names, eg Sprackling ('The man with the creaking legs'), Coe (N: *ká* = jackdaw), Kidd (N: *kið* = kid), Scafe (N: *skeifr* = crooked), Scarfe (N: *skarfr* = cormorant), Tait (N: *teitr* = cheerful), Hake (N: *haki* = hook), Corey (N: *kári* = curley; the man's name, Kåre, is still used in Denmark and Norway), Skeat (N: *skjótr* = swift), Couse (N: *kausi* = tomcat), Cates (N: *kati* = cheerful), Clack (N: *klak* = clod), Snarey (N: *snari* = swift), Orr (N: *orri* = blackcock), Frane (N: *fráni* = the bright one), Brockliss (N: *broklauss* = trouserless), and Ofram (N: *úframr* = sluggish). Many other English names based on

Scandinavian sobriquets have long since been discarded, no doubt at a time when their opprobrious allusions were still dimly understood; such were: Crokebain (crow's leg), Gaitscar (goat's hair), Blouthead (soft head), Wanwit (mad) and Skitebrok (dirty breeches).

Of special interest, in that they testify to the vigour of the Scandinavian name-giving tradition in Britain, are the 60-odd Norse names recorded in the Domesday survey that are not attested from Scandinavia itself. Typical of these home-grown Danelaw creations were: Suertebrand (N: *Svartbrandr), Algrim (N: *Álfgrímr), Gamalber (N: *Gamalbjǫrn), Hunchill (N: *Hundkell), Ormchetel (N: *Ormkell), and Sceldfrithe (N: *Skjaldfríðr). One of them, Cytelric (N: *Ketillríkr) survives as the English family name, Ketteridge. A comparable class of names comprised those compounded of a Norse and an English element, as were Swartcol, Cylferth and Thorgifu – the second two surviving as the surnames Kilvert and Turriffe.

The areas where Scandinavian names appear to have been particularly popular at the time of the Norman Conquest include Norfolk, where as many as 40 per cent of the recorded twelfth-century names were of Danish inspiration; and Yorkshire, especially the North and East Ridings, which yielded the following typical examples from the first half of the twelfth century: Ragnilda, Audkill, Gamel son of Suan, Stainulf, Acca son of Thor, Rainkill son of Stainbern, Ketel son of Siward, Ulf, Orm, Colbrand, Ilving, Leising, Turkil son of Thorald, Thorne, Leot, Askil, Halthor, Kille son of Erchel, Swartebrand, Arkil son of Thurkil and Helrandus son of Forni. Scandinavian names also continued to flourish, during the early post-Conquest generations, in parts of Suffolk, which offers such examples as: Dag, Gangulf, Grimulf, Scanche, Suein, Turgod and Ormer, and it is surely no coincidence that the parish of Coney Weston, whose name is a Scandinavian reshaping of an original English Cyningestun (Kingston), numbered among its eleventh-century landowners men with such unambiguously Danish names as Brother, Turchetel, Suein and Odin.

A generation or so after the compilation of the Domesday survey, rent rolls, village inventories and other mid-twelfth century statistical records began to indicate the waning popularity of Scandinavian names in many parts of England. By the end of the century such names were becoming unfashionable even in the hard-core Danish districts of Lincoln, Leicester and the East Riding, where newer continental names such as Richard, Robert, William and John, introduced by the Normans, were becoming increasingly more stylish.

Illustrative of the dwindling use of the Scandinavian names are these late-twelfth-century examples from Lincoln, in which the Christian names are Norman but the patronymics Danish: John filius *Swave* (N: Svafi), Robert filius *Gamel* (N: Gamall), William filius *Ougrim* (N: Auðgrímr), and Simon filius *Toke* (N: Tóki). From this time forward, Danish given-names rapidly drop out of English contexts and none (save for the rare and aristocratic Scottish Torquil) have survived to the present day. Harold is a fairly recent revival, and Eric was given a new lease of life in 1858 with the publication of Dean Farrar's novel, *Eric, or Little by Little*. The girls' names, Ingrid, Greta and Karen are very recent imports from Scandinavia to Britain, where the first two were reinforced by the popularity of the Swedish film actresses, Ingrid Bergman and Greta Garbo. Thora and Gudrun are also familiar to Britons as the Christian names of actresses Thora Hird and Gudrun Ure; Gudrun's appeal may be due to the fact that it is the name of one of the heroines in D. H. Lawrence's novel, *Women in Love*.

A situation very similar to that which existed in some of the most heavily Scandinavianised parts of England seven and eight hundred years ago – when Danish given-names, though still popular, were beginning to become obsolescent – obtains at the present time in certain sections of the American Upper Middle West – an area sometimes referred to as 'The American Danelaw'. Here, where entire communities are of wholly or partially Scandinavian extraction, Swedish and Dano-Norwegian given-names – particularly Nils, Olof, Gustaf, Knut, Anders, Gunnar, Holger, Axel, Hedvig, Sigrid, Ingeborg and Karin (or Karen) – are still in circulation. Just as in twelfth- and thirteenth-century England, however, their popularity is gradually waning as the connections between the second- and third-generation expatriates and the Scandinavian motherland become increasingly more tenuous.

While it is doubtless many hundred years since Scandinavian names were given at the font in England, family names of Norse derivation – dating from the time when their prototypes were still popular as baptismal names in the Danelaw and the north-west – live on.

Only in a minority is the underlying Scandinavian original still transparent. Such are: Ayliffe (Eilafr), Drummond (Drǫmundr),

Hacon (Hákon), Kettle (Ketill), Ivor (Ívarr) and Osborn (Ásbjǫrn). In the majority, the original Scandinavian forms have been obfuscated by various processes of phonic distortion. It is, for example, hard to recognise Qgmundr in Ammon, Sígvatr in Suett, Arnketill in Arkell, Kolbjǫrn in Colcin, Dolgfinnr in Dolphin, Gamall in Gamble, Áslákr in Haslock, Eiríkr in Herrick, Áki in Oakey, Hrafnkell in Rankill, Hróaldr in Rowatt, Sǫrli in Searle, Þórgils in Sturgis, Sveinnbjǫrn in Swinburne or Tóli in Tooley. How many families bearing the name Rayner can be aware that they are the probable namesakes of Ragnar Hairybreeks, the arch-Viking whose sons, the 'Porkers' as he called them, wrought such havoc in ninth-century England? How many Goodrams and Gooderhams know that they share a name with Guthrum, the Danish chieftain who was finally defeated by Alfred at Edington? And how many Haldanes, Aldens and Holdens recognise their connection with Halfdan Ragnarsson, who conquered Northumbria in 870? Not infrequently, a Norse given-name has survived in upwards of a dozen different forms, as has Þórkell, which has seventeen descendants among the English family names, from the obvious Thurkell, Thirkell, Thirkill and Thorkhill to the more disfigured Turkel, Thirtle, Turtle, Tuttle and Toghill.

Despite many claims to the contrary, the various orthographic renditions of early Scandinavian names in English, Norman-French or Latin texts give precious little information about the pronunciation of Norse that prevailed in the Danelaw at the time when they were first committed to vellum. What these spellings do indicate are the various attempts to bring the Scandinavian names into line with the sound systems of the scribal languages. Interestingly, many of the selfsame anglicising processes that led to the disfigurement of Norse names in the Danelaw a thousand years ago have been applied in much more recent times to the names of Scandinavian settlers in North America.

Here, just as in Anglo-Saxon and post-Norman England, unfamiliar Scandinavian sounds and sound clusters are adapted – often ruthlessly – to fit into the procrustean bed of English articulation. The very Scandinavian phonemes that troubled our forebears in the old Danelaw are still distorted, or sidestepped altogether, by English speakers living alongside Scandinavian immigrant families in America.

The clusters *Bj*, *Gj*, *Hj*, *Kj*, *Lj*, *Sj* and *Skj* are invariably deprived of their palatal *j* to yield such examples as Burns for Bjørn and Hart for

Hjort – just as medieval English scribes transliterated Ingjaldr as Ingold and Ásbjǫrn as Osborn or Osbern. During the American Civil War, a Swede named Esbjörn enlisted in the Federal Army as Esbyorn but mustered out as Osborn; his name had suffered a fate identical to that undergone by so many of his namesakes in England a thousand years earlier. Attempts on the part of non-Scandinavian Americans to enunciate both consonants in this type of cluster (as was done by the Baltimore stevedores who broke the name of the Norwegian vessel, *Bjørnstjerne Bjørnson*, down into 'B. Jesus B. Johnson') are rare – and obviously influenced by spelling rather than by sound. Sometimes a compromise is reached, and a Scandinavian palatal is rendered by its nearest English equivalent. In this way, Sjögren, Sørkjel, Skjeldrud, Gjersjø and Kjerret may become Shogren, Surchel, Sheldrew, Jarshaw and Cherry in America.

Somewhat more easily mutatable are the recurrent clusters, *sv*, *tv*, and *kv*, which usually become – in America as in Anglo-Saxon and early medieval England – *sw*, *tw*, and *qu*, giving Swenson or Swanson for Svensson or Svendsen, Tweet for Tvedt, Quarne for Kverne and Lofquist for Löfkvist. In the cluster *kn*, it is the *k* which is lost – giving Newtson for Knutsson.

Among the first features to be plundered from immigrant Scandinavian names in America are those vowel sounds that have no equivalent in English. Norwegian Lønås thus becomes Lonas – both orthographically and in pronunciation – Danish Jørgensen becomes Jorgenson, and Swedish Åhlén loses its diacritics to become Ahlen. A comparable British example from recent times is Haggard, which, at any rate in the case of Rider Haggard's family, began life as the Danish surname Aagaard.

Many Scandinavian surnames in America are translated, element for element, into English – just as the Norse Valþjóf became, in Old English, Walþēof (the prototype of such modern names as Waldo, Walthew, Waddilove, etc). This is particularly the case with Norwegian names based on the immigrant family's place of origin in the old country. Thus, Norskog becomes Norwood, Østerhus becomes Easthouse, Nygard becomes Newton, and Lysaker becomes Lightfield. Similarly, Swedish Sjöstrand and Liljeström are apt to become Seashore and Lillystream.

By far the commonest fate to befall the immigrant Scandinavian name in America is for it to become adjusted, often in the most brutal and insensitive manner, in the direction of what seems, to the untutored ear, its nearest English equivalent. Among the most monstrous of these metamorphoses are Elmer for Hjalmar, Fred for Fridtjof, Earl for Erling, Orin for Arne, Chester for Tjøstolv, Cameron for Kolbjørn, Charlie for Kjetil, and Tom, which has become a general-purpose American substitute for such Scandinavian *Tor-* compounds as Torfinn, Torleiv and Tormod.

Extended to family names, this process has given birth to such abortions as Burkc for Bcrg, Bacon for Bakken, Butler for Botolvson, Hawkins for Håkonsen, Evans for Eivindsen and O'Gordon for Øygaren. Somewhat more intelligently, Swedish Karlsson, Bengtsson and Henriksson, and Dano/Norwegian Nicolaisen (or Nikolajsen) are frequently melted down to Carson, Benson, Henderson and Nicolson.

Crass though the more outrageous of these American mutations may seem, they are no more so than such Domesday distortions as Gert, Welp and Ram for N: Gurðr, Hvelpr and Hrafn, and show most graphically that the modern processes of anglicisation of Scandinavian names through folk-etymology and sound-distortion are almost identical with what they were a thousand years ago.

The traditional English practice of creating patronymic family names by appending the suffix *-son* to a personal name (yielding such surnames as Johnson, Peterson, Thomson and Wilson) has frequently been attributed to Scandinavian influence. And with good reason; for of all the Gothonic-speaking peoples, it is the Scandinavians who have always exploited the method most fully and who have kept it alive to the present day.

In Iceland, 'shifting' patronymics, changing with each generation, are still used for both sexes. Stefán Gunnarsson's son, Björn, will be known as Björn Stefánsson, whilst Stefán's daughter, Gudrún, will be known as Gudrún Stefánsdóttir.

In rural Sweden, shifting patronymics flourished right up until the end of the last century – although the practice was ended by a law passed in 1901 which made it compulsory for every family to settle on a fixed, inheritable surname. Among many of the expatriate Swedes in North America, however, fixed family names were uncommon – at least among those settlers hailing from rural parts of the old country – and the immigrants continued to resort to their traditional method of patronymics as a matter of course, Anders Larsson's son Per being known as Per Andersson, and Per's son Ole as Ole Persson. Indeed, the habit seems to have persisted in the remoter Swedish marches of the Middle West until after World War I, for, as late as 1923, the Swedish Bishop, Nathan Söderblom, was exhorting his quondam compatriots in Nebraska and the Dakotas to cling to their old system of patronymics – though little heed seems to have been taken of his plea.

Patronymics also survived until within living memory in parts of rural Norway; the common practice among the Norwegian peasantry was to name a man or woman not merely after his or her father (as, for example, *Kristin Lavransdatter*, the title of a novel by Sigrid Undset), but also after the farm or hamlet where he or she was born, e.g. Anders Halvorsen Bakkerud, Else Hansdatter Hauggard.

In Denmark, patronymics continued in use among the country people until the early decades of the last century – although they had been abandoned by the majority of the townsfolk some two hundred years earlier – whilst the nobility and the old-established clerical and bourgeois families had been in possession of fixed surnames since as early as the thirteenth and fourteenth centuries. On 28 May 1828, shifting patronymics were declared illegal in Denmark, on account of the inevitable chaos they caused in official statistical records, and the country people were ordered to settle on surnames that could be passed on unaltered down the successive generations of each family. So many of these names were patronymics – Hansen, Jensen, Larsen, Sørensen, etc. – that a further act was promulgated in 1904 enabling families to purchase for 4 kroner a 'proper' surname that was *not* a patronymic. This Act was revoked in 1961. After the 1828 Decree – and a subsequent one issued in 1858 to ensure that the names selected in 1828 were being adhered to – a compromise system developed in many rural areas which enabled an individual to retain his patronym proper and at the same time to possess an officially approved surname. Thus, Peder, son of Hans Jensen, would call himself Peder Hansen Jensen; to his associates in the village he would be known as Peder Hansen, whilst for official purposes he was Peder Jensen. Interestingly, an identical state of affairs existed in fourteenth-century Yorkshire, where only one man in six had a fixed surname, and individuals with double patronymics, such as William Hanson Johanson, son of Hanne Peterson Johanson, were common.

In view of their deeply entrenched allegiance to patronymics, it might seem reasonable to assume that the Scandinavians were responsible for the introduction of the practice to the British Isles – at any rate to England (the various Keltic speakers being themselves inveterate bestowers of patronymics). However, while the habit seems admittedly to have been adhered to longer in the northern and eastern counties than elsewhere, there is ample evidence to show that this particular naming device had been exploited widely in England and Lowland Scotland – even in districts far removed from the main Scandinavian settlement areas – long before the coming of the Vikings. Again, if the Scandinavians were indeed responsible for the introduction of the practice, why are so few of the existing English family names in -*son* compounded with Norse personal names? Examples like Coulson, Swainson, Knottson, Ormeson, Grimson, Gunnson, Iverson and Ingerson, which *do* contain Scandinavian names, are far outnumbered by names like Johnson, Paulson, Nelson, Benson and Anderson which do not. There were, of course, many more patronymics based on Norse names in the Middle Ages, when few of them had ossified into fixed family names. Typical examples from eleventh-century Lincolnshire are Yric Haroldes sunu, Askyl Tokes sune, Outy Grimkelson and Gunilde Thurkilles dohter, whilst twelfth-century Yorkshire offers specimens such as Gamel Grimessune and Ulf Fornessuna. Those that have survived as English surnames, however, probably number less than a dozen.

The English habit of forming patronymics in the traditional Gothonic fashion – doubtless reinforced in places by the identical Scandinavian usage – persisted throughout the Norman period, although names with the native suffixes -*son* or -*sunu* are eclipsed in twelfth- and thirteenth-century texts by the Latin *filius*. From early post-Norman Co. Durham come the following examples, in which both the Christian name and the patronymic are Scandinavian: Sceal filius Colbein (Skjalg Kolbeinsson), Thorkil filius Thoraldi, Suartebrand filius Ulf (Svartbrandr Úlfsson), Snacolf filius Cytel (Snækolfr Ketilsson), Swerus filius Sivardi (Sverri Sigvardsson) and Ulfkil filius Suhain (Úlfkil Sveinsson).

Examples like Orm Gamalson from the Kirkdale inscription, however (see p. 59 above), show clearly that this latinising was merely a scribal convention, and that the common folk still continued to use the native and Scandinavian suffix -*son* among themselves. Names in

-*son* (rather than *filius*) begin to appear again in vernacular texts from the fourteenth century onwards, particularly from the northern counties where the fixing of hereditary surnames took place later than in the south – enabling the traditional method of calling a man the son (and a woman the daughter) of the father (or, occasionally, the mother) to persist.

Family names in -*son* have remained commoner in the north and in the east Midlands than elsewhere in Britain to this day, the densest concentrations occurring in the Scottish Lowlands (where names like Donaldson, Jameson, Davidson, Henderson, Ferguson and Matthieson are common), in Northumberland (home of the Adamsons), Durham, the Lake District, Yorkshire (home of the English Hansons and Christisons – still known as 'Christiansons' and 'Cristensons', just as in Scandinavia, until as late as the fourteenth century), Lancashire, Lincoln and Nottingham. Somewhat fewer of the English family names in -*son* appear to have originated in such peripheral Danelaw shires as Derby, Leicester and Norfolk.

Incidentally, despite appearances, the English surnames Tyson, Jepson (or Jeppeson) and Ibson have no connection with the very similar-looking Danish Thaisen, Jepsen (Jeppesen) and Ibsen. English Tyson is the Old French nickname *tison* = a firebrand, whereas Danish Thaisen contains the Frisian name Taie. Middle English Gepp and Ib were affectionate forms of Geoffrey and Isabel respectively, whereas Jep and Ib in the Danish names are derived from Iæip, a medieval corruption of Jacob.

Cumberland appears to have been one of the last corners of England where 'shifting' patronymics persisted among the peasantry. A deed from as late as 1397 names one 'Richard Thomson, sone of Thomas Johnson', whilst, scarcely a century prior to this date, Scandinavian personal names seem to have still been characteristic of the older generation of Cumbrians. In the year 1285, Stephen son of Gamel, Henry son of Hamund, William Tyrpyn (Þórfinnsson) and Richard Siward (Sigurðsson) were all convicted for poaching deer in the royal forest of Inglewood.

Although it is clear that the use of -*son* as a patronymic suffix is not of direct Norse inspiration, it can hardly be coincidental that the distribution of -*son* surnames in England and Scotland corresponds so precisely with the main areas of other Scandinavian linguistic influence. It is not in the least fanciful to speculate that the presence in these districts of Scandinavians – to whom the appending of the element *-son* was the only known method of patronymic formation – may have reinforced the established native practice. Although the

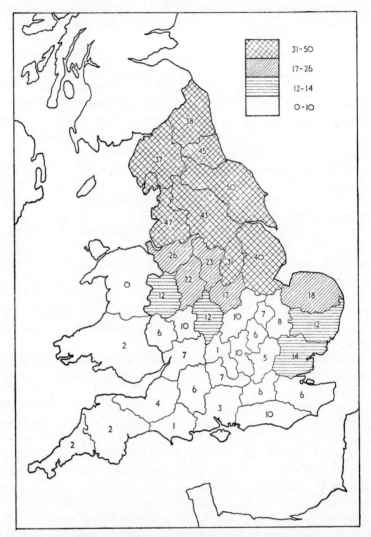

FIG. 12.   Distribution of English family names ending in *-son* (based on the map in *Norge og Vest-Europa i gammel Tid* by Belsheim, 1925, p. 143). The figures give the number of patronymic surnames believed to have originated in each county.

English knew an alternative construction – in which the suffix -*ing* was added to the father's name (e.g. Ælfred Æþelwulfing = Alfred, son of Athelwulf) – it is almost certainly due to Scandinavian reinforcement that the -*son* device prevailed.

Orkney

'Shifting' patronymics were evidently still in general use in Orkney until well into the 1500s, and examples dating from that and the preceding century – such as Hakon Biarnason, Anders Jonson, Niels Jeepsen, Jon Magnusson, Gudbrand Anderson, Hakon Thoresson, Gunnar Gellison and Patrick Tyrgilson – show that Scandinavian personal names continued in popularity among the Orcadians long after the islands had passed into Scottish hands. Only a few Orkney family names of patronymic type containing Scandinavian personal names have survived to the present day, although Swanson (N: Sveinn) is one of the most familiar surnames in the islands. In other cases, the original suffix -*son* has been completely eroded away, Þórfinnsson (recorded in 1601 as Torphison, the name of a man from Sanday) and Ámundarson surviving in Orkney as Turfus and Omond.

Shetland

Still further north, in Shetland, patronymics continued in use among the inhabitants of the more isolated islands until within living memory. The last Shetlander to be called after his father is said to have been James Manson, son of Magnus Robertson, who died on Foula during World War I. Shetland records indicate that, until as late as the seventeenth century, the islanders not only used patronymics with the -*son* suffix as a matter of course, but also kept alive many venerable Scandinavian names. Examples from this period are: Laurence Erickson, Thomas Harraldsoun, Mans Magnusson, Henry Ollasoun, Swannie Guthrumson (Sveinn Guðrumsson), Niels Monson and Manns Enorson (Magnus Einarsson), whilst women's names such as Marete Suensdoter, Agnes Mawnisdotter, Marion Colbeinsdotter, Marion Guthramdottir, and Swinna Petersdottir were familiar in the Shetlands until well into the eighteenth century. -*son* surnames are still very characteristic of Shetland, typical examples being Thomasson, Ollason, Laurenson, Shuardson (N: Sigurðsson), Erasmusson,

Manson and the bizarre Herculeson, said to be a corruption of Hákonsson.

Shetland, incidentally, is the only place in Britain where baptismal names of Norse derivation have persisted in use until our own time; the boys' names Olie, Hakki (a diminutive of Hákon), Tirval (N: Þórvaldr) and Shuard (N: Sigurðr, Norw: Sjurd, Faer: Sjurður) and the girls' names Inga, Hilda and Osla (Norw: Aslaug), have always been popular. In Orkney, on the other hand, it is the revival of interest in the islands' old Scandinavian connections that is responsible for the recent crop of Norse baptismal names like Sigurd, Olaf, Harald, Einar, Ivar and Ingrid.

Mainland Scotland

Scandinavian names were introduced to western Scotland both by the Norse colonists on the mainland and in the Hebrides and through the hybrid Irish/Norse Gall-Gael who settled parts of south-western Scotland from Ireland and the Isle of Man. Among the Gall-Gael, patronymic names were formed in Gaelic fashion, with the affix *Mac-* replacing the Norse suffix *-son*, e.g. Thorfynn Mac Thore for N: Þórfinnr Þórsson. Several patronymics of this type, containing Scandinavian personal names, have persisted as family names in Scotland. Such are MacAulay (N: Óli, a diminutive of Óláfr), MacLeod (N: *ljótr* = ugly), MacCrimmon (N: Hrómundr), MacSiridh (N: Sigríðr), MacIver (N: Ívarr), MacRanald (N: Rǫgnvaldr), Godfrey (N: Guðrǫðr), MacCodrum (N: Guðormr), MacCorquodale (N: Þórketill), MacQueen (Gael: MacSuain for N: Sveinsson), MacUsbaig (N: Óspakr), and MacSorley, derived through the corrupt medieval form 'Sorli Marlady' (thus written by uncomprehending scribes) from Gael: Somhairle (N: *sumarliði* = summer warrior, also the prototype of the Scottish surname Summerlad). Another Scots clan, the Lamonts (Lammonds or MacLamons) take their name from a Norse Lǫgmaðr or Lawman, whilst the Gunns take theirs from Gunni, an affectionate diminutive form of such Norse names as Gunnhildr, Gunnarr, etc. The name MacDougall (Gael: MacDubhgall – son of the black stranger) is based on the Gaelic nickname for a Dane, as is the Irish corruption, Doyle. MacLachlan, on the other hand, refers to the 'Lochlannach', or men from 'Lochlann', i.e. Norway. English, in identical fashion, has preserved surnames that began life as ethnic designations describing the two main species of Viking invader. Dennis (Denns, Dence, Dench, etc) goes back to Old English *denisc* = Danish, whilst Norman and Norris are corruptions of the Old English and Norman French names, respectively, for a Norwegian.

The Isle of Man

Many dozen Scandinavian names appear on the twelfth- and thirteenth-century Manx runestones, where they outnumber Gaelic names by two to one. Today, some 16 per cent of the local Manx surnames are of wholly or partly Norse derivation, and many of these are formed, as are their Scottish counterparts, in the Gaelic fashion, although here the prefix *Mac-* has been eroded to *C-*. Typical examples are: Cowley (N: Óli), Crennell (N: Rǫgnvaldr), Corkill (N: Þórketill), Casement (N: Ásmundr), Castell (N: Ásketill), Cotter (N: Ottarr) and Corlett (N: Þórljótr).

Ireland

Few, if any, family names of Norse inspiration appear to have survived in Ireland, although early documents show that such names as Swein, Torsten, Toki and Torfind were still popular in the old 'Ostman' towns until the end of the twelfth century, as were Aric (N: Eiríkr), Amlaibh (N: Óláfr), Caittil (N: Ketill), Erulb (N: Herjólfr), Iulb (N: Eyjólfr), Hingar (N: Ingvarr) and Tormod (N: Þórmoðr). Ecclesiastical registers from medieval Dublin show that names like Harrold, Olof, Iwyr and Siward were still in circulation until as late as the fourteenth and even the early fifteenth century.

Appendix 1

A selection of Scandinavian loanwords in modern literary English

(Dates in brackets refer to earliest attested occurrence in English literature)

AKIMBO   ME: *in kenebowe*, poss. rel. to Icel: *kengboginn* = crooked

ALOFT   ME < ON: *á* = on + *lopt* = air

ANGER   ME < ON: *angr* = grief, sorrow. Whence adj. *angry*

ASLANT   (1790) Cf Swe dial: *slant* = slippery

AUK   (1678) < ON: *alka*. Taken into standard English from Scots dialect

AWE   ME: *age* < ON: *agi*

AYE   (always, ever – now poetical) ME: *ei, ai* < ON: *ey*

BAFFLE   (1548) Scot: *bauchill* = to ridicule, from adj. *bauch* = ineffective, inferior. Prob. from ON: *bagr* = clumsy, in difficulties, uncomfortable

BAG   ME: *bagge* < ON: *baggi*

BAIT   ME: *baiten* = to make to bite < ON: *beita*

BALDERDASH   (1596) Poss. conn. with Dan: *balder* = clatter, noise + Dan: *daske* = to flap or slap

BAND   (a fastening ligature) ME < ON: *band*

BANG   (to beat violently) (1550) ON: *banga*

BANK   ME: *banke* = a mound of earth, prob. conn. with Dan: *bakke* = hill

BARK   (of a tree) ME < ON: *bǫrkr*

BASK   ME: *basken* < ON: *baðask* = to bath oneself

BASTE   ME: *bastin* < ON: *basta*

BAT   ME: *bakke* (E and Scots dial: *backie*), prob. conn. with Dan: *bakke*, more often *aftenbakke* = evening bat (now chiefly dial)

BAWL   (1556) Cf ON: *baula*, Swe: *böla* = to low

BIG   ME: *bigge*, prob. akin to Norw: *bugge* = an important man

BILLOW   (1552) < ON: *bylgja*

BLATHER   ME < ON: *blaðra* = to talk nonsense. The Scots form is *blether*.

BLEAK   (1538) < ON: *bleikr* = white, pale – a sense still preserved by some E dialects.

BLOAT   = to cure a herring by salting or smoking slightly, whence *bloater*. Sixteenth- and seventeenth century usage: *blote, bloate* = a herring, poss. from ON: *blautr fiskr* = soft fish

BLUNDER   ME: *blundren* < ON: *blunda* = to doze or slumber

BLUNT   ME poss. from same ON source as *blunder*

BLUR   (1620) Poss. conn. with Swe dial: *blura* = to partially close the eyes

BOLE   (stem of a tree) ME: *ból* < ON: *bolr*

BOND   ME: *bond*, a variant of *band* (see above)

BOON   = a favour, petition. ME: *bōne* < ON: *bón*

BOOTH   ME: *bōthe* < ON: *búð*

BORE   (a tidal wave) ME < ON: *bára*

BOTH   Early ME: *bathe* < ON: *báðir*

BOULDER   (1617) Prob. conn. with Swe: *bullersten* = a large rock in a stream

BOUND   = ready, going to (bound for). ME: *boun* < ON: *búinn* = ready

BOW   (of a ship) ME < ON: *bógr*, or Dan: *bov*

BRAD   ME < ON: *broddr* = any pointed piece of hard metal

BRAE   (chiefly Scotland dial) = slope. ME: *brā* = eyebrow < ON: *brá* = eyelid

BRINDLED   1678, previously 'brinded', 'brended', etc. Poss. of Scand derivation

BRINK   ME < ON: *brekka* = slope. Cf Dan: *brink* = edge, brink

BULK   1440 = cargo. Present sense since 1725 < ON: *bulki* = cargo, heap.

BUNCH   ME: *bunche* < ON: *bunki* = heap, pile, cargo

BUNGLE   (1656) Conn. with OSwe: *bunga* = to strike or *bangla* = to work inefficiently

BUNK   See under *bunch*. Used in sense of 'a sleeping place' (i.e. a heap of bedclothes) since 1815

BURR   ME. Cf OSwe: *burr* = burdock, thistle

BUSTLE   (1560) Earlier: *buskle*, from ME: *busken* = to prepare oneself < ON: *búask*

BUTT   (vb) ME: *butten*. Cf Swe dial: *butta, botta*

BY-LAW   ME < ON: *býjarlǫg – býr* = town + *lǫg* = law

CAKE   ME < ON: *kaka*

CALF   (of leg) ME < ON: *kálfi*

CAST   ME: *casten* < ON: *kasta*

CLEFT   ME: *clift, clyft*. May be conn. with ON: *Kluft*. OE: *clyft unattested

CLIP   ME: *clippen* < ON: *klippa*

CLOWN   (1563) Prob. from Icel *klunni* = a clumsy boor

CLUB   ME: *clubbe, clobbe* < ON: *klubba*

CLUMSY   (1597) ME: *clumsen*, E dial: *to clumse* = to be numb with cold. Clearly conn. with Swe dial: *klumsig* = numb with cold, hence: clumsy

COCK   (haycock) ME < ON: *kǫkkr* = lump

COG   (on wheel) ME: *kogge*, app. rel. to Swe: *kugge*, Norw: *kug, kugger*

COSY   (1709) Poss. conn. with Norw: *koselig* = snug

COW   (vb) (1605) ON: *kúga* = to oppress

COWER   ME: *couren*. Cf Norw: *kura*

CRAB APPLE   ME: *crabbe appule*. Cf Swe: *krabbäpple*

CRAWL   ME: *craulen* < ON: *krafla* = to scrabble with the hands. Cf Dan: *kravle* = to crawl

CRAZE   (to break into small, irregular pieces) ME: *crasen*. Cf Swe: *krasa* = to break. Whence adj: *crazy*, which, in its modern sense of 'deranged', 'unsound in mind', dates only from 1859

CROOK   (hook) ME: *crok* < ON: *krókr*

CUB   (1530) Cf Norw: *kub, kubbe* = a block or stump

CUT   ME: *cuttin*, poss. con. with Swe dial: *kåta, kutå* = to cut

DAIRY   ME: *deierie*, from *deie* = dairymaid, female servant < ON: *deigja*

DANGLE   (1590) Of Scand orig. Cf Dan: *dingle*

DANK   ME: *dank*. Cf Swe: *dank* = a marshy place, its meaning in earlier English

DAPPLE   ME: *dappel* < ON: *depill* = a spot, a dog with spots above the eyes

DASH   ME: to knock, drive, thrust, throw. Cf Swe: *daska* = to drub, Dan: *daske* = to strike, beat

DAWN (1499) Earlier *dawning*. Cf Swe and Norw dial: *dagning*, from ON: *daga* = to become day

DAZE ME: *dasen*. Cf ON: *dasask* = to grow weary and exhausted, Swe: *dasa* = to lie idle

DIE ME: *deghen* < ON: *deyja*

DIRT ME: *drit* < ON: *drit* = excrement

DOWN (feathers) ME: *doun* < ON: *dúnn*

DOZE (1647) Prob. from ON: *dusa* = doze. Cf Dan: *døse* = to make dull or drowsy

DRAG ME: *draggin* < ON: *draga*. Cf Swe: *dragga*

DREGS ME: *dreg* < ON: *dregg*

DROOP ME: *droupen* < ON: *drúpa*

DROWN ME: *drounen* < ON: *drukna*

DUDS (clothes) ME: *dudde*, prob. akin to ON: *duða* = to swathe

DUMP (to let fall heavily) ME: *dumpen*, poss. conn. with Norw and Dan: *dumpe* = to let fall heavily. Cf ON: *dumpa* = to thump

EGG (n) ME: *egge* < ON: *egg*

EGG (vb) ME: *eggen* < ON: *eggja*

ELK (1486) < Norw *elg* < ON: *elgr*

FAST (abstinence) ME: *faste* < ON: *fasta*

FAST (a mooring rope) ME: *fest* < ON: *festr* = rope

FELLOW ME: *felaghe* < ON: *félagi*

FIDGET ME: *fiken* < ON: *fíkjask* = to be eager. The modern form, 'fidget', dates, in its verbal sense, only from 1754.

FILLY ME: < ON: *fylja* (a derivative of *fóli* = a foal)

FIR ME: *firre* < ON: *fyri*

FIRTH Scots < ON: *fjǫrðr*

FIT (vb) ME: *fitten* < ON: *fitja* = to knit together

FIZZ Prob. Scand Cf ON: *físa* = to break wind, OSwe: *fisa* = to fizzle

FLAG (plant) ME: *flagge* Cf Dan: *flæg*

FLAG (stone) (1604 – the compound *flagstone* dates from 1730) < ON: *flaggi* = a flat stone

FLAKE ME. Prob. rel. to Norw: *flak* = a piece of flat ice

FLAT ME: *flat* < ON: *flatr*

FLAUNT (1560) Akin to Norw: *flanta* = to gad about

FLAW (a sudden gust of wind) (1513). Cf Norw: *flaga*

FLAW (crack, fault) ME: *flawe* = flake, breach, crack < ON: *flaga* = a flat stone

FLECK   ME: *flek* < ON: *flekkr* = spot

FLEER   (archaic or dial) ME = to sneer or jeer. Cf Swe dial: *flira* = to grin

FLEET   (swift) (1592) Akin to ON: *fljótr* = swift

FLING   ME: *flengen* < ON: *flengja* = to hurl

FLIT   ME: *flitten, flütten* < ON: *flytja*

FLOUNDER   (1450) Cf OSwe: *flundra*

FLUSTER   ME. Cf Icel: *flaustra* = to hurry, bustle

FOG   (long grass left standing in winter) (1450) Cf Norw: *fogg*

FOG   = mist (1544). Cf Dan: *fog*, ON: *fok* = spray, driving snow, Norw: *fuka* = sea fog

FRECKLE   ME: *freken* < ON: *freknur* = freckles

FRO   ME: *fro* < ON: *frá*

FROTH   ME: *frothe* < ON: *froða, frauð*

FULMAR   (1698 – a Hebridean word) < ON: *fúll + már* = 'foul gull', so named because it feeds on floating offal

GABLE   ME < ON: *gafl*

GAD   (fly) From obs. *gad* = spike < ON: *gaddr*

GAINLY   = graceful (mod. sense since 1855). ME: *gayn* = gracious < ON: *gegn* = straight, decent. Nowadays usually found in negative form: 'ungainly'

GAIT   (way of going) ME: *gate* = road < ON: *gata*

GALE   (1547) Cf. Norw: *galen* = bad (of weather)

GANG   (lit. 'going together', modern sense of 'a company of people' from 1632) ME: *gang* = a going < ON: *gang* = a lane or street

GAPE   ME: *gapen* < ON: *gapa*

GARISH   Sixteenth century *gaurish*, from obs. vb *gaure* = to stare, the same as *gaw*, which see under *gawk*

GASP   ME: *gaispen* < ON: *geispa* = to yawn

GAUNT   (1736) Formerly *gant*, prob. Scand Cf Shet: *gant* = a tall, thin person

GAWK   (an awkward person) (1837) Derived from obs. vb: *to gaw* = gape, stare < ON: *gá* = to heed

GAZE   ME: *gasen*. Cf Swe and Norw dials: *gasa* = to stare

GEAR   (clothes) ME: *gere* < ON: *gervi*

GELD   (to castrate) ME: *gelden* < ON: *gelda*

GELDING   ME < ON: *geldingr*

GET   ME: *geten* < ON: *geta*

GIFT   ME < ON: *gipt*

GIG   A whirligig (its orig. E sense), whence, by association, a light carriage. Cf Dan: *gig* = a whirligig

GILL   ME: *gile* < ON: *gjǫlnar* = jaws

GIRTH   ME < ON: *gjǫrð, girði*

GLINT   ME: *glenten* = to gleam, also: to turn aside. Cf Swe dial: *glinta, glänta* = to slide, ON: *glan* = brilliance

GLITTER   ME: *gliteren* < ON: *glitra*

GLOAT   (1575) Poss. from ON: *glotta* = to smile derisively

GLOSS   (1538) Prob. conn. with Icel: *glossi* = a blaze

GNASH   (1496) Northern ME: *gnast* < ON: *gnista* = to gnash, *gnastan* = a gnashing

GRISKIN   (1700) = the lean part of the loin of a bacon pig. Obs. E dial: *grice* = pig < ON: *gríss* = young pig

GROVEL   ME: *o grufe* = grovelling, on the face < ON: *á grúfu* = grovelling, *grúfa* = to grovel

GUESS   ME: *gessen*. Poss. Scand Cf OSwe: *gissa*

GUN   ME: *gonne, gunne*. In 1330 the Swedish woman's name Gunhild was applied to a particularly fine mangonel, or stone-throwing engine (*Una magna balista de cornu quae vocatur Domina Gunilda*) – much as guns were later christened Big Bertha, etc.

GUST   (1588) app from ON: *gustr*, a derivative of *gjusa* = to gush

HAGGLE   (1583) Scots: *hag, haggle* = to chop, from ON: *hǫggva* = to hew

HAIL   (vb) (greet) ME: *hailin* < ON: *heilla*, from adj. *heill* = sound, healthy, whence E *hale*

HAKE   (fish) E dial: *hake*. Cf Norw dial: *hakefisk* = hake

HANDSEL   ME: *handsale* < ON: *handsal* = giving of the hand, especially in a promise

HANK   (vb) = to coil a rope (now chiefly dial.) ME: *hanken* < ON: *hanka*

HAP   = luck, chance, lot. ME: *happe* < ON: *happ* = good luck

HAPPEN   ME: *happen*, from *happe* = chance, luck. Cf Swe dial: *happa*

HAPPY   ME: *happi*, see under HAP

HARBOUR   ME: *herberge* < ON: *herbergi*

HARSH   ME: *harsk*. Cf OSwe: *harsk*

HAWSE   (1497) Earlier *halse, haulse* < ON: *hals* = neck – hence: part of a ship's bows

HIT   ME: *hitten* < ON: *hitta* = to meet with, find, hit upon

HOOT ME: *huten, hoten*. Cf Swe and Norw: *huta*

HUG (1567) Cf ON: *hugga* = to comfort or sooth, as a mother hugging her child

HUSBAND Late OE: *hūsbōnda* < ON: *húsbóndi* = householder

ILL ME: *ille* < ON: *illr*

JADE ME: *jade, iade* = a worn out horse. Scots dial: *yade, yawd*, prob. from ON: *jalda* = a mare

JOLLY ME: *joli, jolif*, from OFr: *joli, jolif*, prob. from ON: *jól* = yule

JOLLY(BOAT) (1727) Cf Dan: *jolle* = a yawl or dinghy

KEG Late ME: *kag* < ON: *kaggi* = a cask

KEMP = coarse hair in wool. ME < ON: *kampr* = whisker, beard

KEN (as in 'beyond one's ken') Obs. E *to ken* = to know or discern < ON: *kenna*

KID ME: *kid* < ON: *kið*

KIER (vat in which cloth is boiled for bleaching, etc) (1573) < ON: *ker* = vat, vessel

KILT ME. Cf Dan: *at kilte op* = to tuck up, Swe: *kilta* = lap

KINDLE ME: *kindlen* < ON: *kyndil* = torch, *kynda* = to set on fire

KINK Ultimately from ON: *kengr* = a bend. Cf also Icel: *kikna* = to bend at the knees

KNIFE ME: *knif* < ON: *knífr*

LAG (non-conducting cover of a boiler) (1672) Swe: *lagg* = rim of a barrel

LAW Late OE: *lagu*, ME: *lawe* < ON: *lǫg* (earlier *lagu*)

LEAK (noun from 1487, vb from 1440) < ON: *leki* (n), *leka* (vb)

LEG ME: *legge* < ON: *leggr*

LILT ME: *lülten*. Cf Norw: *lilla, lirla* = to sing high

LING (types of heather) ME: *lyng* < ON: *lyng*

LINK (n) ME: *linke*, poss. from ON: *hlenkr* (unattested, but Icel: *hlekkur*)

LOFT Late OE from ON: *lopt* = air, heaven, hence *loft*

LOOM (vb) (1591), poss. conn. with ON: *ljóma* = to gleam

LOON (1450), also *loom* (1649) = the Great Northern Diver. ON: *lómr*

LOOSE ME: *lous, loos, laus* < ON: *lauss*

LOW ME: *lah, louh, low* < ON: *lágr*

LUG ME: *luggen*. Cf Swe and Norw: *lugga* = to pull by the hair

LURK Northern ME: *lurken*. Cf Norw: *lurka* = to sneak forth

MARRAM (grass) (1640) ON: *marálm*; *marr* = sea + *halmr* = grass, haulm

MARROW (mate) (now chiefly dial), prob. from ON: *margr* = friendly

MAWKISH (1668) Scots and northern E dial: *mawk* = maggot < ON: *maðkr*

MEEK Late OE: *mēoc*, ME: *mēc* < ON: *mjúkr* = mild, soft, gentle

MIDDEN ME: *midding*. Cf Dan: *mødding*, earlier *møgdynge*, in which *møg* = dung, *dynge* = heap

MIRE ME: *mire* < ON: *mýrr* = swamp

MISTAKE (vb) ME: *mistaken* < ON: *mistaka*

MOULDER (1531) Cf Norw dial: *muldra* = to crumble

MUCK ME: *muk* < ON: *myki* = dung

MUGGY (1731) E dial: *mug* = drizzle, ME: *muggen* = to drizzle < ON: *mugga* = fine rain

NAB (Seventeenth century) E dial: *nap* = to catch or seize. App. of Scand derivation. Cf Swe: *nappa* = to catch or seize. (Also second element in *kidnap*.)

NAG (vb) (1828) Prob. orig. Scots dial. Cf Swe and Norw: *nagga* = to gnaw or irritate

NARWHALE (1658) Dan: *narhval* < ON: *náhvalr*, in which *nár* = corpse (an allusion to its deathly white colour) and *hvalr* = whale

NASTY Late ME: *nasky*, prob. Scand. Cf Swe dial: *nasket, naskug* = dirty

NAY ME: *nei* < ON: *nei*

NICK (n) (1483) a small notch. Cf OSwe: *nock*

NIGGLE (1599) Orig.: 'to cheat pettily' – now – 'to be over elaborate on petty details'. App. Scand. Cf Norw dial: *nigla*

NUDGE (1675) Cf Norw dial: *nuggja* = to push gently

OAF (1625) Earlier *awf* < ON: *álfr* = elf

ODD ME: *odde* < ON: *oddi* = point or tip, hence the 'odd' or third angle of a triangle. From *oddr* = the point of a weapon

OUTLAW Late OE: *utlaga* < ON: *útlagi* = one who is outside the law

PADDOCK (a toad – archaic and dial). ME: *padde* < ON: *padda*

PIXY (1630) Earlier and dial form 'Pisky'. Cf Swe dial: *pyske* = goblin

PROD (1535) ME and E dial: *brod* = a goad < ON: *broddr*

PURL (1586) = to ripple, eddy. Cf Swe: *porla*, Norw: *purla* = to ripple, murmur

QUEASY (1545) Cf Norw: *kveis* = a hangover

QUIRK (1547) Poss. rel. to Norw. dial: *kvark* = throat

RACK (a mass of wind-driven clouds) ME: *rak* < ON: *reka* = to drive or thrust

RAFTER Late OE: *ræfter* < ON: *raptr*

RAG ME: *ragge* < ON: *rǫgg* = shagginess, a tuft

RAISE ME: *reisen* < ON: *reisa*

RAKE (vb) ME. Cf Icel: *raka* = to rake, Swe: *raka* = to scrape

RANSACK ME: *ransaken* < ON: *ransaka* = to search (*saka*) a house (*rann*) for stolen goods

REEF (chain of rocks) ME: *riff* < ON: *rif*

RID (vb) ME: *rüden* < ON: *ryðja* = to clear land

RIFT ME: *rift*. Cf Dan: *rift* = cleft, ON: *ript* = breach

RIP (1477) Poss. Scand. Cf Swe: *reppa*, Dan: *rippe*, *reppe*. May equally well be Dutch or Low German

RIVE (rend, tear) ME: *riven* < ON: *rífa*

ROE (fish eggs) Late ME: *rowne* (E dial *roan*) < ON: *hrogn*

ROOT ME: *rote* < ON: *rót*

ROTTEN ME: *rotin* < ON: *rotinn*

ROUT (roaring, shouting) Scots and northern E dial: *rowt* = to roar or shout < ON: *rauta*

ROW (small metal plate or ring for a rivet to pass through) (1440) < ON: *ró*

RUB ME: *rubben*, poss. LGmn but equally likely conn. with Norw: *rubba*, Dan: *rubbe*

RUCK (to crease) (1812). Cf ON: *hrukka* (vb)

RUCK (a crease) (1787). Cf ON: *hrukka* (n)

RUG (1551) Cf Norw: *rugga* = a coarse rug, Swe: *rugg* = ruffled hair

RUGGED ME: *rugged*, *ruggi*. Cf Swe: *ruggig* = hairy, *rugga* = to roughen, Swe. dial: *rugget* = shaggy

RUMP ME. Cf MDan: *rumpe*, MSwe, Norw: *rump*

SAG Late ME: *saggen*, poss. conn. with Norw. dial: *sakke* = to subside

SAITHE (1632) From Scots < ON: *seiðr* = the coal-fish

SALE ME: *sale* < ON: *sala*

SCAB ME: *scabbe*. Cf. Swe: *skabb*

SCALL (rough, scaly eruption on the skin – now obsolescent) ME, prob. from ON: *skalli* = a bald head

SCALP Northern ME: *scalp* < ON: *skalpr* = sheath

SCANT Late ME: *scant* < ON: *skamt* (adj *skamm* = short, with neuter suffix -*t*), hence also E: *to scamp* (on one's work)

SCARE ME: *skerren* < ON: *skirra* (from adj *skjarr* = shy, timorous)

SCATHE (vb) Me: *scathen* < ON: *skaða*

SCATHE (n) ME: *scathe* < ON: *skað*

SCHOONER (1716) From Scots and northern E dial vb: *to scoon* = to skim along the water, a variant of *to scun* = to fly, hurry < ON: *skunda*

SCOFF ME: *scof* < ON: *skop, skaup* = a scoff or jibe

SCOLD (n) ME: *scald, scolde* = a person given to ribaldry and then to fault-finding < ON: *skáld* = poet. The verb first appeared in the late ME period.

SCORCH ME: *scorken* < ON: *skorpna* = to dry up, E: *scorch* prob. influenced by MFr: *escorchier* = to dry up

SCORE (vb) ME: *scoren* < ON: *skora* = to make an incision, to count by tallies

SCOUT (to reject contemptuously, to scoff at) (1605). Cf ON: *skúta* = to gibe, *skúti* = a scolding

SCOWL ME: *scoulen*, app. of Scand orig. Cf Dan: *skule*

SCRAP ME: *scrapp* < ON: *skrap*, properly 'something scraped off' – ON: *skrapa* = to scrape

SCRAPE ME: *schrapen* < ON: *skrapa*

SCRAWNY, SCRANNY From northern E dial: *scranny*, poss. Scand. Cf Norw dial: *skran* = thin, desiccated, Swe dial: *skran* = weak

SCREAK ME: *scriken* < ON: *skrækja*

SCREAM ME: *scremen* < ON: *skræma* = to terrify

SCREE (1781) ON: *skríða* = a landslide, from vb *skríða* = to slip or slide

SCREECH ME: *skrichen* < ON: *skrækja*

SCRUB Analogues in Scand. Cf Dan: *skrubbe*, Swe: *skrubba*, although poss. from MDut: *schrobben, schrubben*

SCRUFF (1790), SCUFF (1787) = back of the neck, rel. to ON: *skopt* = hair

SCUFFLE (1579) possibly Scand. Cf Swe: *skuffa* = to push

SCULL (a type of oar, whence the verb to scull), via Scots *scull* = a shallow wicker basket, from ON: *skjóla* = a basket

SCURF Late ME: *scurf* < ON: *skurfur* (pl.). Cf OSwe: *skorver*

SEEMLY ME: *sēmelīch* < ON: *sæmiligr*

SHEER ME: *schēre*, prob. from ON: *skærr*

SHRIKE (a type of bird of prey) (1544). Cf Icel: *skríkja*, Norw: *skrike*, Swe: *skrika* = jay

SHRILL, SKIRL (vb) Cognate with Norw: *skrylla*, Swe: *skrälla*

SHRUG Late ME: *schruggen*. Cf Dan: *skrugge* = to stoop or crouch, Swe dial: *skrugga* = to walk with a stoop

SILT ME: *sylt*, app. Scand. Cf Norw. dial: *sylt* = a salt water swamp

SIMPER (1563), app. of Scand inspiration. Cf Dan dial: *simper*, *semper* = coy, affected

SKATE (fish) (1656) < ON: *skata*

SKEP (coarse round basket of wicker or wood) ME: *skeppe* < ON: *skeppa*

SKI (1885) Norw: *ski* < ON: *skíð* = a billet of wood. (The identical OE: *scíd* yields modern E: *shide* = a thin board.)

SKID (a plank set under a structure or on a rollway) (1609) ON: *skíð* = a billet of wood. Whence the vb to *skid* (1674)

SKILL (expertise) ME: *schile* < ON: *skil* = discernment, rel. to vb *skilja* = to divide, part or separate

SKIMP (1775) A variant of vb *to scamp* (see under *scant*)

SKIN ME: *skin* < ON: *skinn*

SKIP ME: *skippen* < ON: *skopa* = to leap, run. Cf OSwe: *skoppa*, *skuppa*

SKIRL (1665) See under *shrill*

SKIRT ME: *skyrt* < ON: *skyrta* = shirt, kirtle. Cf Swe: *skört* = skirt, Dan: *skjort* = shirt

SKIT (vb = to leap aside, jump about – 1611), prob. conn. with ON: *skytta*, *skyti* = a marksman. The sense 'to ridicule or caricature' dates from 1781. From the vb come *skit* = a flirtatious girl (or an easily frightened horse), to *skite* = to dash about or act objectionably, and *skittles*.

SKIVE (to split or pair leather) (1825) < ON: *skífa*

SKUA (1678) < ON: *skúfr*

SKULK ME: *skulken*, app. Scand. Cf Norw: *skulka* = to lurk, Swe: *skolka*, Dan: *skulke* = to play truant

SKULL ME: *skulle*. Cf Norw: *skulle*, Swe: *skalla*

SKY ME: *skie* = cloud < ON: *ský*

SLAB   (mire) – now chiefly dial (1611). Cf obs. Dan: *slab*, Swe dial: *slabb*

SLAM   (1691) Cf Norw: *slemma, slemba, slam* = a sharp slap or blow

SLANG   (1756) From E dial *to sling* = to abuse or cheek. Cf Norw: *å slengja kjeften* = to use slang (lit: 'to sling the jaw')

SLANT   ME: *slenten* = to slope. Cf Norw dial: *slenta* = to slope, Swe: *slinta* = to slide

SLAT   (to hurl, toss, pitch – now chiefly dial.) ME < ON: *sletta* = to throw

SLAUGHTER   ME: *slaghter, slauhter* < ON: *slátr* = butcher's meat

SLAVER   ME: *slaveren* < ON: *slafra*. Cf Swe: *slabbra*

SLEEK   See *slick*

SLEIGHT   ME: *sleght* < ON: *slægð* = cunning, skill, slyness

SLICK   ME: *slike* < ON: *slíkr* = smooth

SLOUCH   (n from 1515, vb from 1754), formerly also *slouk*. Prob. conn. with Norw dial: *slauk* = an indolent person, Swe dial: *slugga, slogga* = to be slow and languid

SLUG   ME: *slugge* = a sluggard, poss. Scand. Cf Norw dial: *sluggje* = a slow, cumbersome person

SLUSH   (Seventeenth century) Also *sludge, slutch*, prob. Scand. Cf Swe: *slask* = wetness, liquid filth, *slaska* = to wallow or paddle

SLY   ME: *slegh, sleih, sli* < ON: *slægr*

SMATTERING   (1538) ME: *smateren* = to speak in a superficial manner. Cf Swe: *smattra* = to chatter

SNAG   (1577) < ON: *snagi*, Norw: *snag* = a sharp point

SNEER   ME: *sneren*, Cf Dan: *snærre* = to grin (like a snarling dog)

SNIPE   ME: *snype* < ON: *snípa*

SNUB   (vb) ME: *snubben* < ON: *snubba* = to chide or reprove

SNUG   (1595) Poss. reached us via Dut: *snugger* = clever, smart. Cf obs. Dan: *snyg* = tidy

SPAN-NEW   ME: *spōn-neōwe* < ON: *span-nýr*, lit. 'chip new', as fresh and clean as a chip newly chopped off

SPIKE   ME < ON: *spíkr*

SPRAY   (A young or small shoot) ME. Cf Dan: *sprag*

SPUD   ME: *spudde* = a digging knife < ON: *spjót* = a spear. The modern sense of 'potato' dates from *c* 1860 – prior to that time *spud* was also applied to anything, or anybody, short and stumpy.

SQUAB   (Small fish or young pigeon) (1640) Cf Swe dial: *skvabb, kvabb* = anything soft, thick and quivery; *skvabba, kvabba* = a fat woman

SQUABBLE   (1602) Cf Swe dial: *skvabbla* = to quarrel
SQUALL   (1719) Cf Swe dial: *skval* = a violent gushing of water
SQUEAK   Late ME. Cf Swe: *skväka* = to croak
SQUIB   (A fire cracker) (1525). ME: *squibben, squippen* = to move
   swiftly < ON: *svífa* = to dart
STACK   ME: *stacke* < ON: *stakkr*
STAG   ME: Cf ON: *steggi* = any male bird, Icel: *steggi* = tomcat
STAGGER   ME: *stakeren* < ON: *stakra*
STEAK   Late ME < ON: *steik* = a slice of roast meat on a spit
STERN   (of a vessel) ME: *steorne* < ON: *stjórn*
STILT   ME: *stilte*. Cf Dan: *stylte*
STITHY   (anvil) ME: *stithe* < ON: *steði*
STOUP   (drinking vessel), late ME < ON: *staup*
STUMP   ME: *stumpe, stompe* < ON: *stumpr*
STUNTED   OE: *stunt* = dull, stupid. Modern sense influenced by ON:
   stuttr = short
SWAGGER   Cf Norw: *svagga* = to walk unsteadily
SWAY   ME: *sweiyen* < ON: *sveigja*
SWIRL   Cf Norw: *svirla*, Dan: *svirre* = to whirl
SWIVEL   Late ME < ON: *sveifla* = to turn
TAG   (n) Late ME. Cf Swe: *tagg* = a point, Norw: *tag* = a jagged
   point
TAKE   ME: *taken* < ON: *taka*
TANG   ME: *tang*. Orig. E sense = a tongue, then a fang, later = the
   'tang' (point) of a knife. Mod. sense of a 'sharp, lingering taste on
   the tongue' is from 1440 < ON: *tangi* = a pointed projection
TANG   (1547) seaweed. < Norw: *tang*, Dan: *tang*
TANGLE   (1536) seaweed < Norw: *tångel, tongul*. ON: *þǫngull*
TANGLE   (vb) Obs. E: *tagle*, poss. Scand. Cf Swe dial: *taggla*
TAT   (to make a knotted lace) Cf Icel: *tæta* = to tease wool
TATTER   Late ME: *tater*, of Scand orig. Cf Icel: *tötrar* = tatters
TEEM   To pour, lit. 'to empty', ME: *temen*, ON: *tœma*, from adj:
   iómr = empty
TERN   (1678) ON: *þerna*
THEIR   ME: *thair* < ON: *þeira*
THEM   ME < ON: *þeim*
THEY   ME: *thei* < ON: *þeir*
THOUGH   ME: *thoh* < ON: *þó*
THRALL   ME: *thral* < ON: *þræll*

THRIFT ME < ON: *þrift* = the result of grasping for oneself, hence, by extension, a thriving condition, hence good management, hence frugality

THRIVE ME: *thriven* < ON: *þrífast* = to grasp for oneself. Cf Dan: *trives* = to thrive

THROE ME: *thrawe* < OE: *þrauu*, poss. influenced by ON: *þrá* = an extreme pang of pain

THRUST ME: *thristen* < ON: *þrýsta*

THURSDAY ME: *thoresdai* < ON: *þórsdagr*. Replaced earlier E: *Thundersday*

THWART ME: *thwert* < ON: *þvert*, neuter of *þverr* = transverse

TIGHT ME: *thyht, tigt* < ON: *þéttr*

TIKE ME: *tyke* = mongrel < ON: *tík* = bitch

TILL (= to) ME: *til* < ON: *til*

TIPPLE (1560), poss. direct from Norw: *tipla* = to tipple

TIT (bird of the genus *Parus*) (1706), prob. Scand. Cf Icel: *tittur* = titmouse, Norw dial: *tita* = small object

TOSS (1506) Cf Norw dial: *tossa* = to scatter

TRASH (1518) Cf ON: *tras* = fallen twigs, rubbish, Norw dial: *tras* = twigs, *trask* = rubbish

TUSSOCK (1550) Derivative of a Scand word attested by Dan: *tusse*, Swe: *tuss* = a wad, ball of wool, and Swe dial: *tuss* = a handful of hay

TWIDDLE (1540) Echoic and poss. Scand in origin

UGLY ME: *uglike*, from vb *uggen* = to feel disgust (E dial: *to ug*) < ON: *ugga* = to fear, *uggligr* = dreadful

VOLE (1805) Short for *volemouse*. Cf Norw: *vollmus* = field mouse

WAIVE ME: *weyve* < OFr: *gaiver, guever* < prob. from ON: *veifa* = to vibrate

WALL-EYED ME: *wawil-eyid* < ON: *vagleygr, vagl* = beam + *eygr* = eyed

WAMBLES (nausea), ME: *wamblen* = to feel nausea, evidently Scand. Cf ON: *váma* = nausea

WAND ME: *wand* < ON: *wondr* = a slender, supple stick cut from a tree

WANT ME: *wanten* < ON: *vanta* = to lack

WEAK ME: *wayke* < ON: *veikr*

WHIM (1821) Seems to be Scand, poss. ultimately traceable back to ON: *hvíma* = to let one's eyes wander

WHIN   Late ME, rel. to ON: *hvein* = a marshy field

WHIRL   Late ME < ON: *hvirfla*

WHITLOW   Late ME and E dial: *whickflaw, quickflaw*, lit. a flaw (qv) or inflammation of the 'quick' (ON: *kvikr*) of the finger

WHORE   ME: *hore* < ON: *hóra*

WHOREDOM   ME: *hordom* < ON: *hórdomr*

WICKER   ME: *wyker, wekir* = osier. Cf Swe: *vicker* = willow

WINDLASS   ME: *wyndas* < ON: *vindáss*, lit. 'winding pole', ME is from Icel: *vindiláss*

WINDOW   ME: *windoge* < ON: *vindaugr*, lit. an 'eye' of the wind

WING   ME: *wenge* < ON: *vængr*

Appendix 2

A selection of British surnames of probable or partial Scandinavian origin

AGG, AGGS < ODan: Aggi, mod. Dan: Agge, short form for names with Ag- as their first element, e.g. ON: Qgmundr, Qgvaldr, etc.

ALGAR, ALGER, ALGORE, AUGAR, ALJER, AUGER, AUGUR, AGAR, ELGAR, ELGER, etc. Some may be from OE: Ælfgar or Ealhhere, although, as most of these names come from countries where Scandinavian influence was strong, their common source is more likely to be ON: Álfgeirr

ALLEY, ALLY < ODan: Alli, OSwe: Alle

ALLGOOD, AUGOOD < ODan and OSwe: Algot, Algut

ALLGRIM < ON: Álfgrímr

AMMON, AMMONDS, AMON, AMOND < ON: Qgmundr, OSwe: Aghmund

ANGER, ANGEAR, ANGIER, AUNGER, AINGER < probably a Norman version of ON: Ásgeirr

ANKETELL, ANKETTLE, ANQUETIL, ANKILL, ANTELL, ANTILL < Norman form of ON: Ásketill

ANNAND < ODan and OSwe: Anund

ANTIN, ANKIN, ANNAKIN, ANNIKIN < Norman version of ON: Áskell

ARBORN, ARBON, ARBOURNE < ON: Arnbjǫrn

ARKELL, ARKILL, ARKLE, ARCKOLL, ARKCOLL < ON: Arnkell

ARTHUR, ARTHURS, ARTHARS, ARTER Although most of these reflect the Keltic name Arthur, some may be corruptions of ON: Arnþórr, ODan: Azur

ASHBURNER Some north-country forerunners of this name appeared in Scandinavian form, e.g. Askebrenner, Askbrinner, containing ON: askr = ash + a derivative of ON: brenna = to burn. South-country forms contain the native: æsc + a derivative of beornan = to burn

13

ASHKETTLE < ON: Ásketill

ASKELL, ASTELL, ASTIL, ASTILL, ESKELL, HASKEL, HASKELL < ON: Áskell

ASKIN, ASKINS, ASTIN, ASTINS, ASHKEN, HASKIN, HASKINS, HASKINGS, HASTIN, HASTINGS < Norman form of ON: Ásketill

AUTIE, AUTY, AWTY, ALTY < ODan: Auti, perhaps a version of the German name Otto

AXTELL < ON: Ásketill

AYLIFF, AYLIFFE, ELLIF < either ON: Eilífr or Eíleifr

AYLOFF < ODan: Elaf

BAIN, BAINE, BAINES, BAINS, BAYNES, BAYNS < ME: *beyn, bayn* < ON *beinn* = straight, direct, hospitable

BARNE, BARNES While many Barnes are of native English origin (OE: *beorn* = warrior) those from the old Danelaw areas may be based on ON: Bjǫrn (lit. 'bear') or ON: *barn* = child

BARNFATHER, BANFATHER < ON: Barnfaðir = a child's alleged father

BASK < ME: *beisk* < ON: *beiskr* = bitter, acrid

BLAMIRE, BLAMIRES, BLAMORE, BLAYMIRE < ON: *blár mýrr* = dark swamp; thus 'dweller by the dark swamp' – as at Blamires in the West Riding

BLAND < ON: Blanda

BOATSWAIN, BOESON < Late OE: *bātswegen* < ON: *bátsveinn* = boat man

BODFISH First element ME: *butte*, conn. with Swe: *butta* = turbot

BOLT, BOLTE, BOULT Poss. conn. with ON nickname Boltr, which might have been applied to a short, thickset person

BOND, BONDS, BONDY, BOUND, BOUNDS, BOUNDY, BUNDAY, BUNDEY, BUNDY < ON: *bóndi* = peasant, husbandman, later serf, unfree tenant

BOOTH, BOOTHE < ODan: *bōth* = cowhouse, herdsman's hut. An occupational name for a cowman or herdsman. Also occurs as BOOTHMAN

BOTTLE, BOTTELL < ON: Bóthildr

BRAND, BRANT, BRAUND, BRAUN, BRAUNS, BRONT < ON: Brandr

BRENNER A possible derivative of ON: *brenna* = to burn. The meaning may be 'burner of lime' charcoal or bricks'

BRIGG, BRIGGS Dweller by the bridge (ON: *bryggja*)

BROCKLESS, BROCKLISS < ON: Broklauss = breechless, without breeches. A nickname also found at Brocklesby in Lincs

BROTHERS < ON: Bróðir

BYRNE, BYRNES, BIRN An Irish name, sometimes reflecting native Gaelic: Ó Broinn = descendant of Bran (raven), sometimes Norse: Bjǫrn (lit. 'bear')

CARL, CARLE < Either ON: *karli* or ME: *carl* = countryman, husbandman, free peasant; later: villain, bondman, churl, ill-mannered fellow < ON: *karl* = man

CARMAN < ON: Karlmaðr = male, man

CARR, KERR, KER, etc < ME: *kerr* = brushwood, wet ground < ON: *kjarr*

CASEMENT (Manx) Mac + ON: Ásmundr

CASTELL, CAISTELL (Manx) Mac + ON: Áskell

CATES, KATES < ON: Kati = the merry one (nickname)

CLACK < ODan: Klak

COE, COO < ME: *co, coo*, Midland form corr. to northern: *ka* = jackdaw < ON: *Ká*

COLBAN < ON: Kolbeinn

COLBRAN, COLBRON, COLBRUN, COALBRAN < ON: Kolbrandr

COLE, COLES, COALES Often from ON: Koli, short form for names with Kol- as their first element, such as: Kolbeinn, Kolgrímr, Kolbrandr, etc

COLEMAN, COLMAN, COLLMAN, COULMAN < ON: Kalman, introduced to north-west England by Norwegians from Ireland, who adopted it from the Gaelic Colmán, earlier Columbán

COLESON, COLSON, COULSON, COULSEN < ON: Koli, ODan: Kol

COLL, COLLE, COLLS, COULL, COULE, COULES, COWL, COWLE, COWLES < ON: Kollr, Kolr

COLLING, COLLINGE, COLLINGS, COLING, COWLING < ON: Kollungr

COPEMAN, COOPMAN, COUPMAN < ON: Kaupmaðr = merchant

COPSEY < ON: Kupsi

COREY, CORY < Either ON: Kori or Kári

CORKHILL, CORKILL (Manx) Mac + ON: Þórketill

CORLETT (Manx) Mac + Þórljótr

CORP, CORPE < ON: *korpr* = raven

COTTER (Manx) Mac + ON: Óttarr

COUSE < ON: Kausi = nickname meaning 'tom cat' – also found at Cowesby in the North Riding

COWLES see COLL

CRELLIN (Manx) Mac + ON: Rǫgnvaldr

CROOK, CROOKE < ON: Krókr = nickname meaning 'hook', 'Something crooked' – referring either to a hunchback or to a sly or cunning person

CRUIKSHANK First element ON: krókr = something crooked or bent

DOLPHIN, DUFFIN < ON: Dolgfinnr

DOWSING May be a derivative, + suffix -ing, of ODan: Dūsi, which also occurs in the placename Dowsby

DRAKE, DRAKES, DRAKERS Sometimes derived from ODan: draki = dragon

DRENG, DRING < OE: dreng < ON: drengr = young man. In the Danelaw = 'free tenant holding by service and rent and military duty'

DRUMMOND < ON: Drómundr

DUNNABY A partly Anglicised form (OE: dūne = down) of a Scandinavian phrase, 'niðr í bý' (the man who lived) down in the village

EASTERBY First recorded (thirteenth century) in its original Scandinavian form 'Austebi', 'Oust in by', etc, reflecting ON: austr í bý (the man who lived) east in the village

FARMAN < ON: Farmaðr, ODan: Farman

FASTOLF < ON: Fastulfr

FATHERS, FADDER < ODan: Fathir

FELL, FELLS Dweller on a fell or mountain (ON: fjall, fell)

FELLOW, FELLOWS See under FELLOW in glossary of Scandinavian loanwords in modern literary English

FINN, FYNN, PHIN, PHINN < ON: Finnr = a Finn or Lapp

FISK, FISKE < ON: fiskr = fish, used as a byname

FLATT Dweller on the level ground (ON: flatr)

FLOOK < ON: Flóki

FOLK, FOLKE, FOULKES, FOLKES, FOKES, FOWKES, FOOKES, etc Occasionally from ON: Folki, otherwise from OFr: Fulco, Fouques < OHGmn: Fulco, Folco, literally 'folk', 'people'

FOOT, FOOTE Sometimes from ON nickname: fótr = foot, otherwise from the corresponding native form

FOWKES see FOLK

GAIT, GAITES, GAITE, GAITT, etc < ON: geitr = goat (used as a nickname)

GAITER, GAYTER, GAYTOR, GEATER, GEATOR < ME: *gayte* < ON: *geit* = goatherd

GAMBELL, GAMBLE, GAMBLES, GAMMELL, GAMMIL < ON: *gamall* = old

GAMLIN, GAMLANE, GAMLEN, GAMBLIN, GAMBLING   As above + Fr diminutive suffix *-in*

GAPP   ON: *gap* = gap or breach in a hedge or wall. In East Anglian dialect, 'gap' refers to a dweller by a gap in the cliffs

GAREY, GEARY < ON: *geiri* = spear

GARTH < ON: *garðr* = paddock, enclosure. As a personal name, 'one in charge of a paddock or enclosure'

GATE, GATES   When it hails from the most heavily Scandinavianised counties, the name often refers to a dweller by a road (ON: *gata*)

GATER   In the north country, 'dweller by a road' (ON: *gata*)

GELDING, GILDING < ON: *geldingr* = a gelded person, eunuch – an opprobrious nickname

GEMMELL, GEMMILL   Late Scots pronunciation of Gammell

GILDING   see GELDING

GILL   Either from ON: *gilli* = servant (itself of Irish origin, Old Irish: *gilla*), or from ME: *gill* < ON: *gil* = ravine, thus 'dweller by the gill'

GIPP < ON: Gípr = drunkard

GODMAN, GODDMAN, GOODMAN, GOUDMAN, GUTMAN < ON: Guð-mundr, although often the native 'good man'

GOODBAIRN, GOODBAN, GOODBAND = good child (ON: *barn*). A name confined to the parts of Britain most densely settled by Scandinavians

GOODERHAM, GOODRAM, GOODRUM < ON: Guðþormr

GOODLAKE, GOODLUCK, GULLICK, GUTLACK, etc. Although usually OE: Guðlac, occasionally ON: Guðleikr

GOODREAD, GOODRED, GOODREDS, GOODERED < ON: Guðrøðr

GOODSWEN, GOODSWIN, GOUDSWEN   ME: *god swain* = good servant, second part ON: *sveinn* = boy, servant

GOOK < ON: *gaukr* = cuckoo (used as a nickname)

GOOKEY < ON: Gauki (nickname)

GRAVE, GRAVES, GREAVEY   Either directly from ON: Greifi, a byname meaning, literally, 'earl' or 'count', or from ON: *greifi* = steward – whence also GRAVESON, GRAYSON, etc.

GRICE, GRISE, GRISS   Often from OFr: *gris* = grey (haired), although sometimes from ON: *griss* = pig

GRIME, GRIMES, GRIMM, GRIMME   Often from OE: *grim* = grim, fierce, otherwise from ON: Grímr

GRIMMET, GRIMMETT, GRUMMITT, GRUMMETT < ON: Grímhildr, although OHGmn: Grimbald is a frequent alternative origin

GRIMSON   Son of ON: Grímr

GRIPP < ON: Grípr

GULL < ON: *gulr* = pale, wan

GUN, GUNN < ON: Gunni, pet form of Gunnhildr, or from other names with Gunn- as their first part

GUNNELL < ON: Gunnhildr

GUNNER   Although some GUNNERS go back to ME: Gonner = a gunner, the majority stem from ON: Gunnvǫr (ODan: Gunwor, Gunnor), a favourite woman's name with the Normans

GUNSON   Son of Gunni

GUTMAN   see GODMAN

HACKETT, HAGGETT, HAGGITT, ACKET, ACKETTS   An Anglo-Norman diminutive of ON: Haki

HACKLING, HACLIN, ACKLING   Double diminutive (-*el* + -*in*) of ON: Haki

HACON < ON: Hákon

HAGAN, HAGEN, HAIN, HAINES, HAYNES, HAYNE, etc < ODan: Haghni

HAKE, HAKES, HACK < ON: Haki

HALDANE, HALDEN, HALDIN, HALLDING HOLDANE < ON: Halfdanr. (The Dan man's name HALFDAN is pronounced 'HOLDEN' in South Jutland.)

HANKE, HANKS < ON: Anki, a diminutive of some name the first element of which was Arn-, such as Arnbjǫrn, Arngrímr, etc. ₁From an unrecorded ON: *Arnkarl comes Dan: Anker

HARFOOT < ON: Harfótr = hare foot – nickname for a swift runner. Cf Harald Harefoot, one of the sons of Canute the Great

HASKELL   see ASKELL

HASKIN   see ASKIN

HASLOCK, HASLUCK < ON: Áslakr

HASTIE, HASTY   From Asti, Norman pet form of Asketin < ON Ásketill

HASTINGS   see ASKIN

HAWARD < ON: Hávarðr

HAYNES   see HAGAN

HEMMING, HEMMINGS < ON: Hemmingr

HERRICK < ON: Eiríkr

HILDEBRAND, HILDERBRAND   Usually from OHGmn: Hildebrand, though occasionally from ON: Hildibrandr

HILGER < ODan: Hildiger

HOGBEN, HOGBIN   Yorks dial: Hug-bone = haunch bone < ON: *huka* = to crouch, sit bent, sit on the haunches

HOLD, HULD < ON: *hǫldr* = a nobleman, next in rank beneath a jarl

HOLM, HOLME, HOLMES, HOLMS   Dweller by a holm (ON: *holmr* = a piece of land partly surrounded by streams, or flat land in a fen). A less likely origin lies in 'holm oak', an archaic and provincial name for the evergreen oak (*Quercus ilex*)

HOW, HOWE, HOWES, HOO, HOUGH, HOUF, HUFF, etc.   Usually traceable to ON: *haugr* = mound

HULM, HULME, HUME < ODan: *hulm*, equivalent to ON: *holmr*

HUNN   An East Anglian surname possibly derived from ON: *húnn* = a young bear

IDDISON   see IDDON

IDDON, IDDINS < ON: Iðunn, also the name of a goddess in Norse mythology

INGALL, INGOLD, INGLE, INGLES, HINGLE < ON: Ingjaldr

INGELL, INGELS, INGLE, INGLES, HINGLE < ON: Ingólfr

INGER, INKER, INGERSON < ON: Yngvarr

INGREY < ON: Ingiríðr

IREMONGER, IRONMONGER   Many of the predecessors of these names from the Danelaw districts contained the Scandinavian *jarn* for the native *iron*, e.g. 'Yernmonger'

IVOR, IVERS, IVERSON < ON: Ívarr

KAY, KAYE, KEAY, KEEYS, KEY, KEYES, KEYSE, etc.   Most of the Lowland Scots, Yorkshire and Lancashire KAYS take their name from the dialect word: *kae* = jackdaw < ON: *Ká*. Those from Cheshire, Derby, Staffs, Norfolk and Suffolk may take theirs from another Scandinavian nickname, 'Kei', which survived in the dialects of these areas in the sense of 'left' until last century. The word survives, as *kej*, in Danish dialects. Its origin is to be sought in ON: *keikr* = bent over backwards (Norw dial: *keik*), and it has persisted, in neuter form (with suffixed -*t*) in the standard Danish: *kejthaandet* = left-handed. As a byname, the word probably signified 'clumsy' as well as left-handed. Many of the KAYS, of course have nothing to do with either ON: *ká* or ON: *keikr*, and may be traced back to such alternative sources as 'quay', 'key' (-maker) or a Keltic corruption of Latin Caius (properly Gaius), whence also Dan. Kai, Kaj.

KEDGE, KETCH E dial: *kedge* = brisk, lively, prob. conn. with Norw: *kjekk*, Swe: *käck* = bold, brisk

KEED, KID, KIDD, KIDDE, KIDDS, KYD, KYDD < ME: *kide* = kid < ON: *kið*

KELL, KELLS < OSwe: Kæl, short form of ON: Ketill

KERR see CARR

KERSHAW, KERSAW Resident near a church wood (ON: Kirkjaskógr, as at Kirkshaw, Lancs)

KETTERIDGE, KETTRIDGE, KITTERIDGE, KITTREDGE, etc Anglo-Scandinavian hybrid consisting of ON: Ketill + OE: *-rīc*

KETTLE, KETTLES, KETTLESS, KETTEL, KETTELL, KITTEL, KITTLE, etc < ON: Ketill (Dan: Ketel – still used thus in South Jutland. Otherwise shortened to: Keld, Kjeld.)

KILL < ODan: Kille, Killi

KILVERT < Unattested ON: *Ketilfrøðr

KIRK, KIRKE, KERK, KYRKE, etc Dweller by the church (ON: *kirkja*)

KIRKMAN, KIRMAN, KERMAN Custodian of a church (ON: *kirkja*)

KNOTT < ON: Knútr

KNOTTSON Son of Knútr

KYDD see KEED

LAKER < ME: *leyker* = player, actor < ON: leikari

LAMBIE, LAMBY, LAMMIE, LAMPEY < ON: Lambi

LAMMOND, LAMOND, LAMONT < ON: *lǫgmaðr* = lawman

LANGBAIN < ON: Langabeinn = long legs, used as a nickname

LATHE, LEATH, LEATHES Worker at the barn(s) (ON: *hlaða*)

LAWMAN < ON: *lǫgmaðr* = lawman

LAX < ON: *lax* = salmon

LEGG, LEGGE < ON: *leggr* = legg, used as a nickname

LUND, LUNT, LOUND, LOUNT Dweller by a grove (ON: *lundr*)

MACASGILL, MACASKILL, MACCASKILL, etc Gaelic Mac + ON: Áskell

MACAULAY, MACAULIFFE, MACALLEY, MACALLY, etc Gaelic: Mac + ON: Óli or Ólafr

MACCORQUODALE, MACCORKINDALE Gaelic: Mac + ON: Þórketill

MACCRINDELL, MACCRINDLE, MACCRANALD Gaelic: Mac + ON: Rǫgnvaldr

MACIVER, MACIVOR, MACCURE, MACKEEVER, etc   Gaelic: Mac + ON: Ívarr

MACK   Maccus, Old Irish adaptation of ON: Magnus, which itself is the Latin *magnus* = great

MACLEOD, MACCLOUD   Gaelic: Mac + ON: *ljótr* = ugly

MAGNUS, MAGNUSSON, MANUS, MCMANUS < ON: Magnus, whence also mod. Dan: Mogens

MAIN   In north-east Scotland, often from ON: Magnus

MANSON   Son of Magnus

MEEK, MEEKE, MEEKS < ON: *mjúkr* = humble, meek

MUNDAY, MUNDY < ON: Mundi

MYER, MYERS, MIER, MIERS   Often 'dweller by the marsh' (ON: *mýrr*)

ODD, ODDE   Possibly ON: Oddi

OKEY, OAKEY   Often from ODan: Aki, short form of *Anager or *Anur

OLLIFF, OLIFF < ON: Óleifr, Óláfr

OMAN, OMOND < ON: Hámundr

ORME, ORMES, ORAM, ORUM, ORROM < ON: Ormr

ORMESON   Son of Ormr

ORR < ON: Orri = blackcock (used as nickname)

OSBORN, OSBORNE, OSBOURN, OSBURN, OSBAND, ORSBORNE, HOSBURN, HOSBONS, etc < ON: Ásbjǫrn

OSGOOD, HOSEGOOD, HOSGOOD, HORSEGOOD < ON: Áusgautr

OSMOND, OSMUND, OSMAN, OSMANT, OSMENT, OSMINT < ON: Ásmundr

OSWALD, OSSWALD, OSWELL < ON: Ásvaldr. Some are possibly from OE: Ōsweald, whence also Dan: Osvald

OTHEN < ON: Auðun, ODan: Øthin

OTTER < ON: Ottarr

OUTLAW < ON: *útlagi* = an outlaw

OVERBECK   Dweller beyond the stream (ON: *bekkr*)

PAW, POE, POWE < ON: Pá = peacock, used as a nickname

RANKILL < ON: Hrafnkell

RAVEN, RAVENS, REVAN, REVANS, REVENS < ON: Hrafn

RAVENHILL < ON: Hrafnhildr

RAWBONE, RABONE, RAWBINS, RAYBON < ON: *rábeinn* = roe leg, a nickname for one with legs as fleet as those of a roe

REANEY < ON: Hrafnhaugr = raven hill

REYNOLD, REYNOLDS, RENNELL, etc   Often via OFr: Reinald from ON: Ragnaldr (ODan: Regnald)

RIGG Dweller by the ridge (ON: *hryggr*)

ROGER, ROGERS, RODGERS, etc The name was introduced from Normandy, where OHGmn: Rodger was reinforced by ON: Hróðgeirr

ROLF, ROLFE, ROLES, ROLL, ROLLE, ROFF, ROAF, ROOF, ROUF, ROVE, ROWE, ROWLES, RULF, etc < ON: Hrólfr

RONALD, RONALDS, RANALD Scots equivalent of E: Reynold, but derived from ON: Rǫgnvaldr

ROWAT, ROWATT, ROWETT < ON: Hróaldr

ROWE see ROLF

SAFFELL, SAFFILL, SAFFLE, SAFHILL < ON: *sæfugl* = seabird (especially the cormorant). Not recorded as a personal name in Scandinavia, but common in England after the Norman Conquest

SANDAL, SANDALL < ON: *Sandúlfr

SANDEY, SANDY, SANDAY < ON: Sandi

SANK May be from *Samki, an unattested pet form of *Sandúlfr or from *Sanni, an unattested pet form of Sandi

SARL, SARLL, SAREL, SARELL Anglo-Scandinavian or Norman Sarle, Sarli from ON: Sǫrli

SCALE, SCALES, SCHOLES, SCOLES Dweller by the hut(s) or shed(s), ON: *skáli*

SCARFE, SCARF < ON: *skarfr* = cormorant

SCHOFIELD, SCHOEFIELD, SCHOLEFIELD, SCHOLFIELD, SCOLFIELD, SCO-FIELD Dweller by the hut (ON: *skáli*) in the field

SCHOLAR, SCHOLER, SCHOLLAR, SCOLLARD, SCOULARD, SCOULER Dweller by the shieling (ON: *erg*) with a hut (ON: *skáli*)

SCHOLES see SCALE

SCHOLEY, SCHOOLEY Dweller by the lowlying land (OE: *ēg*) with a hut (ON: *skáli*)

SCHOOLCRAFT, SCOWCRAFT Dweller by the croft (OE: *croft*) with a hut (*skáli*)

SCOWLE < ON: Skúl, Skúli

SEAGRIM, SEAGRIN < ON: Sægrímr

SEARCH, SARCH, SARGE, SEAWRIGHT, SERRICK, SARK, SURRAGE, SUR-RIDGE Often from ON: Sigríkr

SEARL, SEARLE, SEARLES Often from ON: Sǫrli, although a frequent alternative source is OHGmn: Sarilo

SECKER A derivative of ON: *sekkr* = sack, thus 'a maker of sacks or sackcloth'

SEWARD, SEWARDS, SEWART, SEAWARD, SAWARD, SAWORD, SAYWARD, SUART Those from the Danelaw frequently go back to ODan: Sigwarth

SEWELL, SEWILL Often from ON: Sigvaldr

SHACKEL, SHACKELL, SHACKLE, SHACKLES, SKAKLE, etc Anglo-Scandinavian Skakel < ON: Skǫkull, a byname meaning, literally, 'car pole'

SIGGERS, SIGER Often traceable to ON: Sigarr

SIMMONDS, SIMMONS, SIMMANCE, SIMMANS, SIMMEN, SIMMENS, SEMENS, SIMONDS, etc Many from OHGmn: Sigmund, others from Hebrew: Simon, but a number traceable to ON: Sigmundr

SIRED, SIRETT, SYRATT, SYRETT, etc Often traceable to ON: Sigríðr, although more usually a derivative of OE: Sigeræd

SKEAT, SKEATS, SKETT, SKEET < ON: *skjótr* = swift, fleet

SKEGG < ON: Skeggi = 'bearded one' – as at Skegness

SKEPPER A derivative of ON: *skeppa* = basket, thus 'basket maker'

SKILL < ON: *skil* = reason, discernment

SKILLMAN < ON: *skilamaðr* = trustworthy man

SKIN < ON: *skinn* = skin

SKINNER A derivative of ON: *skinn* = skin

SKIPP < ON: *skeppa* = basket, probably 'basket maker'

SLACK Dweller in the shallow valley (ON: *slakki*)

SLAY, SLEE, SLEIGH, SLEATH, SLY < ON: *slægr* = clever, cunning

SLING cf Norw: *sleng* = idler

SMITHWHITE, SMORTHWAITE, SMORFIT, SMURTHWAITE, SMURFIT, SMALL-THWAITE Dweller at the small clearing (ON: Smár Þveit)

SNAREY, SNARY < ON: Snari, from *snarr* = swift

SNELL Although most SNELLS are from OE: *snel* = smart, active, bold, those from Yorks and Norfolk may go back to ON: *snjallr*, meaning the same

SOTHEBY, SUDDABY, SUTHERBY < ON: *suðr í bý* (the man who lived) 'south in the village'

SPRACKLING, SPRATLING, SPRANKLING < ON: *sprakaleggr* = man with creaking legs

STACK < ON: *stakkr*, either a 'stacker' or a person hefty as a haystack

STEIN, STEYN, STAIN, STAINES, STAINS, etc < ON: Steinn

STIGAND, STIGANT, STIGGINS < ON: Stígandr

STORR < ON: *storr* = big

STORRS Dweller by the brushwood or young plantation (ON: *storð*)

STOTT, STOTE, STOAT < ME: *stott* = bullock, conn. with Swe: *stut*

STURGE, STURGES, STURGIS, TURGOOSE < ON: Þórgils

STYAN, STYANCE, STYANTS < ON: Stígandr

SUETT < ON: Sighvatr

SUMMERLAD, SOMMERLAT < ON: Sumarlíðr

SURRIDGE see SEARCH

SWAIN, SWAINE, SWAYN, SWAYNE < ON: *sveinn* = boy, servant

SWAN, SWANN Sometimes an anglicised version of ON: Sveinn

SWANNELL, SWONNELL < ON: Svanhildr

SWANSON (Orcadian) Son of Sveinn

SWART < ON: *svartr* = swarthy

SWINBURN < ON: Sveinbjǫrn

SYKES, SIKES < ON: *sík* = watercourse

TAIT, TEYTE < ON: *teitr* = cheerful, gay

THACKER A derivative of ON: *þak* = thatch, thus 'thatcher'

THEAKER A derivative of ON: *þekja* = to cover, thus 'one who roofs buildings'

THOROLD, TURRAL, THURRALL < ON: Þóraldr or Þórvaldr

THORY, TORY < ON: Þórir

THRALE, THRALL < ON: *þræll* = villein, serf, bondman

THURBAN, THURBURN, THORBURN, TURBIN, TARBIN < ON: Þórbjǫrn

THURGAR, THURGER < ON: Þórgeirr

THURGOOD, THORGOOD, THURGATE < ON: Þórgautr

THURKLE, THURTLE, THIRKILL, TURTLE, TUTTLE, TURGILL, TOGHILL, etc < ON: Þórkell

THURLOE < ON: Þórlaugr

THURMAN < ON: Þórmundr

TOD, TODD ME. and northern E dial: *tod* = fox, poss. conn. with an Icel byname, *tóa* = fox

TOGHILL see THURKLE

TOLL, TOLLES, TOWLE Anglo-Scandinavian < Toll, pet form of ON: Þórleifr

TOLLFREE, TOLEFREE, TURFERY, TURFREY, TUFFREY < ON: Þórfrøðr, OSwe: Thorfridh

TOOK, TOOKE, TOKE, TUKE < ON: Tóki, short form of Þórkell

TOOKEY, TUCKEY < ON: Tóki, see under TOOK

TOOLEY, TOLEY < ON: Tóli, Tolli, short forms of Þórleifr
(NB. Bermondsey's Tooley Street, however, is not based on Þórleifr.
It is a corruption of (Sain)t Óli – an affectionate name for the eleventh-
century Norwegian king, Olaf Haraldsson, who was canonised shortly
after his death at the battle of Stiklestad. He is also remembered in
Britain in the names of innumerable streets, from Fulham to Lerwick,
and in many churches dedicated to 'St Olave' – the best known being
in Stepney.)

TOOP, TOOPE < ODan: Topi

TOVELL, TUFFIELD, TUFFILL < ON: *Tófahildr, a hypothetical Anglo-
Scandinavian name

TOVEY, TOOVEY, TUVEY < ON: Tófi, short form for names beginning
with Þór-

TRAIN < ON: *tran* = crane (the bird). Away from Scotland and the
North country, TRAIN is more likely a derivation of ME: *trayne* <
OFr: *traine* = a trap or snare for catching wild animals – thus 'a
hunter or trapper'

TRIGG < ON: *tryggr* = true, faithful, trustworthy

TUBB, TUBBS < ON: Tubbi, short form of Þórbjǫrn

TUCK < Anglo-Scandinavian *Tukka, pet form of ON: Þórketill

TURK   Often a nickname, 'Turk', dating from the time of the Third
Crusade. Sometimes, however, a possible pet form of ON: Þórketill

TURKENTINE, TURKETINE   Turk (see above) + two Norman diminutive suffixes, -et, -in

TURPIN < ON: Þórfinnr

TURREFF, TURRIFF   Anglo-Scandinavian compound, ON: Þórr +
OE: *gifu*

TURRILL < ON: Þórhildr

TUTTLE   see THURKLE

ULPH < ON: Ulfr

UNCLE, UNCLES < ON: Ulfkell, Ulfketill

WAITHMAN < ON: *veiðimaðr* = hunter

WAKE < ON: *vakr* = watchful

WALTHEW, WALDO, WADDY, WADLOW, WADDILOVE < via OE:
Wælþéof from ON: Valþjófr

WATMOUGH, WHATMOUGH, WHATMORE, WHATMUFF   Second element
is ME: *maugh* < ON: *mágr* = brother-, father- or son-in-law.
First element is Wat-, short form of Walter

WESTABY, WESTOBY < ON: *vestr i bý* (the man who lived) west in the village

WICKING, WICKINGS < ON: Víkingr = viking

WIGGER   In thirteenth-century Suffolk, Wigor was a fairly familiar peasant name, deriving from ON: Vígarr. Some Wiggers are traceable back to this Scandinavian source

WIGGETT, WICKETT, WICKETTS < ODan: Vigot

WITHER, WITHERS < ON: Viðarr

WRAGG, WRAGGE < ODan: Wragg

WROE, WRAY   Dweller in the nook, corner or isolated place (ON: *vrár*)

WYMAN, WYMANS, WEYMAN, WHYMANT, WHAYMONT, etc   In the old Danelaw area, the name may reflect the ON: Vígmundr

Glossary of terms not explained in the text

ACCIDENCE Variations in the form of a word to express distinctions of number, gender, case, tense, mood, etc

APICAL A sound produced with the apex or tip of the tongue as articulator

ASPIRATION The addition to a stop consonant of a perceptible puff of breath

BACK VOWEL A vowel whose point of articulation is in the rear of the oral cavity, and which is pronounced with the back part of the tongue arched towards the soft palate, i.e.: O, U, A

BORROWING The process whereby one language absorbs words, expressions and sometimes also sounds and grammatical forms from another, and adapts them to its own use

BYNAME A name additional to the main one, usually a descriptive epithet, fanciful sobriquet or nickname

CALQUE A word or expression whose meaning is modelled on that of a prototype in another language to which it is felt to be an equivalent, e.g. Danish *stumtjener* < English *dumbwaiter*; French *gratte-ciel* < English *skyscraper*

COGNATES Words in two or more languages from the same original source

COMPARATIVE METHOD A method consisting of laying side by side speech forms from various languages to determine their similarities and differences, their common and divergent lexical features, phonological and morphological correspondences and ultimately the relationship among the languages in question, and the probable structure of their assumed common parent tongue

CONTACT VERNACULAR A makeshift language in current use for everyday contacts between people of different language backgrounds. Also known as 'hybrid' or 'mixed' language

DIPHTHONG A sound made by gliding uninterruptedly from the position of one vowel to that of another, e.g. AI, OI, EU, etc

DORSAL = VELAR

EDDA A collection of traditional Scandinavian myths and heroic legends, written down in Iceland in *c* AD 1250

EPENTHESIS The interpolation in a sound group of a sound whose usual purpose is to ease a difficult transition between two other adjacent sounds

FLEXION = ACCIDENCE

FORTIS see LENIS

FRICATIVE A consonant produced by friction caused by the air moving through a sustained narrow passage somewhere in the mouth. May be voiceless, as F, Þ, S and SH, or voiced, as V, Ð, Z and ZH

FRONT ROUNDED VOWEL A front vowel produced with rounded lips, as Y (Ü) and Ø

FRONT VOWEL A vowel whose point of articulation is in the front part of the oral cavity, and which is produced with the mass of the tongue pushed towards the front of the mouth and the front part of the tongue arched towards the palate, as E, I

FUTHARK See under RUNES

GLOSS An interlinear or marginal notation in a manuscript giving a translation of a word or passage

GUTTURAL = VELAR

HYDRONYMICS River names

INDO-EUROPEAN A widespread constellation of related language families, at present comprising Gothonic, Keltic, Italic, Baltic, Slavic, Albanian, Armenian, Iranian and Indic. The Indo-European nucleus is presumed, on linguistic grounds, to have lain somewhere in east-central Europe between the Baltic and the Black Sea, and Indo-European languages are thought to have radiated outwards from this cradleland in all directions by means of ethnic movements, cultural diffusion, or both

INFLECTION The addition of certain endings to the base of a word to express grammatical relationships, functions and aspects

ISOPHONE A line marking the boundaries within which a given speech sound is to be found

JOMSVIKINGS Members of a community of Scandinavian warriors based at Jomsborg, an island fortress founded by the tenth-century Danish king, Harald Bluetooth, in the mouth of the river Oder

LENIS   A stop produced with a weaker, laxer articulation than its FORTIS counterpart. Usually unaspirated, i.e. B, D, G as against P, T, K

LOAN WORD   A borrowed or adopted word from another language

MORPHOLOGY   The study of the smallest meaningful units of a language, and of their formation into words

NYNORSK, LANDSMÅL or NEW NORWEGIAN   A modern literary form of Norwegian, artificially constructed of elements drawn from various indigenous dialects

OCCLUSIVE   A consonant that momentarily stops the flow of sound. Also called a STOP or PLOSIVE

OGHAM (pronounced 'awm')   An ancient alphabet of twenty characters used by the Goidelic-speaking Kelts of Ireland and implanted by them in Scotland

ONOMASTICS   The study of the meanings and derivations of names

PALATAL   Any type of consonant sound formed by placing the front or blade of the tongue against the hard palate, thus imparting to the consonant the timbre of I, e.g. Kj is a palatalised K, Gj a palatalised G

PHONEME   A minimal unit of distinctive sound

PHONOLOGY   The sound system of a language

PIDGIN   A hybrid version of a language, usually characterised by simplified grammar and by limited and often mixed vocabulary, and used chiefly for intergroup communication. A pidgin is an auxiliary language that has no speech community of its own but arises from casual contacts among people having no common speech background. An example is 'Russenorsk', a hybrid jargon of Russian and Norwegian parentage, used in certain Arctic ports of Norway until c 1917 as a vehicle of communication between Russian herring fishers and Norwegian merchants. See also CONTACT VERNACULAR

PLOSIVE = OCCLUSIVE

PRIMITIVE NORSE (Dan: URNORDISK)   The form of North Gothonic spoken in Scandinavia until c AD 500, and first attested in runic inscriptions from the second century AD

PROSODY   The general term embracing all the 'musical' or contour features of an utterance, such as accent, pitch, cadence and pauses

14

RECONSTRUCTION, LINGUISTIC   Determining, by means of a comparison of attested languages or forms, an earlier, unrecorded state of a language

RIKSMÅL, BOKMÅL   A form of Norwegian based on literary Danish

RISING DIPHTHONG   A diphthong in which the final vowel element is more prominent than the preceding, as in French *nuit*

RUNES   The twenty-four (later sixteen) characters of the runic alphabet (or FUTHARK) used by most of the Gothonic peoples from the second century AD and surviving in parts of up-country Sweden until the eighteenth century. The runes are believed to have been inspired by some Graeco-Roman script encountered by Gothonic wanderers (possibly Heruleans) in the neighbourhood of the Black Sea

SPIRANT = FRICATIVE

STOP = OCCLUSIVE

STRESS   Special emphasis on a sound or sound group

SUBSTRATE, SUBSTRATUM   A language displaced as the dominant tongue in its area by another language or languages, but possibly continuing to be responsible for certain changes and tendencies in the languages that have submerged it

SYNCOPE, SYNCOPATION   The loss of a medial vowel, due generally to stress accent elsewhere in the word, e.g. Primitive Norse: Harjuwulaf R > Old Icelandic: Hálfr (man's name)

SYNTAX   The combination and arrangement of words into phrases, clauses and sentences

TABOO, LINGUISTIC   The substitution of certain words by euphemistic or circumlocutory terms or phrases for superstitious, moral or social reasons, e.g. Shetland 'Haaf' usage: *bønhus* (prayerhouse) for *kirk*

TENUIS   A devoiced plosive consonant

TOPONYMICS   The study of placenames

VARANGIANS or VAERINGS   Scandinavian rovers who, in the ninth and tenth centuries AD, overran parts of Russia and reached Constantinople. Varangian warriors formed the nucleus of the bodyguard of the Byzantine emperors

VELAR   A consonant formed by the back of the dorsum of the tongue against the velum or soft palate. Also called DORSAL or GUTTURAL

Bibliography

Ethnogeny and early history of the Gothonic-speaking peoples

COON, C. *The Races of Europe*, 1939

GEIPEL, J. *The Europeans*, 1969

KLINDT–JENSEN, O. *Denmark before the Vikings*, 1957

LUNDMAN, B. *Raser och folkstockar i Baltoskandia*, Uppsala, 1946

——— *Baltoskandias antropologi*, Uppsala, 1967

SCHÜTTE, G. *Our forefathers – the Gothonic nations*, Cambridge, 1933

STARCKE, V. *Denmark in World History*, Philadelphia, 1962

STERN, P. *Prehistoric Europe*, 1969

WEIBULL, C. 'Den äldsta grännsläggningen mellan Sverige och Danmark', in *Historisk tidskrift för Skåneland*, VII, 1917.

Language history and language mixture

BLOOMFIELD, L. *Language*, 1933

DAUZAT, A. *La géographie linguistique*, Paris, 1948

FEIST, S. 'The origin of the Germanic languages and the Indo-Europeanizing of northern Europe', in *Language*, 8, 1932

HAAS, M. *The prehistory of languages*, The Hague, 1970

HALL, R. *Pidgin and Creole languages*, Cornell University Press, 1966

HAUGEN, E. 'The analysis of linguistic borrowing', in *Language*, 26, 1950

HOENIGSWALD, H. *Language change and linguistic reconstruction*, University of Chicago Press, 1965

LEHMANN, W. *Historical linguistics – an introduction*, New York, 1962

LOEWE, R. *Germanische Sprachwissenschaft*, Berlin and Leipzig, 1933

MALMBERG, H. *The origin of the Scandinavian nations and languages*, Copenhagen, 1958

MEILLET, A. *The comparative method in historical linguistics*, Paris, 1967

PAUL, H. *Prinzipien der Sprachgeschichte*, Halle, 1920

PROKOSCH, E. *A comparative Germanic grammar*, Philadelphia, 1938

SAPIR, E. *Language*, Oxford, 1921

SCHÖNFELDER, K. 'Zur Theorie der Sprachmischung, der Mischsprachen und des Sprachwechsels', in *Wissenschaftliche Zeitschrift der Karl Marx Universität*, 1953

TOVAR, A. 'Linguistics and prehistory', in *Word*, Vol 10, 1954

VILDOMEC, V. *Multilingualism*, Leyden, 1963

VOGT, H. 'Language contacts', in *Word*, Vol 10, 1954

WEINREICH, U. *Languages in contact*, The Hague, 1953

The Viking expansion

ARBMAN, H. *The Vikings*, 1961

BRØGGER, A. *Ancient emigrants – a history of the Norse settlements in Scotland*, Oxford, 1929

BRØNDSTED, J. *The Vikings*, (Pelican Books), 1960

CAPPER, D. *The Vikings of Britain*, 1937

CHARLES, B. *Old Norse relations with Wales*, Cardiff, 1934

COLLINGWOOD, W. *Scandinavian Britain*, 1908

EKWALL, E. 'The proportion of Scandinavian settlers in the Danelaw', in *Saga Book of the Viking Society*, XII, 1937–45

—— 'The Scandinavian settlement' in Darby, H. C. (ed), *An historical geography of England before 1800*, 1936

FISHER, R. and TAYLOR, G. 'Scandinavian influence on Scottish ethnology', in *Nature*, 145, 1949

FOOTE, P. and WILSON, D. *The Viking achievement*, 1970

HEINBERG, A. *Danske i England, Skotland og Irland*, Copenhagen, 1934

JONES, G. *A history of the Vikings*, Oxford, 1968

KENDRICK, T. *A history of the Vikings*, 1930, reprinted 1968

KLINDT–JENSEN, O. *The Vikings in England*, Copenhagen, 1948

BIBLIOGRAPHY 217

LAURING, P. *Danelagen*, Copenhagen, 1957
LUND, N. *De danske vikinger i England*, Copenhagen, 1967
MARSTRANDER, C. 'Det norske landnåm på Man', in *Norsk tidsskrift for sprogvidenskap*, 1932
MAWER, H. *The Vikings*, Cambridge, 1913
MEGAW, B. *The Norse heritage of the Isle of Man*, Cambridge, 1950
SAWYER, P. *The Age of the Vikings*, 1962
SHETELIG, H. *Vikingeminder i Vesteuropa*, Oslo, 1936
—— *An introduction to the Viking history of western Europe*, Oslo, 1940
STEENSTRUP, J. *Nordmœnnerne IV – Danelagen*, Copenhagen, 1882
STENTON, F. *The Danes in England*, Oxford, 1927
—— 'The Scandinavian colonies in England and Normandy', in *Transactions of the Royal Historical Society*, 4th series, xxvii, 1945
VOGT, L. *Dublin som norsk by*, Oslo, 1896
WADSTEIN, E. *Norden och kontinenten i gammal tid*, Uppsala, 1944
WAINWRIGHT, F. *Danes and Norwegians in England*, 1952
—— *Early Scandinavian settlement in Derbyshire*, 1947
—— *The Northern Isles*, 1962
WALSH, A. *Scandinavian relations with Ireland during the Viking period*, Dublin, 1927
WARD, G. *The first Danes come to England*, 1949
WATKIN, I. 'A Viking settlement in Little England beyond Wales: ABO blood-group evidence', in *Man*, LX, 1960
WILSON, D. *The Vikings and their origins*, 1970
WORSAAE, J. *Minder om de Danske og Nordmœndene i England, Skotland og Irland*, Copenhagen, 1851

The Scandinavian languages

General
HOLMBERG, B. and JANZÉN, A. *Att studera nordiska språk*, Stockholm, 1963
WALSHE, M. *Introduction to the Scandinavian languages*, 1965
WESSÉN, E. *De nordiska språken*, Stockholm, 1965

Individual Scandinavian languages

Old West Norse

CHAPMAN, K. *Icelandic–Norwegian linguistic relationships*, Oslo, 1962

Icelandic

EINARSSON, S. *Icelandic*, Baltimore, 1967
JÓNSSON, F. *Det islandske sprogs historie i kort omrids*, Copenhagen, 1918

Faeroese

HELGASON, J. 'Færøiske studier', in *Maal og Minne*, 1924
LOCKWOOD, W. *An introduction to modern Faeroese*, 1955

Norwegian

LUNDEBY, E. and TORVIK, I. *Språket vårt gjennom tidene*, Oslo, 1956
SKARD, V. *Norsk språkhistorie*, Oslo, 1962

Swedish

WESSÉN, E. *Svensk språkhistoria*, Stockholm, 1945

Danish

OXENVAD, E. *Vort sprog*, Copenhagen, 1943
SARAUW, G. *Dansk fra oldtid til nutid*, Copenhagen, 1937
SKAUTRUP, P. *Det danske sprogs historie*, Copenhagen, 1953

Scandinavian dialectology

BRØNDUM-NIELSEN, J. *Dialekter og dialektforskning*, Copenhagen, 1951
KOLSRUD, S. *Nynorsken i sine målføre*, Oslo, 1951
LARSEN, A. *Oversigt over de norske bygdemål*, Oslo, 1948
WESSÉN, E. *Våra folkmål*, Stockholm, 1954

Shetland and Orkney Norn

FLOM, G. 'The transition from Norse to Lowland Scotch in Shetland, 1600–1850', in *Saga Book of the Viking Society*, X, 1926

JAKOBSEN, J.   'Nordiske minder, især sproglige, på Orknøerne', in *Maal og Minne*, 1911
——— 'Om Orknøernes historie og sprog', in *Danske Studier*, xvi, 1919
——— *Det norrøne sprog på Shetland*, Copenhagen, 1897
——— *Old Shetland dialect and placenames of Shetland*, 1926
——— *An etymological dictionary of the Norn language in Shetland*, 1932
MARWICK, H.   *The Orkney Norn*, Oxford, 1927

Caithness Norn

THORSON, P.   *Katanes og norrønt mål*, Oslo, 1936
——— 'The Third Norn Dialect – that of Caithness', in *Saga Book of the Viking Society*, 1954

Scandinavian influence on Scots and Irish Gaelic

CHRISTENSEN, R.   'Norse influence on Celtic Scotland', in *Maal og Minne*, 1938
——— 'Sudrøy-Norn', in *Maal og Minne*, 1938
HENDERSON, G.   *The Norse influence on Celtic Scotland*, Glasgow, 1910
KRISTENSEN, M.   *Om nogle dialektejendommeligheder i Vesterøernes sprog*, Oslo, 1924
MARSTRANDER, C.   'Det norske substrat i skotsk-gelisk', section of an article entitled 'Okklusiver og substrater', in *Norsk tidsskrift for sprogvidenskap*, Oslo, 1932
——— *Bidrag til det norske sprogs historie i Irland*, Oslo, 1915
SOMMERFELT, A.   *Norse-Gaelic contacts*, Oslo, 1951

Scandinavian influence on English

BAUGH, A.   *A history of the English language*, 1965
BJÖRKMAN, E.   *Scandinavian loanwords in Middle English*, Halle, 1900

BROOK, G. *English dialects,* 1963

EKWALL, E. *How long did the Scandinavian language survive in England?,* Copenhagen, 1930

FLOM, G. *Scandinavian influence on southern Lowland Scotch,* New York, 1900

—— 'Norse elements in the English dialects', in *Saga Book of the Viking Club,* Vol. VII, 1911

JESPERSEN, O. *Growth and structure of the English language,* Oxford, 1938

SERGEANTSON, M. *A history of foreign words in English,* Oxford, 1968

SKEAT, W. *The Scandinavian element in English,* Oxford, 1891

THORSON, P. *Anglo-Norse studies,* Amsterdam, 1936

WALL, A. *A contribution towards the study of the Scandinavian element in the English dialects,* Halle, 1898

The Scandinavian element in Channel Island French

FABRICIUS, A. *Danske minder i Normandiet,* Copenhagen, 1897

SPENCE, N. *A glossary of Jersey French,* Oxford, 1960

Placenames

EKWALL, E. 'The Scandinavian element', in *Introduction to the survey of English placenames,* Cambridge, 1924

—— *English river names,* Oxford, 1968

—— *The Oxford Dictionary of English placenames,* 1951

HALD, K. *Vore stednavne,* Copenhagen, 1965

JAKOBSEN, J. *The placenames of Shetland,* 1936

LINDKVIST, H. *Middle English placenames of Scandinavian origin,* Uppsala, 1912

MARWICK, H. *Orkney farm-names,* Kirkwall, 1952

MAWER, A. 'The Scandinavian settlements in England as reflected in placenames', in *Acta. Phil. Scand.* 7, 1932

NICOLAISEN, W. 'Norse placenames in south-west Scotland', in *Scottish Studies,* iv, 1960

OFTEDAL, M. 'Norse placenames in the Hebrides', in *Annen Viking Kongress,* ed. K. Falck, Oslo, 1955

RATTER, W. *Our Shetland placenames*, Lerwick, 1947

TAYLOR, A. 'British and Irish placenames in Old Norse literature', in *Annen Viking Kongress*, ed. K. Falck, Oslo, 1955

Personal names

BJÖRKMAN, E. *Nordische Personennamen in England in frühmittelenglischer Zeit*, Halle, 1910

FEILITZEN, O. VON. *The Pre-Conquest names of Domesday Book*, Uppsala, 1937

HORNBY, R. *Danske navne*, Copenhagen, 1951

JENSEN, G. *Some observations on Scandinavian personal names in English placenames*, 1962

――― *Scandinavian personal names in Lincolnshire and Yorkshire*, Copenhagen, 1968

KÖPKE, J. *Altnordischen Personennamen bei den Angelsachsern*, Berlin, 1909

LÖFVENBERG, M. *Studies on Middle English local surnames*, Lund, 1942

REANEY, P. *The origins of English surnames*, 1967

SKEIDSVOLL, A. *Norske manns- og kvinnenamn*, Oslo, 1944

STENTON, F. *Danelaw charters*, 1920

TENGVIK, G. *Old English bynames*, Uppsala, 1938

WESSÉN, E. *Nordiska namnstudier*, Uppsala, 1927

WHITELOCK, D. 'Scandinavian personal names in the Liber Vitae of Thorney Abbey', in *Saga Book of the Viking Society*, XII, 1945

Index

Page numbers in *italic type* indicate illustrations

DATE DUE

GAYLORD   PRINTED IN U.S A